Probability and Statistics

Probability and Statistics

Dr. M. Venkata Krishna

Professor and Head
Department of Mathematics
University College of Engineering
Osmania University
Hyderabad – 500 007

BSP BS Publications
An unit of **BSP Books Pvt., Ltd.**

4-4-309, Giriraj Lane, Sultan Bazar,
Hyderabad - 500 095 - A.P.
Phone : 040 - 23445605, 23445688

Published by :

BSP BS Publications
An unit of **BSP Books Pvt., Ltd.**

4-4-309, Giriraj Lane, Sultan Bazar,
Hyderabad - 500 095 - A.P.
Phone : 040 - 23445605, 23445688
e-mail : info@bspbooks.net
www.bspublications.net

Printed at

Adithya Offset Process (I) Pvt. Ltd.
Hyderabad.

Price : Rs. 195.00

ISBN : 978-81-7800-240-8

Dedicated to

My Parents

Preface

Probability and Statistics is a core subject of study for all branches of Engineering and Technology. It is also important course of study for MCA students under various Universities. The present book is the outcome of the author's rich experience in classroom teaching to students of Engineering at Osmania University and other institutions.

The subject matter is divided into nine chapters for easy understanding of various concepts and theory, aided by many solved examples. Some problems are left for the students to solve.

I am thankful to all my colleagues who have helped in the preparation of manuscript of the book.

I also want to express my appreciation to Naresh, the production incharge at BS Publications, Manoj Jha for constant motivation and Sri Nikhil Shah and Sri Anil Shah, Directors for agreeing to publish the book under BSP banner.

Any suggestions for future improvement of the book will be gratefully accepted.

Dr. M. Venkata Krishna

Contents

Chapter 2

Random Variables

Chapter 3

Distributions

Chapter 4

Testing of Hypothesis I

Chapter 9

Stochastic Processes

Probability

1

1.1 Introduction

This chapter is devoted to a study of Probability–what it is and some of the basic concepts of the theory. The theory of probability is a science concerned with random events. The theory was originated in the middle of seventeenth century and is associated with the names of Huygens, Pascal, Fermat and Jarnes Bernoulli. The analytical theory of probability was developed by De Moivre, Laplace, Gauss and Poisson. During recent decades the theory of probability in modern science has grown immeasurably. Today, probability theory is extending its influence and practical application to many spheres. In this chapter we shall discuss some preliminaries.

We know that statistics is concerned with inferences about population based on sample information. In this chapter we assume that the population is known, and calculate the chances of obtaining various samples from the population. In probability we use population information to infer the probable nature of the sample.

Many experiments do not yield exactly the same results, when performed repeatedly. For Example, if we toss a coin, we are not sure if we will get "heads" or " tails" and if we roll a six-faced die, we have no way of knowing which of the six possible outcomes 1, 2, 3, 4, 5 or 6 will turn up. The outcomes of these experiments are associated with uncertainties and the experiments of this type are called probabilistic experiments. The outcome of a probabilistic experiment cannot be predicted in advance and any prediction made involves uncertainty. Probability is a concept which tends the measure the degree of this uncertainty.

The general meaning of the term probability is "chance" or "possibility". This term is used in this sense when we say that "most probably it will rain tomorrow" or "it is likely that England wins this tournament this time" then the probability is used in qualitative sense. When we say that " there is 50 per cent chance of rain tomorrow" it is expressed as a percentage and the term probability (chance) in this case is used quantitative sense. In general probability is the chance same thing will happen. Probabilities are expressed fraction or as decimals between 0 and 1. Before going to deal with the definition and theory of probability it is necessary to understood the following concepts.

1.2 Basic Concepts

1.2.1 Experiment

***Definition* 1.1** An experiment is an act or process that leads to a single outcome that cannot be predicted with certainty.

Our definition of the term "experiment" is broader than that used in physical sciences. Experiments are usually denoted by upper case letters of alphabet.

Tossing a coin is an experiment.

Recording the monthly sales of a business firm is an experiment.

Counting the number of defective parts in a box of parts is an experiment.

Single performance of an experiment is called a trial. A result of an experiment is called an outcome. Each experiment may yield one or more outcomes. When these are not predetermined but subject to chance, we have a random experiment. Probability is concerned with the analysis of random experiment.

***Definition* 1.2:** An experiment whose outcome cannot be predicted with certainty is called a random experiment.

***Example* 1:** Counting the number of misprints in a page is a random experiment.

***Example* 2:** Reading the daily temperature on a thermometer is a random experiment.

1.2.2 Simple Event

***Definition* 1.3:** A simple event is an outcome of an event that cannot be decomposed with a simpler outcome.

A simple events is a single outcome of an experiment and it cannot be broken into smaller events. A simple event is also called an elementary event. Getting a head or a tail when a coin is tossed is a simple event.

1.2.3 Event

***Definition* 1.4:** An event is a collection of one or more simple events.

Event will be designated by capital letters A, B, C, etc. Events can be decomposed into simpler outcomes. Consider the experiment in which a die is tossed. Getting an even number is an event of the experiment. It can be decomposed with simple events. Events which are not simple are also called compound events.

1.2.4 Exhaustive Event

***Definition* 1.5** Events are said to be exhaustive when they include all possible outcomes of an experiment.

***Example*:** In throwing a die, the events 1, 2, 3, 4, 5, 6 are exhaustive.

***Definition*:** 1.6 (Exhaustive number of events) The total number of possible outcomes of an experiment in any trial is known as the exhaustive number of events (or cases).

Example: In throwing a die the exhaustive number of cases is 6.

1.2.5 Sample Space

We now introduce a convenient mathematical device for developing the theory of probability. It is customary to refer to a set of points which represents all the possible outcomes of an experiment as a sample space of the experiment.

***Example*:** Consider an experiment in which two coins are tossed. If we are interested simply in whether the coins fall alike (both heads or both tails) or differently (one head and one tail), then we have two possible outcomes, L (like) and D (different). In this case the set of possible outcomes is

$$S' = \{L, D\}$$

If we are interested in the number of heads or the number of tails then the set of possible outcomes is

$$S'' = \{(2, 0), (1, 1), (0, 2)\}$$

Where, (2, 0) denotes 2 heads and no tail

(1, 1) denotes 1 head and 1 tail

(0, 2) denotes the showing of two tails

Again, if we are interested in whether each individual coin falls heads (H) or tails (T), the set of all possible outcomes may be written as

$$S''' = \{(H, H), (H, T), (T, H), (T, T)\}$$

Each of the sets S', S'', S''' is a set of all possible outcomes of the experiment in which the coins are tossed. Each set is called a sample space of the experiment. There may be many possible sample spaces of an experiment.

***Definition* 1.7** A sample space of a random experiment is a set of the elements such that every outcome of the experiment corresponds to exactly one element of the set.

A sample space of an experiment is denoted by S and is also called an event space of the experiment. A sample S of an experiment is the collection of all its simple events and any subset of S is an event. If a sample space S is finite sample space if it has finite number of elements. If S is not finite then it is called an infinite sample space, finite sample spaces are also called discrete spaces.

1.2.6 Equally Likely Events

***Definition* 1.8** Outcomes of an experiment are equally likely if there is no reason for an event to occur in preference to any other event.

***Example*:** In drawing a card from a well shuffled pack of cards, there are 52 equally likely possible outcomes.

1.2.7 Mutually Exclusive Events

***Definition* 1.9** Events are said to be mutually exclusive if the occurrence of one preludes occurrence of the others.

In tossing a coin, the events Head (H) and Tail (T) are mutually exclusive.

In other words two events E_1 and E_2 are mutually exclusive if there is no point in common in between the points belonging to E_1 and E_2 i.e., events E_1 and E_2 are called mutually exclusive if their joint occurrence is impossible.

1.2.8 Impossible Event

***Definition* 1.10** An event which is certain not to occur is called an impossible event.

An impossible is denoted by ϕ.

***Example*:** Consider an experiment in which two dice are rolled simultaneously. Getting a total score of 15 is an impossible event.

1.2.9 Certain Event

***Definition* 1.11** An event which is certain to occur is called a certain event or sure event.

***Example*:** If S denotes sample space of an experiment, then S is a certain event.

1.2.10 Complement of an Event

***Definition* 1.12** The complement of any event E is the event that E does not occur.

The complement of an event is denoted by E^C or $\bar{E}$ or E'

***Example*:** Let E {2,4, 6} be an event when a die is thrown, then, $E^C = \{1. 3, 5,\}$.

1.2.11 Symbolic Notation

If E_1, E_2 and E_3 are any three events, then

(i) $E_1 \cap E_2$ denotes the event of simultaneous occurrence of both the events E_1 and E_2.

(ii) $E_1 \cup E_2$ denotes the event of occurrence of at least one of the events E_1 and E_2.

(iii) $E_1 - E_2$ the occurrence of the event E_1 and E_2. It is also denoted by $E_1 \cap \bar{E}_2$.

(iv) $E_1^C \cap E_2^C$ denotes the occurrence of neither E_1 and E_2.

(v) $E_1 \cup E_2 \cup E_3$ denotes the occurrence of at least one events E_1, E_2 or E_3.

(vi) $E_1 \cap E_2 \cap E_3$ denotes the occurrence of all three events E_1, E_2 or E_3.

(vii) $\left(E_1 \cap E_2^C\right) \cup \left(E_2^C \cap E_2\right)$ denotes the occurrence of exactly one of E_1 and E_2.

(viii) $(E_1 \cap E_2) \cup (E_2 \cup E_3) \cup (E_3 \cup E_1)$ denotes at least two of E_1, E_2, E_3 occur.

(ix) $\left(E_1 \cap E_2^C \cap E_3^C\right) \cup \left(E_1^C \cap E_2^C \cap E_3^C\right) \cup \left(E_1^C \cap E_2^C \cap E_3^C\right)$ denotes the event in which only one of E_1, E_2, E_3 occur.

1.3 Pictorial Representations of Sample Spaces, Events and their Relationships

1.3.1 Venn Diagram

A graphical method called Venn diagram is useful for representing sample space and its sample points. A venn diagram is a useful device to our consideration of relationships that may exist between subjects of a given universe. A sample space of an experiment is shown as a closed curve labelled S. The figure contains a set of points, called sample points, with each point representing a simple event.

***Example* 1:** Consider an experiment in which a corn is tossed. If S denotes a sample space, then

$$S = \{H, T\}$$

The venn diagram in Fig. 1.1 represents S

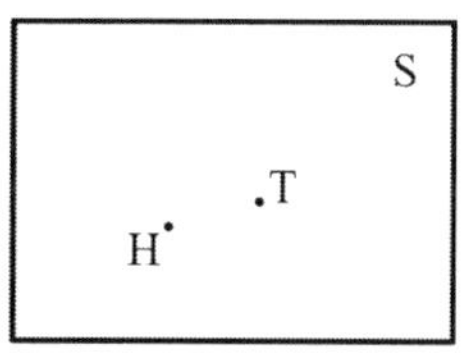

Fig. 1.1

***Example* 2:** A die is rolled and S denotes the set of all possible outcomes (sample space), then

S = {1, 2, 3, 4, 5, 6} is shown in Fig. 1.2.

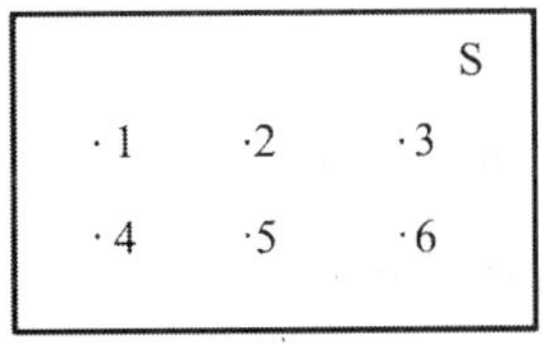

Fig. 1.2

***Example* 3:** If E_1 and E_2 are two events of a sample space S such that E_1 is a subject of E_2, then the venn diagram to represent this is shown in Fig. 1.3.

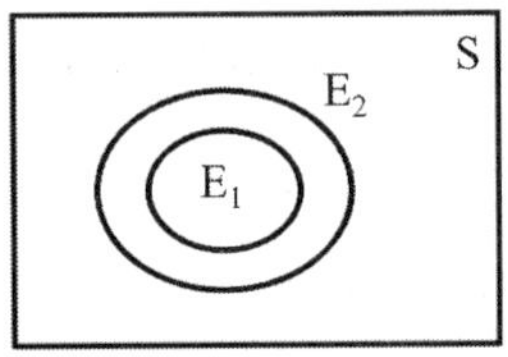

Fig. 1.3 $E_1 \subset E_2$

1.3.2 Tree Diagram

Sample spaces of random experiments can also be described graphically in terms of tree diagram. Few Examples are given below:

***Example* 1:** A bag contains twenty red balls. If three balls are drawn at random: one after the other without replacement, list the sample space by means of a tree diagram.

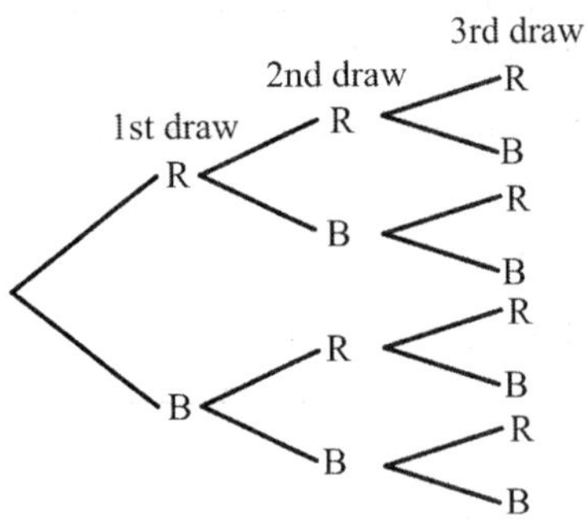

Fig. 1.4 Tree diagram

here, we have S = {RRR, RRB, RBR, RBB, BRR, BRB, BBR, BBB}

***Example* 2:** List the sample space to study the distribution of boys and girls in a family of two children.

The following combinations are possible

Boy-boy, Boy-girl, Girl-boy, Girl-girl

$\therefore \qquad S = \{BB, BG, GB, GG\}$

We have the following diagrams.

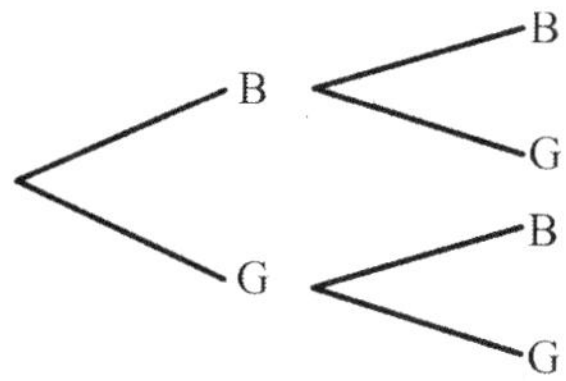

Fig. 1.5

1.4 Definition of Probability

***Definition* 1:** The probability that an event E will occur is the ratio of the number of sample points that correspond to the occurrence of E to the total number of sample points.

In symbols P(E) denotes the probability that E will occur when the experiment is performed and if n(E) denotes the number of sample points giving rise to E and n denotes the total number of sample points,

Then
$$P(E) = \frac{n(E)}{n}$$

The above definition of probability is the general definition of probability. There are many different definitions of probability. The definitions may be divided into three groups.

1.5 Types of Probability

There are three basic ways of classifying probability, namely

1. Classical approach
2. Relative frequency approach
3. Subjective approach

1.6 Classical Probability

***Definition* 2:** Let n be the number of all possible outcomes of a random experiment all of which are equally likely, of which let m be favourable to the event E. Then the probability of E denoted by P(E) is

$$P(E) = \frac{\text{Number of outcomes favourable to the event E}}{\text{Total number of outcomes in the experiment}}$$

i.e., $$P(E) = \frac{\text{Number of outcomes favourable to E}}{\text{Total number of outcomes in S}} = \frac{m}{n}$$

where S is the sample space of the experiment.

The above definition of probability is called the classical definition or Laplacian definition of probability. It is also called the mathematical definition. The probability is known as a "Prior Probability".

1.6.1 Properties of Classical Probability

If *E* is an event of a sample space S, then

(i) P(E) is a pure number

(ii) $0 \leq P(E) \leq 1$

(iii) If $E_1, E_2, \ldots, E_K$ are K mutually exclusive and exhaustive events in the sample space S. Then

$$\sum_{i=1}^{K} P(E_i) = 1$$

i.e., P(S) = 1

(iv) The probability of an impossible event is zero

i.e., $P(\phi) = 0$

(v) If $E_1 \subseteq E_2$ then $P(E_1) \leq P(E_2)$

(vi) If $E_1 \subset E_2$, then $P(E_2\ E_1) = P(E_2) - P(E_1) = P(E_2 - E_1)$

The advantage of the classical definition of probability is that it can be applied 'a priori' or without experimentation. The method fails when the number of possible outcomes is infinite and the outcomes are not equally likely.

In the classical definition, the term 'favourable is' rather used loosely–what is favourable to one player is unfavourable to his opponent. A favourable event is also called 'successful event'. The terms 'favourable' and 'success' can be applied to any particular kind of outcome.

1.6.2 Probability of Failure

Suppose an event E can happen in m ways out of total n possible equally likely outcomes. Then the number of times the event E does not occur is (n – m). The probability of non-occurrence of the event E denoted by $P(E^C)$ (or $P(\bar{E})$)is given

$$P(E^C) = \frac{n-m}{n}$$

Note:

(i) From the definition

$$P\left(E^C\right) = \frac{n-m}{n}$$

$$= \frac{n}{n} - \frac{m}{n}$$

$$= 1 - \frac{m}{n}$$

$$= 1 - P(E)$$

$\therefore$ $$P(E) + P(E^C) = 1$$

(ii) $$P(E) = 1 - P(E^C)$$

(iii) The probability of the occurrence of the event E is called the probability of its success and is usually denoted by p.

(iv) The probability of non-occurrence of the event E is called the probability of its failure. It is denoted by q.

We have $p + q = 1, 0 \le p \le 1, 0 \le q \le 1, p = 1 - q$ and $q = 1 - p$

1.7 Relative Frequency Approach

By introducing relative frequency approach, some of the deficiencies of the classical probability could be removed.

Let an experiment be conducted a larger number of times under essentially homogeneous and identical conditions. If n denotes the number of times the experiment is conducted out of which m are favourable to an event E, then the probability of the event E is

$$P\left(E\right) = \underset{n\to\infty}{Lt} \frac{m}{n}$$

This definition is known as Statistical or Empirical or A posteriori definition of probability. In this approach n is never infinity and for large values of n the statistical probability will tend to be equal to the mathematical probability.

Solved Examples

***Example* 1:** A coin is tossed once. Find the probability of getting a Head.

***Solution*:** Coin is tossed once. Therefore, the number of equally likely cases =2

(The equally likely cases are head and a tail)

$\therefore$ n = 2

Number of favourable cases = 1

$\therefore$ m = 1

Probability of getting a head = $\frac{m}{n}$

$$P(\text{Head}) = \frac{m}{n} = \frac{1}{2}$$

***Example* 2:** Two coins are tossed once. Find the probability of getting (a) one head (b) at least one head.

Solution: The sample space of possible outcomes when two coins are tossed simultaneously is

$$S = \{HH, HT, TH, TT\}$$

where HH denotes the case in which both coins turn up head; HT denotes the outcome that the first coin turns up head (H) and the second coin turns up tail (T), and so on.

Number of points in the sample space = 4

$\therefore$ n = 4

***Example* 3:** A die is rolled. List a sample space and find the probability in which an event number appears on the die.

(A die has six faces marked with the numbers 1, 2, 3, 4, 5 and 6)

***Solution*:** We have S = {1, 2, 3, 4, 5, 6}

Number of elements in S = n(S) = n = 6

Let E be the event of getting an events number

$\therefore$ $E = \{2, 4, 6\}$

$\therefore$ $m = n(E) = 3$

$\therefore$ $P(E) = \frac{m}{n} = \frac{3}{6} = \frac{1}{2}$

***Example* 4:** A pair of dice is tossed and the two numbers appearing on the top are recorded.

(a) Describe the sample space, and

(b) Find the probability of the event in which the sum is 10 or more.

***Solution*:** There are six possible numbers 1, 2, 3, 4, 5 and 6 on each die. The total number of possible outcomes when a pair of dice is tossed is $6 \times 6 = 36$

$\therefore \quad n = 36$

We have

S = {(1, 1), (1, 2), (1,3), (1,4), (1, 5), (1,6), (2, 1), (2, 2), (2, 3), (2, 4), (2, 5), (2, 6), (3, 1), (3, 2), (3, 3), (3, 4), (3, 5), (3, 6), (4, 1), (4, 2), (4, 3), (4, 4), (4, 5), (4, 6), (5, 1), (5, 2), (5, 3), (5, 4), (5, 5), (5, 6), (6, 1), (6, 2), (6, 3), (6, 4), (6, 5), (6, 6)}

(a) Let *A* be the event in which exactly one head turns up

$\therefore$ A = {HT, TH}

$\therefore$ Number of cases favourable to the event A = 2

$\therefore$ $m = 2$

$$\therefore \quad P(A) = \frac{m}{n} = \frac{2}{4} = \frac{1}{2}$$

(b) Let B denote the event in which at least one head turns up

$\therefore$ B = {HH, HT, TH}

$\therefore$ Number of cases favourable to B = 3

$\therefore$ m = 3

$$\text{and,} \quad P(B) = \frac{m}{n} = \frac{3}{4}$$

***Example* 5:** A coin is tossed thrice. Find the probability of getting all tails.

Solution: Sample space for the experiment is

S = {HHH, HHT, HTH, THH, TTH, THT, HTT, TTT}

Number of points in the sample space i.e., n(S) = n = 8

(a) Let E be the event of getting all tails.

$\therefore$ E = {TTT}

n(E) = m = 1

$$\therefore \quad P(E) = \frac{m}{n} = \frac{1}{8}$$

(b) Let *E* be the event in which the sum of the numbers obtained is 10 or more.

$\therefore$ E = {(4, 6), (5, 5), (6, 4), (5, 6), (6, 5), (6, 6)}

The number of cases favourable to E = 6

i.e., m = 6

$$\therefore \qquad P(E) = \frac{m}{n} = \frac{6}{36} = \frac{1}{6}$$

***Example* 6:** What is the chance that a leap year selected at random will contain 53 Sundays?

***Solution*:** A leap year has 366 i.e., 52 weeks and 2 days.

The two days may be

(i) (Sunday, Monday)

(ii) (Monday, Tuesday)

(iii) (Tuesday, Wednesday)

(iv) (Wednesday, Thursday)

(v) (Thursday, Friday)

(vi) (Friday, Saturday) and

(vii) (Saturday, Sunday)

Total number of cases = 7

i.e., n = 7 out of the 7 possibilities given above only two are favourable viz (i) and (vii)

∴ Number of favourable cases = 2

i.e., m = 2

Let E denote the event in which a leap year will have 53 Sundays.

$$\therefore \qquad P(E) = \frac{m}{n} = \frac{2}{7}$$

***Example* 7:** A single card is drawn from an ordinary pack of 52 cards. Find the probability that

(a) The card is a king

(b) The card is a heart

(c) The card is a face card

Solution: One card is drawn from 52 cards in 52 ways

∴ Number of points in the sample space 52

n (S) = n = 52

(a) Number of kings in a pack = 4

Number of ways a king can be drawn from 4 kings = $4_{C_1} = 4$

m = 4

∴ Probability that the card drawn is a king = P(King)

$$\frac{4}{52} = \frac{1}{13}$$

(b) There are 13 hearts in a pack of cards:

Number of ways a card of hearts can be drawn from the 13 cards $13c_1 = 13$

∴ m =13

Hence, the probability that the card drawn from the pack is a heart

$$= \frac{13}{52} = \frac{1}{4}$$

(c) Number of cards in a pack = 4 kings + 4 queens + 4 jacks = 12

Number of ways in which a face card is drawn from the pack = $12_{C_1} = 12$

∴ Probability that a card drawn from the pack is a face card = $\frac{12}{52} = \frac{3}{13}$

***Example* 8:** A group of scientific men reported 11705 sons and 11527 daughters. If this is for sample from the population, what is the probability that a child to be born will be a boy.

Solution: Total number of cases in which a child is born

= Number of sons + Number of daughters

= 11705 + 11527 = 23232

∴ The probability that a child to be born will be a boy

$$= \frac{11705}{23232}$$

***Example* 9:** If E and $\bar{E}$ denote the happening and not happening of an event and if $P(\bar{E}) = \frac{1}{5}$, find P(E).

***Solution*:** We have $P(\bar{E}) = \frac{1}{5}$

∴ $$P(E) = 1 - P(\bar{E}) = 1 - \frac{1}{5} = \frac{4}{5}$$

***Example* 10:** From a set of 17 cases numbered 1, 2, 3,..., 17 one card is drawn at random. Find the chance that the number on the card is divisible by 3 or 17.

Solution: Number of cards = 17

The number of ways drawing one card from the 17 cards = $17_{C_1} = 17$

$\therefore$ n = 17

Let E be the event in which the card drawn is divisible by 3 or 5

Favourable cases are 3, 5, 6, 9. 10, 12, 15

Number of favourable cases = m = 7

$$P(E) = \frac{m}{n} = \frac{7}{17}$$

***Example* 11:** A bag contains 7 white, 5 black and 4 red balls. If two balls are drawn out random, find the probability that

(i) both balls are black (ii) one ball is black and the other is red

***Solution*:** Total number of balls in the bag

= 7 white + 5 black + 4 red

= 16

The total number of ways of drawing two balls from 16 balls

$$= 16_{C_2} = 120$$

(i) Number of black balls in the bag = 5

Number of ways drawing 2 black balls from the 5 black balls = $5_{C_2} = 10$

The probability of drawing 2 black balls from the bag = $\frac{10}{120} = \frac{1}{12}$

(ii) Number of black balls in the bag = 5

Number of red balls in the bag = 4

Number of ways drawing a black ball and a red ball from the bag

$$= 5_{C_1} \times 4_{C_1} = 5 \times 4 = 20$$

$\therefore$ The probability of drawing a red and a black ball from the bag $= \frac{20}{120} = \frac{1}{6}$

***Example* 12:** In a throw with a pair of dice, what is the chance of throwing a doublet.

***Solution*:** Numbers of dice thrown = 2

$\therefore$ Number of points in the sample spacc = n(S) = n = 6 × 6 – 36

Let E be the event of getting a doublet.

$\therefore$ E = {(1, 1), (2, 2), (3, 3), (4, 4), (5, 5), (6, 6)}

Number of cases favourable to the event E = 6

We have m = 6

$$\therefore \qquad P(E) = \frac{m}{n} = \frac{6}{36} = \frac{1}{6}$$

***Example* 13:** Nine cards are labelled 0, 1, 2, 3, 4, 5, 6, 7, 8. Two cards are drawn and put on a table in a successive order and then the resulting number is read. Find the probability that the number is even.

Solution: The evenness of a number is defined by last digit which must be even. There are five numbers which are even: they are 0, 2, 4, 6, 8.

If the last digit is anyone of the above digits, then the resulting number is even

$\therefore$ Then the required probability is $\dfrac{5_{C_1}}{9_{C_1}} = \dfrac{5}{9}$

***Example* 14:** E and F be events in a sample space S such that P(E) = 0.3, P(F) = 0.2 and $P(E \cap F) = 0.1$. Find $P(\bar{E} \cap F)$ and $P(E \cap \bar{F})$

Solution:
$$F = (E \cup \bar{E}) \cap F = (E \cap F) \cup (\bar{E} \cap F)$$

where $(E \cap F)$ and $(\bar{E} \cap F)$ are mutually exclusive.

$$\therefore \qquad P(F) = (E \cap F) + P(\bar{E} \cap F)$$

$$\text{or} \qquad 0.2 = 0.1 + P(\bar{E} \cap F)$$

$$\text{i.e} \qquad P(\bar{E} \cap F) = 0.1$$

Similarly, we have

$$E = (E \cap F) \cap (E \cap \bar{F})$$

Where $E \cap F$ and $E \cap \bar{F}$ are mutually exclusive.

$$\therefore \qquad P(E) = P(E \cap F) + P(E \cap \bar{F})$$

$$\text{or} \qquad 0.3 = 0.1 + P(E \cap \bar{F})$$

$$\text{i.e} \qquad P(E \cap \bar{F}) = 0.2$$

1.8 Odds in Favour and Odd against an Event

Let S be a sample space and A be an event of S. Then $P(A) : P(A^C)$ is the odds in favour of the event A and $P(A^C) : P(A)$ is odds against the event A. If $P(A) = m/n$, then $P(A^C)$ i.e., $P(\bar{A}) = (n - m)/n$

$\therefore$ The odds is favour of the event A is

$$m/n : (n - m)/n$$

i.e., $$m : n - m$$

and the odds against the event is $n - m : m$

If the odds in favour of an event A are a to b (i.e., a : b)

Then $$P(A) = P(A^C) = a : b$$

i.e., $$\frac{P(A)}{P(A^C)} = \frac{a}{b}$$

$$\Rightarrow \quad b\,P(A) = a\,P(A^C)$$

$$\Rightarrow \quad b\,P(A) = a\,(1 - P(A))$$

$$\Rightarrow \quad b\,P(A) = a - a\,P(A)$$

$$\Rightarrow \quad a\,P(A) + b\,P(A) = a$$

$$\Rightarrow \quad (a + b)\,P(A) = a$$

$$\therefore \quad P(A^C) = \frac{a}{a+b}$$

Similarly, we can prove that

$$P(A^C) = \frac{b}{a+b}$$

***Example* 1:** If the odds against a certain event are given as 7 to 3, what is the probability of the event?

***Solution*:** We have $P(A^C) : P(A) = 7 : 3$

$$\therefore \quad P(A^C) = \frac{7}{7+3} = \frac{7}{10}$$

and, $$P(A) = 1 - P(A^C) = 1 - \frac{7}{10} = \frac{3}{10}$$

***Example* 2:** If the dice are rolled, find the odds in favour of throwing a sum of 8.

Solution: Let E be the event in which the sum obtained is 8.

Favourable cases are: (2, 6), (3, 5), (4, 4), (5, 3), (6, 2)

Number of favourable cases = 5

$\therefore$ m = 5

Number of points in the sample spaces = 6 × 6 = 36

$$\therefore \qquad P(E) = \frac{5}{36} \text{ and } P(E^C) = 1 - \frac{5}{36} = \frac{31}{36}$$

$$P(E) : P(E^C) = 5/36 : 31/36 = 5 : 31$$

$\therefore$ Odd in favour of throwing a sum of 8 is 5 to 31

Exercise 1.1

1. Define the terms:

(a) Simple event (b) Event

(c) Complementary event (d) Mutually exclusive event

Give Examples.

2. Define the terms

(i) Probability (ii) Impossible event (iii) Certain event

3. What is the probability of getting a head on one toss of coin'?

Ans. $\frac{1}{2}$

4. From a well-shuffled deck of cards. If a card is drawn, find the probability that it is an honours card 5/13.

5. A cubical die is thrown. Find the probability of obtaining an odd number.

Ans. $\frac{1}{2}$

6. A coin is tossed twice. Find the probability of getting (i) one tail, (ii) two tails, (iii) at least one head (iv) at least one tail.

Ans. (i) 1/2 (ii) 1/4 (iii) 3/4 (iv) 3/4

7. Three coins are tossed. Find the probability of getting at least one head.

Ans. 7/8

8. What is the probability of getting a number greater than 3 when a die is rolled once?

Ans. 1/2

9. Find the probability of obtaining a score of 8 with 2 dice in a single throw.

Ans. 5/36

10. Two dice are tossed. Find the chance that the sum of the numbers obtained is 7.

Ans. 1/6

11. If a die is thrown, what is the probability that the upper face shows

(a) 5 dots, (b) more than 5 dots (c) an even number of dots

Ans. (a) 1/6 (b) 1/6 (c) 1/2

12. When two dice are rolled, find the probability that the total score on the two dice show up even numbers.

Ans. 7/12

13. When two unbiased dice are rolled simultaneously. what is probability that both dice show up even numbers.

Ans. 1/4

14. There are p white balls and q black balls in an urn. A ball is drawn at random from the urn. Find the probability that the ball is also white.

Ans. $p/p + q$

15. A box contains 3 red and 4 yellow balls. Two balls are drawn from the box at random. What is the probability that the two balls are of different colours.

Ans. 2/7

16. When an unbiased coin is tossed five times, find the probability of getting 'Head' at least once.

Ans. 31/32

17. From a set of 17 cards 1, 2, 3, …, 17, one card is drawn at random. Find the chance that its number is divisible by 3 or 7.

Ans. 6/17

18. Dialing a telephone an old man forgets the last two digits; remembering only that these are different dialled at random. Find the probability that the number is dialled correctly.

Ans. 1/90

19. Find the probability that in a family of 4 children there will be at least one boy.

Ans. 15/16

20. Three bulbs are chosen at random from 15 bulbs of which 5 are defective. Find the probability that none is defective.

Ans. 24/91

21. The population of the amount of 500 personal loans made by a bank during the year 1999 can be described as follows.

Amount of loan in rupees			
under 2000	2000 – 3999	4000 – 6999	7000 or more
24	102	290	84

for the purpose of checking accuracy of the banks records an auditor will randomly select one of these loans for inspection (where each loan has an equal chance of being selected)

(a) What is the probability that the loan selected will be Rs. 7,000 or more?

(b) What is the probability that the loan will be less than Rs. 4,000?

Ans. (a) 0.168 (b) 0.252

22. From 30 tickets marked with the first numbers, one ticket is drawn at random. Find the chance that it is a multiple of 5 or 7.

Ans. 1/3

23. A man's pocket contains 5 fifty paise coins, 4 twenty five paise coins and ten paise coins, A boy is asked to draw two coins at random. What is probability of the boy drawing maximum possible amount?

Ans. $5_{C_2} / 13_{C_2}$

***Hint*:** To get the maximum possible amount, the boy should draw 2 fifty paise coins, Therefore, the required probability is $5_{C_2} / 13_{C_2}$.

24. If a pack of cards is distributed among four people A, B, C and D, what is the probability that A may get the cards of the same colour (suit).

Ans. $4_{C_1} / 52_{C_{13}}$

25. A card is drawn from a pocket of 100 cards numbered 1 to 100. Find the probability of drawing a number which is a square.

Ans. 1/10

26. A card is drawn from a pocket of 100 cards numbered 1 to 100. Find the probability of drawing a number divisible by 13.

Ans. 7/100

27. A die is rolled. Find the probability of

(a) getting 4 (b) getting a number greater than 4

Ans. (a) 1/6 (b) 2/6 = 1/3

28. In a single throw with two dice, find the probability of throwing 11.

Ans. 1/18

29. An unbiased coin is tossed five times. Find the probability of getting at least one tail. Also find the odds in favour of getting at least one tail.

Ans. 31/32; 31 : 1

30. Three cards are drawn from a pack of cards. Find the chance that they are an ace, a king and a queen.

Ans. $4_{C_1}.4_{C_1}.4_{C_1} / 52_{C_3} = 64 / 52_{C_3}$

31. If odds in favour of an event be 3 : 5, find the probability of occurrence of the event.

Ans. 3/8

32. If odds against an event is 3 : 4, find the probability of occurrence of this event.

Ans. 4/7

33. A bag contains 5 green and 7 red balls. Two balls are drawn at random from the bag. What is probability the one is green and the other is red?

Ans. 35/66

34. In a lottery, there are 10 prizes and 25 blanks. Find the probability of getting a prize.

Ans. 2/7

35. A bag contains 4 white and 5 black balls. A ball is drawn at random from the bag. Find the probability that the ball drawn is white.

Ans. 4/9

36. A bag contains 8 red and 5 white balls. Three balls are drawn at random. Find the probability that–

(i) all the three balls are white (ii) all the three balls are red

(iii) one ball is red and two balls are white

Ans. (i) 5/143 (ii) 28/143 (iii) 40/143

37. A child who cannot read plays with blocks labelled with letters of the alphabet. He takes five blocks from which the word "table" is formed. Then **he** scatters them in an arbitrary fashion. Find the probability that he will again **form** the same word.

Ans. 1/120

38. A box contains n enumerated articles. All the articles are taken out one by one at random. Find the probability that the number of the selected balls are successive: 1, 2, 3, ..., n.

Ans. 1/n!

39. There are a white and b black balls in an urn. A ball is drawn from the urn and put aside. The ball is white. Then one more ball is drawn. Find the probability that the ball is also white.

Ans. (a – 1)/(a + b – 1)

40. There are two boxes containing standard elements for replacement. The first box contains a sound elements and b faulty ones and the second box contains c second a faulty elements. Find the probability that?

(i) both elements are sound

(ii) the two elements are of different quality

(iii) both elements are faulty

Ans. (i) ac/(a + b) (c + d) (ii) (ad + bc)/(a + b)(c + d) (iii) bd/(a + b)(c + d)

1.9 Axioms of Probability

Let S be a sample space, E be the class of events and let P be a real valued function defined on E. Then P is called a probability function. P(A) is called the probability of event A if the following axioms hold.

P_1: For event A : $0 \leq P(A) \leq 1$

P_2: $P(S) = 1$

P_3: If A and B are mutually exclusive events, then

$$P(A \cup B) = P(A) + P(B)$$

P_4: If $A_1, A_2, \ldots,$ is a sequence of mutually exclusive events, then

$$P(A_1 \cup A_2 \cup \ldots) = P(A_1) + P(A_2) + \ldots$$

***Theorem* 1.1**: If ϕ denotes an impossible event, then

$P(\phi) = 0$

***Proof*:** Let S be a sample space and A be any event of S

Then $A \cap \phi = \phi$ and $A \cup \phi = A$

$\therefore \quad P(A \cup \phi) = P(A)$

$\Rightarrow \quad P(A) + P(\phi) = P(A)$

$\Rightarrow \quad P(\phi) = 0$

***Theorem* 1.2:** If A^C is the complement of an event S then

$$P(A^C) = 1 - P(A)$$ [JNTU, 2005, 2008]

***Proof*:** Let A be an event of S. Then we have

$$A \cup A^C = S$$

A and $S - A = A^C$ are mutually exclusive events

$\therefore \quad P(A \cup A^C) = P(S)$

$\Rightarrow \quad P(A) + P(A^C) = 1$

$\Rightarrow \quad P(A^C) = 1 - P(A)$

***Theorem* 1.3:** If $A \subseteq B$ then $P(A) \leq P(B)$

***Proof*:** B can be written as

$$B = A + (B - A)$$

where A and B – A are mutually exclusive

$$P(B) = P(A) + P(B - A)$$

$\Rightarrow \quad P(B) - P(A) \geq 0$

$\Rightarrow \quad P(B) \geq P(A)$

i.e., $\quad P(A) \leq P(B)$

***Theorem* 1.4:** If A and B are any two events of S

Then $\quad P(A - B) = P(A) - P(A \cap B)$

***Proof*:** A can be written as the union of two mutually exclusive event A – B and $A \cap B$ such that

$$A = (A - B) \cup (A \cap B), \text{ therefore}$$

$$P(A) = P(A - B) + P(A \cap B)$$

i.e $\quad P(A) - P(A \cap B) = P(A - B)$

Hence, proved

The probabilities of compound events can be calculated from the probabilities of simpler events, using two basic rules of probability, namely i) Addition rule and (ii) Multiplication rule. These rules are called fundamental theorems of probability.

***Theorem* 1.5** (Addition theorem): If A and B are arbitrary events in a sample space S, then

$$P(A \text{ or } B) = P(A \cup B) = P(A) + P(B) - P(A \cap B)$$

[JNTU 2004, 2005, 2006, 2007]

***Proof*:** The event $A \cup B$ can be decomposed into two mutually exclusive events $A - B$ and B as follows.

$$A \cup B = (A - B) \cup B$$

$$\therefore \quad P(A \cup B) = P(A - B) + P(B)$$

$$\Rightarrow \quad P(A \cup B) = P(A) - P(A \cap B) + P(B)$$

$$\left[\because A - B = A - (A \cap B)\right]$$

$$\Rightarrow \quad P(A \cup B) = P(A) + P(B) - P(A \cap B)$$

Addition theorem for mutually exclusive events

***Theorem* 1.6**: If A and B are mutually exclusive events in a sample space, then

$$P(A \cup B) = P(A) + P(B)$$

***Proof*:** If A and B are mutually exclusive, then we have

$$P(A \cap B) = 0$$

We can write

$$P(A \cup B) = P(A) + P(B) - P(A \cap B), \qquad \text{(Th. 1.5)}$$

$$\Rightarrow \quad P(A \cup B) = P(A) + P(B)$$

***Corollary*:** For any events A, B and C

$$P(A \cup B \cup C) = P(A) + P(B) + P(C) - P(A \cap B) - P(B \cap C)$$
$$-P(C \cap A) + P(A \cap B \cap C)$$

[JNTU 2005]

***Proof*:** $P(A \cup B \cup C) = P\left[A \cup (B \cup C)\right]$

$$= P(A) + P(B \cup C) - P\left[A \cap (B \cup C)\right]$$

$$= P(A) + \left[P(B) + P(C) - P(B \cap C)\right] - P\left[(A \cap B) \cup (A \cap C)\right]$$

$$= P(A)+P(B)+P(C)-P(B\cap C)-\left[P(A\cap B)+P(A\cap C)P((A\cap B)\cap(A\cap C))\right]$$
$$= P(A)+P(B)+P(C)-P(B\cap C)-P(A\cap B)-P(A\cap C)+P(A\cap B\cap C)$$
$$= P(A)+P(B)+P(C)-P(A\cap B)-P(B\cap C)-P(C\cap A)+P(A\cap B\cap C)$$

Note:

(i) If A, B and C are mutually exclusive, then

$$P(A\cup B\cup C)=P(A)+P(B)+P(C)$$

(ii) If A_1, A_2, …, A_n are mutually exclusive, thert

$$P(A_1\cup A_2\cup\ldots\cup A_n)=P(A_1)+P(A_2)+\ldots+P(A_n)$$

***Example* 1**: The probability that at least one of the events A and B occur is 0.7 and they occur simultaneously is 0.2. Find $P(A^C) + P(B^C)$

Solution: We have $P(A \cup B) = 0.7$ and $P(A \cap B) = 0.2$

By addition theorem

$$P(A\cup B)=P(A)+P(B)-P(A\cap B)$$

$\Rightarrow$ $\quad 0.7 = 1 - P(A^C) + 1 - P(B^C) - 0.2$

or $\quad 0.7 = 2 - [P(A^C) + P(B^C)] - 0.2$

hence $\quad P(A^C) + P(B^C) = 2 - 0.7 - 0.2 = 1.1$

***Example* 2:** Two events A and B have probabilities 0.25 and 0.50 respectively. The probability that both A and B occur is 0.14. Find the probability that neither A nor B occurs.

Solution: We have $P(A) = 0.25$, $P(B) = 0.50$, and $P(A \cap B) = 0.14$

$$P(A\cup B)=P(A)+P(B)-P(A\cap B)$$
$$= 0.25 + 0.50 - 0.14$$
$$= 0.61$$

$\therefore$
$$P(A^C\cap B^C)=P\left[(A\cup B)^C\right]=1-P(A\cup B)$$
$$= 1 - 0.61$$
$$= 0.39$$

***Example* 3:** If $P(A)=\frac{3}{8}$, P(B) = $\frac{1}{2}$, and $P(A\cap B)=\frac{1}{4}$, then find

(i) $P(A\cup B)$ (ii) $P(\bar{A})$ (iii) $P(\bar{B})$ (iv) $P(A^C\cap B^C)$

Solution:

(i) $P(A\cup B)=P(A)+P(B)-P(A\cap B)$

$$=\frac{3}{8}+\frac{1}{2}-\frac{1}{4}=\frac{5}{8}$$

(ii) $P(A^C)=1-P(A)=1-\frac{3}{8}=\frac{5}{8}$

(iii) $P(B^C)=1-P(B)=1-\frac{1}{2}=\frac{1}{2}$

(iv) $P(A^C\cap B^C)=P\left[(A\cup B)^C\right]$

$$=1-P(A\cup B)$$

$$=1-\frac{5}{8}=\frac{3}{8}$$

***Example* 4:** If A and B are mutually exclusive events such that P(B) =2P(A), find P(A).

Solution: A and B are mutually exclusive, P(B) = 2P(A), $A \cup B = S$

∴ $P(S) = P(A \cup B)$

i.e $1 = P(A) + P(B) = P(A) + 2P(A)$

or $3P(A) = 1$

Hence $P(A) = 1/3$

***Example* 5:** A bag contains 4 red, 6 black and 7 green balls. A ball is drawn at random from the bag. What is the probability that it is either a red or a black ball?

Solution: Total number of balls in the bag = 4 red + 6 black + 7 green = 17

Number of ways of drawing a ball from 17 balls = 17_{C_1}

∴ n(S) = 17

Let A denote the event of drawing a red ball and B denote the event of drawing a black ball from the bag.

Number of ways of drawing a red ball from the four red balls = $4_{C_1} = 4$

$$\therefore \qquad P(A) = \frac{4}{17}$$

Number of ways of drawing a black ball from the six black balls = $6_{C_1} = 6$

$$\therefore \qquad P(B) = \frac{6}{17}$$

The event A and B are mutually exclusive

$$\therefore \qquad P(A \cup B) = P(A) + P(B) = \frac{4}{17} + \frac{6}{17} = \frac{10}{17}$$

***Example* 6:** From a pack two cards are drawn at random. What is the probability that either both are black or both Aces?

Solution: Two cards can be drawn from pack in 52_{C_2} different ways

$\therefore$ Number of points in the sample space = 52_{C_2}

Let A be the event of the drawing 2 black cards and B denote the event of drawing 2 Aces. There are 26 black cards in the pack. The number of ways in which 2 black cards can be drawn $= 26_{C_2}$

There are 4 Aces in the pack.

Number of ways in which 2 aces can be drawn from 4 aces = 4_{C_2}

$$\therefore \qquad P(A) = \frac{26_{C_2}}{52_{C_2}}, \text{ and } P(B) = \frac{4_{C_2}}{52_{C_2}}$$

There are 2 black aces in the pack, and the 2 aces can be drawn 2_{C_2} ways.

$$\therefore \qquad P(A \cap B) = \frac{2_{C_2}}{52_{C_2}} = \frac{1}{52_{C_2}}$$

$$P(A \cup B) = P(A) + P(B) - P(A \cap B)$$

$$= \frac{26_{C_2}}{52_{C_2}} + \frac{4_{C_2}}{52_{C_2}} - \frac{1}{52_{C_2}}$$

$$= \frac{165}{663}$$

***Example* 7:** A, B, C are mutually exclusive and exhaustive events associated with a random experiment. If P(B) = $\frac{3}{2}$ P(A) and P(C) = $\frac{1}{2}$ P(B), then find P(A).

Solution: A, B, C are mutually exclusive and exhaustive events. Therefore, we have

$$S = A \cup B \cup C$$

and $$P(S) = P(A) + P(B) + P(C)$$

i.e $$1 = P(A) + \frac{3}{2}P(A) + \frac{1}{2}P(B)$$

or $$1 = P(A) + \frac{3}{2}P(A) + \frac{1}{2}.\frac{3}{2}P(A)$$

or $$1 = \frac{13P(A)}{4}$$

Hence $$P(A) = \frac{4}{13}$$

Exercise 1.2

1. Let A and B be events with P(A) =0.6, P(B) = 0.3 and P(A $\cap$ B) = 0.2. Find $P(A \cup B)$.

Ans. 0.7

2. A single card is drawn from an ordinary deck of 52 cards. Find the probability that the card drawn is a face card or a heart.

Ans. 11/16

3. A card is drawn at random from a pack. Find the chance that the card drawn is either a spade or a diamond.

Ans. 1/2

4. Card is drawn at random from a pack of cards. Find the chance that the card drawn is either a black card or an ace.

Ans. 7/13

5. Find the probability of getting a king or a queen in a single draw from a well-shuffled pack of cards.

Ans. 2/13

6. In a single throw of three dice, find the probability of getting a total of 17 or 18.

Ans. 1/54

7. A card is drawn at random from a well-shuffled pack of 52 cards. Find the probability that it is neither an ace nor a king.

Ans. 11/ 13

8. A card is drawn at random from a pack 52 cards. Find the probability of drawing a jack, queen or a king.

Ans. 3/13

9. If A and B be events in a sample space S such that. P(A) = 0.5, P(B) = 0.3 and $P(A \cap B) = 0.2$, then find $P(A \cup B)$

Ans. 0.6

10. If A and B be mutually exclusive events in a sample space S such that P(A) = 0.4 and P(B) = 0.5, the find

(a) $P(A \cup B)$ (b) $P(\bar{A})$ (c) $P(\bar{B})$ (d) $P(\bar{A} \cap \bar{B})$

Ans. (a) 0.9 (b) 0.6 (c) 0.5 (d) 0.1

11. One number is chosen from numbers 1 to 100. Find the probability that it is divisible by 4 or 6.

Ans. 33/100

12. In a class of 200 students, 120 take mathematics, 110 take physics and 40 take both mathematics and physics. If a student is selected at random from this class find the probability that the student chosen takes mathematics or physics.

Ans. 19/20

13. A drawer contains 50 bolts and 150 nuts. Half of the bolts and half of the nuts are rusted. If one item is chosen at random, what is the probability that it is rusted or a bolt?

Ans. 5/8

14. In a certain college 25% of the students failed in mathematics, 15% failed in chemistry and 10% failed in both mathematics and chemistry. A student is selected at random. What is the probability that he failed in mathematics or chemistry?

Ans. 0.30

15. One ticket is drawn at random from a bag containing 25 tickets numbered 1 to 25. Find the probability that it is a multiple of 5 or 7.

Ans. 8/25

16. A bag contains 5 green, 8 red and 6 white balls. If a ball is drawn from the bag, find the chance that the ball drawn is either red or white.

Ans. 14/19

17. A bag contains 4 green, 6 black and 9 white balls. A ball is drawn at random. What is the probability that it is either a green or a black ball?

Ans. 10/19

18. In a throw of two dice, find the probability that neither a doublet nor a total of 9 will appear.

Ans. 13/8

19. Two cards are selected at random from 10 cards numbered 1 to 10. Find the probability p that the turn is odd if the

(i) Two cards are drawn simultaneously

(ii) Two cards are drawn one after the other without replacement

(iii) Two cards are drawn one after the other with replacement

Ans. (i) $\frac{5_{C_1}.5_{C_1}}{10_{C_2}}$ (ii) $\frac{5}{9}$ (iii) $\frac{1}{2}$

20. A and B throw alternatively with a pair of ordinary dice. A wins if he throws 6 before B throws 7 and B wins if he throws 7 before A throws 6. If A begins find his chance of winning.

Ans. 30/61

1.10 Conditional Probability

Let A and B denote the events associated with a random experiment. Then the probability of occurrence of B, under the condition that A has already occurred and P(A) ≠ 0, is called the conditional probability of *B* relative to *A*. It is denoted by P(B/A).

In particular, if S is a finite equiprobable space, A and B are two events of S then

$$P(B \cap A) = \frac{n(B \cap A)}{n(S)}, \quad P(B) = \frac{n(B)}{n(S)}$$

$$\therefore \quad P(B/A) = \frac{n(A \cap B)}{n(A)} \qquad (\because n(B \cap A) = n(A \cap B))$$

$$= \frac{\text{Number of ways A and B occur}}{\text{Number of ways A can occur}} = \frac{P(A \cap B)}{P(A)}$$

1.11 Independent and Dependent Events

Consider an experiment in which a coin is tossed twice. The result in the second throw in this experiment is in no way affected by the result in the first throw i.e., the results of the events have no effect on each other. Such events are called independent events.

If A and B are independent events, then P(B/A) = P(B) and P(A/B) = P(A) i.e., A and B are independent, whenever one is independent of the other.

***Definition* 1:** Two events are independent, if the occurrence of one does not depend upon the occurrence of the other.

***Definition* 2:** If two events A and B are not independent, then they are called dependent events.

Theorem (Multiplication Theorem)

Let A and B be two events associated with the same random experiment. Then

$$P(A \cap B) = P(A)P(B/A) \qquad \text{where } P(A) \neq 0$$

***Proof*:** From the definition

$$P(B/A) = \frac{P(B \cap A)}{P(A)}$$

$$\Rightarrow \qquad P(B \cap A) = P(A)P(B/A)$$

$$\text{or,} \qquad P(A \cap B) = P(A)P(B/A) \qquad (\because A \cap B = B \cap A)$$

Corollary

If $A_1, A_2, \ldots, A_n$ are n events related to an experiment, then

$$P(A_1 \cap A_2 \cap \ldots \cap A_n) = P(A_1)P(A_2/A_1)P(A_3/A_1 \cap A_2)\ldots P(A_n/A_1 \cap A_2 \cap \ldots A_{n-1})$$

***Theorem* 1.7:** Two events A and B associated with the same sample space or a random experiment are independent if and only if

$$P(A \cap B) = P(A) \cap P(B)$$

Note: If A and B are mutually exclusive, then $P(A \cap B) = 0$. In general, mutually exclusive events can never be independent.

Definition: Two events A and B are said to be dependent if $P(A \cap B) \neq P(A \cap B)$ and $P(A \cap B) \neq 0$.

Example: Consider a trial in which two cards are drawn in succession. If the first card is not replaced, the probability that the first drawn card to be a king is $\frac{4}{52}$

When the card is not replaced, the number of cards remaining in the pack for second draw is (52 – 1) = 51.

$\therefore$ The probability that the second card drawn to be a queen is $\frac{4}{52}$

Here, the probability is affected, this is a case of dependent events.

Addition theorem for independent events.

***Theorem* 1.8:**

If $A_1, A_2, \ldots, A_n$ are n independent events, then

$$P(A_1 \cup A_2 \cup \ldots \cup A_n) = 1 - P(A_1^C)P(A_2^C)\ldots P(A_n^C)$$

***Example* 1:** If A and B are two independent events in a sample space, then show that

(i) $P(A \cup B) = P(A) + P(B) - P(A)P(B)$

(ii) A and B^C are independent

(iii) A^C and B are independent

(iv) A^C and B^C are independent

Solution: A and B are independent

$\therefore$ $$P(A \cap B) = P(A)P(B)$$

(i) $$P(A \cup B) = P(A) + P(B) - P(A \cap B)$$

$$= P(A) + P(B) - P(A)\, P(B)$$

(ii) $$P(A \cap B^C) = P(A) - P(A \cap B) = P(A) - P(A)P(B)$$

$$= P(A)\,[1 - P(B)] = P(A)\, P(B^C)$$

$\therefore$ A and B^C are independent.

(iii) $$P(A^C \cap B) = P(B) - P(A \cap B) = P(B) - P(A)P(B)$$

$$= P(B)\,[1 - P(A)] = P(B) - P(A^C)$$

$\therefore$ A^C and B are independent.

(iv)
$$P(A^C \cap B^C) = P(A \cup B)^C$$
$$= 1 - P(A \cup B)$$
$$= 1 - [P(A) + P(B) - P(A)P(B)]$$
$$= 1 - P(A) - P(B) + P(A)P(B)$$
$$= 1[1 - P(A)] - P(B)[1 - P(A)]$$
$$= [1 - P(A)][1 - P(B)]$$
$$= P(A^C)\, P(B^C)$$

$\therefore$ A^C and B^C are independent.

***Example* 2:** Let A and B be independent events such that P(A) = 0.3 and P(B) = 0.4. Find

(i) $P(A \cap B)$ (ii) $P(A \cup B)$ (iii) $P(A^C \cap B)$ (iv) $P(A \cap B^C)$ (v) $P(\bar{A} \cap \bar{B})$

Solution:

(i) A and B are independent

$\therefore$
$$P(A \cap B) = P(A).P(B)$$
$$= (0.3)\,(0.4) = 0.12$$

(ii)
$$P(A \cup B) = P(A) + P(B) - P(A \cap B)$$
$$= 0.3 + 0.4 - 0.12$$
$$= 0.58$$

(iii)
$$P(A^C \cap B) = P(A^C)P(B) = (1 - 0.3)(0.4)$$
$$= (0.7)\,(0.4)$$
$$= 0.28$$

(iv)
$$P(A \cap B^C) = P(A)P(B^C) = P(A)(1 - P(B))$$
$$= (0.3)\,(1 - 0.4)$$
$$= (0.3)\,(0.6) = 0.18$$

(v)
$$P(A^C \cap B^C) = P(A^C)P(B^C) = (1 - P(A))(1 - P(B))$$
$$= (1 - 0.3)\,(1 - 0.4) = (0.7)\,(0.6)$$

Thus
$$P(\bar{A} \cap \bar{B}) = 0.42$$

***Example* 3:** A man and his wife appear for an interview for two posts. The probability of husband's selection is 1/7 and that of wife's selection is 1/5. What is probability that

(a) both of them will be selected

(b) only one of them will be selected

(c) none of them will be selected

(d) at least one of them will be selected

Solution: Let A be the event in which husband is selected and B be the event in which wife is selected.

Then we have

P(A) = 1/7 and P(B) = 1/5

$$\therefore \qquad P\left(A^C\right)=1-P(A)=1-\frac{1}{7}=\frac{6}{7}$$

$$P\left(B^C\right)=1-P(B)=1-\frac{1}{5}=\frac{4}{5}$$

A and B are independent

(a) P(both are selected) = $P(A\cap B)$

$$= P(A)\ P(B) = \frac{1}{7}.\frac{1}{5}=\frac{1}{35}$$

(b) P(only one of them will be selected)

$$=P\left(A\cap B^C\right)+P\left(A^C\cap B\right)$$

$$=P(A)P\left(B^C\right)+P\left(A^C\right)P(B)$$

$$=\frac{1}{7}.\frac{4}{5}+\frac{6}{7}.\frac{1}{5}=\frac{10}{35}=\frac{2}{7}$$

(c) P(none of them is selected) = $P\left(A^C\cap B^C\right)$

$$= P(A^C)\ P(B^C)$$

$$=\frac{6}{7}.\frac{4}{5}=\frac{24}{35}$$

(d) P (at least one of them will be selected)

$$= 1 - P(\text{None will be selected})$$

$$=1-\frac{24}{35}=\frac{11}{35}$$

***Example* 4:** John and Jane took their driving tests today. The probability that John passes the test is 3/5 and the probability that Jane passes the test is 7/10. What is the probability that both pass their driving tests?

Solution: Let A denote the event in which John passes the test and B denote the event in which Jane passes the driving tests

Clearly, A and B are independent events.

We have $P(A)\ \frac{3}{5}$ and $P(B) = \frac{7}{10}$ (given)

$\therefore$ The probability that both pass the driving test

$$= P(A \cap B)$$

$$= P(A)\ P(B) = \frac{3}{5} \cdot \frac{7}{10} = \frac{21}{50}$$

***Example* 5:** A can solve 90 per cent of problems given in a book, and B can solve 70 per cent of the problem. What is the probability that at least one of them will solve a problem selected at random from the book?

Solution: We have

$$P(A) = \frac{90}{100} = 0.9 \text{ and } P(B) = \frac{70}{100} = 0.7$$

$$P(A^C) = 1 - P(A) = 1 - 0.9 = 0.1$$

and, $$P(B^C) = 1 - P(B) = 1 - 0.7 = 0.3$$

A and B are independent events.

$\therefore$ Probability that at least one can solve the problem $= 1 - P(A^C)\ P(B^C)$

$$= 1 - (0.1)\ (0.3)$$

$$= 1 - 0.03$$

$$= 0.9$$

***Example* 6:** An urn contains 4 white and 3 green balls, 2 balls are drawn from the urn one after the other and the ball drawn is not replaced. Find the probability that the first drawn ball is white and the second ball is green.

Solution: Number of balls in the urn = 4 white + 3 green

= 7

Number of white balls = 4

Probability that the first ball drawn is white = 4/7

When the first drawn ball is not replaced, the number of balls remaining in the urn

$= 7 - 1 = 6$

The probability the second ball drawn from the urn is green $= \frac{3}{6} = \frac{1}{2}$

$\therefore$ The required probability $= \frac{4}{7} \cdot \frac{1}{2} = \frac{2}{7}$

***Example* 7:** A bag contains 6 red and 5 black balls. A bail is drawn at random from the bag and without replacing it another ball is drawn from the bag. Find the probability that both the balls drawn are red.

Solution: Total number of balls in the bag = 6 red + 5 black

$= 11$

Let A denote the event of drawing the first red ball and B the event of drawing the second red ball (after the first red ball)

Number of ways of drawing 1 ball from 11 balls $= 11_{C_1} = 11$

The first red ball can be drawn from the 6 red balls in 6_{C_1} ways

$$\therefore \qquad P(A) = \frac{6_{C_1}}{11_{C_1}} = \frac{6}{11}$$

Number of balls remaining after drawing first ball $= 11 - 1 = 10$

Number of ways of drawing 1 ball from the 10 balls $= 10_{C_1} = 10$

Number of red balls remaining in the bag after the event A $= 6 - 1 = 5$

Number of ways drawing 1 red ball from the 5 red balls $= 5_{C_1} = 5$

$$\therefore \qquad P(B/A) = \frac{5}{10} = \frac{1}{2}$$

$$P(A \cap B) = P(A)P(B/A) = \frac{6}{11} \cdot \frac{1}{2} = \frac{3}{11}$$

***Example* 8:** Find the probability of drawing a spade on each of the consecutive draws from a well-shuffled pack of 52 cards without replacement.

Solution: Let A denote the event in which a spade is drawn in the first draw and B denote the event in which a spade is drawn in the second draw.

Number of spades in a pack = 13

$$\therefore \qquad P(A) = \frac{13_{C_1}}{52_{C_1}} = \frac{13}{52} = \frac{1}{4}$$

When the card drawn is not replaced, the number of cards remaining in the pack

$$52 - 1 = 51$$

Number of spades for the second draw = 13 – 1 = 12

$$\therefore \qquad P(B/A) = \frac{12_{C_1}}{51_{C_1}} = \frac{12}{51} = \frac{4}{17}$$

∴ Required probability

$$P(A \cap B) = P(A)P(B/A)$$

$$= \frac{1}{4} \cdot \frac{4}{17} = \frac{1}{17}$$

***Example* 9:** Find the probability of drawing two aces in succession from a pack of 52 cards; if the first drawn card is replaced.

Solution: Let A denote the even in which the first card drawn is an ace and B denote the event in which the card drawn after the event A is an ace. The cards drawn are replaced, therefore, the events A and B are independent.

Number of cards in a pack = 52

We have 4 aces in the pack

$$\therefore \qquad P(A) = \frac{\text{Number of favourable cases}}{\text{Total number of possible cases}}$$

$$= \frac{4}{52} = \frac{1}{13}$$

Numbers of cards in the pack after the first drawn card is replaced = 52

Numbers of aces available for the second draw = 4

$$P(B/A) = P(B) = \frac{4}{52} = \frac{1}{13}$$

Probability of drawing 2 aces in succession with replacement

$$= P(A \cap B)$$

$$= P(A)\,P(B) = \frac{1}{13} \cdot \frac{1}{13} = \frac{1}{169}$$

***Example* 10:** A speaks truth in 60% of the cases and B speaks truth in 70% of the cases. Find the probability that they will say the same thing while describing the same thing.

Solution: Let E_1 denote the event: "A speaks truth"

E_2 denote the event: "B speaks truth"

$\therefore$ $E_1 \cap E_2$ is the event in which both A and B speak truth and, $E_1^C \cap E_2^C$ is the event in which both A and B will not speak truth.

We have

$$P(E_1)\frac{60}{100}=\frac{6}{10},\ P(E_1^C)=\frac{4}{10},\ P(E_2)=\frac{70}{100}=\frac{7}{10},\ P(E_2^C)=\frac{3}{10}$$

$$\therefore \quad P\left[(E_1 \cap E_2)\cup(E_1^C \cap E_2^C)\right]=P(E_1 \cap E_2)+P(E_1^C \cap E_2^C)$$

$$=P(E_1).P(E_2)+P(E_1^C)P(E_2^C)$$

$$=\frac{6}{10}.\frac{7}{10}+\frac{4}{10}.\frac{3}{10}$$

$$=\frac{54}{100}=\frac{27}{50}$$

***Example* 11:** A_1 and A_2 are two events with probability 0.25 and 0.5 corresponding to A_1 and $A_1 \cup A_2$ respectively. Find the probability of A_2 if,

(a) A_1 and A_2 are mutually exclusive

(b) A_1 and A_2 are independent

(c) A_2 contains A_1

Solution: We have $P(A_1) = 0.25$, $P(A_1 \cup A_2) = 0.5$

i.e., $$P(A_1) = \frac{1}{4} \text{ and } P(A_1 \cup A_2) = \frac{1}{4}$$

(a) A_1 and A_2 are mutually exclusive

$$\therefore \quad P(A_1 \cap A_2)=0$$

and, $$P(A_1 \cup A_2)=P(A)+P(A_2)$$

$$\therefore \quad \frac{1}{2}=\frac{1}{4}+P(A_2)$$

or $\frac{1}{2}-\frac{1}{4}=P(A_2)$

hence $P(A_2)=\frac{1}{4}$

(b) A_1 and A_2 are independent

$\therefore$ $P(A_1 \cap A_2)=P(A_1)P(A_2)$

from addition theorem

$$P(A_1 \cup A_2)=P(A_1)+P(A_2)-P(A_1 \cap A_2)$$

or $P(A_1 \cup A_2)=P(A_1)+P(A_2)-P(A_1)P(A_2)$

or $\frac{1}{2}=\frac{1}{4}+P(A_2)-\frac{1}{4}P(A_2)$

or $\frac{1}{2}-\frac{1}{4}=\left(1-\frac{1}{4}\right)P(A_2)$

i.e $\frac{1}{4}=\frac{3}{4}P(A_2)$

hence $P(A_2)=\frac{1}{3}$

(c) A_2 contains A_1

i.e., $A_1 \subseteq A_2$

we have $A_1 \cup A_2 = A_2$

and, $P(A_1 \cup A_2)=P(A_2)=\frac{1}{2}$

Hence, $P(A_2) = \frac{1}{2}$ when $A_1 \leq A_2$.

***Example* 12:** A, B, C are independent events and P(A) = 0.3, P(B) = 0.2 and P(C) = 0.1. Find the probability that at least one of the events happen.

Solution: A, B, C are independent

$\therefore$ A^C, B^C, C^C are also independent

We have P(A) = 0.3, P(B) = 0.2, P(C) = 0.1 (given)

$P(A^C) = 1 - P(A) = 1 - 0.3 = 0.7,$

$$P(B^C) = 1 - P(B) = 1 - 0.2 = 0.8$$

and, $$P(C^C) = 1 - P(C) = 1 - 0.1 = 0.9$$

$\therefore$ $$P\left(A^C \cap B^C \cap C^C\right) = P\left(A^C\right)P\left(B^C\right)P\left(C^C\right)$$

$$= (0.7)\,(0.8)\,(0.9)$$

Probability that at least one of the events happen

$$= 1 - P\left(A^C \cap B^C \cap C^C\right)$$

$$= 1 - (0.7)\,(0.8)\,(0.9)$$

$$= 1 - 0.504$$

$$= 0.496$$

***Example* 13:** If $P\left(A^C \cap B^C\right)$ = 1/3, $P\left(A \cap B\right)$ = 1/2 and P(B) =2 P(A), find P(A).

Solution: $$P\left(A^C \cap B^C\right) = 1/3 \qquad \text{...(given)}$$

$\Rightarrow$ $$P\left(A \cup B\right)^C = 1/3$$

or $$1 - P(A \cup B)^c = 1/3$$

or $$1 - P(A \cup B) = 1/3$$

or $$P\left(A \cup B\right) = 1 - 1/3 = 2/3$$

or $$P\left(A\right) + P\left(B\right) - P\left(A \cup B\right) = 2/3$$

or $$P\left(A\right) + 2P\left(A\right) - \frac{1}{2} = 2/3$$

or $$3P\left(A\right) = \frac{2}{3} + \frac{1}{2}$$

or $$3P\left(A\right) = \frac{7}{6}$$

hence $$P\left(A\right) = \frac{7}{18}$$

***Example* 14:** If A and B are the events having P(A) = $\frac{1}{2}$, P(B) = $\frac{1}{3}$ and $P\left(A \cap B\right) = \frac{1}{4}$, find the following

(a) P(A/B) (b) P(B/A) (c) $P(A^C/B^C)$ (d) $P(B^C/A^C)$

Solution:

(a) $$P(A/B) = \frac{P(A \cap B)}{P(B)} = \frac{1/4}{1/3} = \frac{3}{4}$$

(b) $$P(B/A) = \frac{P(A \cap B)}{P(A)} = \frac{1/4}{1/2} = \frac{1}{2}$$

(c) $$P(A^C \cap B^C) = P(A \cup B)^C = 1 - P(A \cup B)$$

$$= 1 - [P(A) + P(B) - P(A \cap B)]$$

$$= 1 - \left[\frac{1}{2} + \frac{1}{3} - \frac{1}{4}\right] = \frac{5}{12}$$

$\therefore$ $$P(A^C / B^C) = \frac{P(A^C \cap B^C)}{P(B^C)} = \frac{5/12}{1 - P(B)} = \frac{5/12}{1 - 1/3} = \frac{5/12}{2/3} = \frac{5}{8}$$

(d) $$P(B^C / A^C) = \frac{P(A^C \cap B^C)}{P(A^C)} = \frac{5/12}{1 - P(A)} = \frac{5/12}{1 - 1/2} = \frac{5/12}{1/2} = 5/6$$

***Example* 15:** The odds against A solving a problem are 8 to 6 and the odds in favour of B solving the same problem are 14 to 10. What is the probability that if both of them try, the problem will be solved?

***Solution*:** Let E_1 be the event in which A solves the problem and E_2 be the event in which B solves the problem.

We have $$P(E_1^C) : P(E_1) = 8 : 6$$

$\therefore$ $$P(E_1^C) = \frac{8}{8+6} = \frac{8}{14} = \frac{4}{7}$$

and, $$P(E_1) = \frac{6}{8+6} = \frac{6}{14} = \frac{3}{7}$$

and, $$P(E_2^C) = \frac{10}{14+10} = \frac{10}{24} = \frac{5}{12}$$

$$P(E_2) = \frac{14}{14+10} = \frac{14}{24} = \frac{7}{12}$$

E_1 and E_2 are independent therefore E_1^C and E_2^C are also independent.

The probability that none of A and b can solve the problem

$$=P\left(E_1^C \cap E_2^C\right)=P\left(E_1^C\right).P\left(E_2^C\right)$$

$$=\frac{4}{7}.\frac{5}{12}=\frac{5}{21}$$

$\therefore$ The probability that the problem is solved

$$=P\left(E_1 \cup E_2\right)=1-P\left(E_1^C\right)P\left(E_2^C\right)$$

$$=1-\frac{5}{21}$$

$$\therefore\ P\left(E_1 \cup E_2\right)=\frac{16}{21}$$

Exercise 1.3

1. If P(A) = 2/5, P(B) = 1/3 and P(A $\cup$ B) = 1/2, find P(A/B) and P(B/A).

Ans. P(A/B) = 7/10, P(B/A) = $\frac{7}{12}$

2. Given P(A) = 1/4, P(B/A) = 1/2 and P(A/B) = 1/4, Find if

(i) A and B are mutually exclusive

(ii) A and B are independent

Ans. (i) Not mutually exclusive (ii) A and B are independent

3. If A and B are independent events and P(A) = 2/3, P(B) = 3/5, find $P(A \cup B)$.

Ans. 13/1 5

4. In a school 25% of the students failed in first language, 15% of the students failed in second language and 10% of the students failed in both.

If a student is selected at random find the probability that

(a) he failed in first language if he had failed in second language

(b) he failed in second language if he failed in first language

(c) he failed in either of the two languages

Ans. (a) $\frac{2}{3}$ (b) $\frac{2}{5}$ (c) $\frac{3}{10}$

5. Find the probability of drawing 4 white and 2 black balls in two drawings in succession without replacement from a bag containing 1 red, 4 black and 6 white balls.

Ans. $\dfrac{6_{C_4}}{11_{C_4}} \cdot \dfrac{4_{C_2}}{7_{C_2}}$

6. There are 6 red and 5 black balls in a bag. A ball is drawn from the bag at random and without replacing it another ball is drawn. What is the probability that both the balls drawn may be red?

Ans. $\dfrac{6_{C_1}}{11_{C_1}} \cdot \dfrac{5_{C_1}}{10_{C_1}}$

7. An urn contains 2 white and 4 black balls. A second urn contains 5 white and 7 black balls. A ball is transferred from A to B and then a ball is drawn from B. Find the probability that it is white.

Ans. 16/39

***Hint*:** Probability when the transferred ball is white = 2/13

Probability when the transferred ball is black = 10/39

Required probability = $\dfrac{2}{13} + \dfrac{10}{39} = 16/39$

8. Two sets of candidates are competing for the positions on the Board of Directors of a company. The probabilities that the first and second sets will win are 0.6 and 0.4 respectively. If the first set wins, the probability of introducing a new product is 0.8 and the corresponding probability if the second set wins is 0.3. What is the probability that the new product is introduced?

Ans. 0.60

9. A solar water heater manufacturing company consists of two parts, namely the heating panel and the insulated tank. In the manufacturing process, 9% are likely to be defective in the panel and 5% are likely to be defective in the insulated tank. If an assembled unit is installed in a house, what is the probability that it is not defective.

Ans. 0.8645

10. A bag contains 19 tickets; numbered from 1 to 19. A ticket is drawn and then another ticket is drawn without replacement. Find the probability that both tickets show even numbers.

Ans. 4/9

11. If P(A) = 0.4, P(B) = p, P(A ∪ B) = 0.6 and A, B are given to be independent events, find the value of p.

Ans. 1/3

12. A purse contains 2 silver and 4 copper coins. A second purse contains 4 silver and 3 copper coins. If a coin is pulled out at random from one of the two purses, what is the probability that it is a silver coin.

Ans. 19/42

13. A bag contains 4 white, 7 black and 5 red balls. Three balls are drawn one after another without replacement. Find the probability that the ball drawn are white, black and red, respectively.

Ans. 1/24

14. There are three men aged 60, 65 and 70 years. The probability to live 5 years more is 0.8 for a 60–year old, 0.6 for a 65–year old and 0.3 for 70–year old person. Find the probability that at least two of the three will remain alive 5 years hence.

Ans. 0.612

15. A candidate is selected for interview for three posts. For the first post, there are 3 candidates; for the second post there are 4 candidates and for the third post there are 2 candidates. What is the chance of his getting selected at least for one post?

Ans. 3/4

1.12 Bayes's Theorem

In this section we discuss total probability formula and Bayes's theorem which is one of the most interesting applications of the probability theory.

1.12.1 Total Probability Formula

If E_1, E_2, …E_n are mutually exclusive events (hypotheses) of which one must occur, then for event A

$$P(A) = P(E_1).P(A/E_1) + P(E_2)P(A/E_2) + ... + P(E_n).P(A/E_n)$$

i.e., $$P(A) = \sum_{i=1}^{n} P(E_i)P(A/E_i) \quad .....(1)$$

where $P(E_i)$ is the probability of event E_1, and $P(A/E_i)$ is the conditional probability of the event A Formula (1) is known as the total probability formula (or rule of Elimination) E_1, E_2, …E_n are n mutually exclusive events which can lead to event A.

***Example* 1:** A purse contains 2 silver and 4 copper coins. A second purse contains 4 silver and 3 copper coins. If a coin is pulled out at random from one of the two purses, what is the probability that it is a silver coin.

Solution: Assume that an event A {coin pulled out is a silver coin}

E_1 = {the first purse is selected}

E_2 = {the second purse is selected}

We have

$$P(E_1)=\frac{1}{2} \text{ and } P(E_2)=\frac{1}{2}$$

$$P(A/E_1)=\frac{2}{6}=\frac{1}{3} \text{ and } P(A/E_2)=\frac{4}{7}$$

By the total probability formula, we have

$$P(A)=P(E_1)P(A/E_1)+P(E_2)P(A/E_2)$$

$$=\frac{1}{2}.\frac{1}{3}+\frac{1}{2}.\frac{4}{7}$$

$$=\frac{1}{6}+\frac{2}{7}=\frac{7+12}{42}=\frac{19}{42}$$

$\therefore$ The required probability $=\dfrac{19}{42}$

***Example* 2:** There are three identical urns. The first urn contains a white and b black balls. The second urn contains c white and d black balls and the third urn contains only white balls. A ball is drawn at random from one of the urns. Find the probability that the ball is white.

Solution:

Let A = {an appearance of white ball}

E_1 = {the first urn is selected}

E_2 = {the second urn is selected}

and, E_3 = {the third urn is selected}

We have
$$P(E_1)=\frac{1}{3},\ P(E_2)=\frac{1}{3},\ P(E_3)=\frac{1}{3}$$

$$P(A/E_1)=\frac{a}{a+b},\ P(A/E_2)=\frac{c}{c+d} \text{ and } P(A/E_3)=1$$

By total probability formula, we have

$$P(A) = P(E_1)P(A/E_1) + P(E_2)P(A/E_2) + P(E_3)P(A/E_3)$$

$$= \frac{1}{3}.\frac{a}{a+b} + \frac{1}{3}\frac{c}{c+d} + \frac{1}{3}.1$$

$$= \frac{1}{3}\left[\frac{a}{a+b} + \frac{c}{c+d} + 1\right]$$

1.12.2 Bayes's Theorem

The theorem was originally developed by Rev. Thomas Bayes in 1763. It gives a probability rule relating a posteriori probability to a priori probability. Bayes's theorem is also called inverse probability theorem. The theorem makes it possible to revise probabilities, when new information concerning a random experiment is available

Theorem

Let E_1, E_2, ..., E_n be n mutually exclusive and exhaustive events with non-zero probabilities of a random experiment. If A is any arbitrary event (or the sample space) of the same experiment with P(A) > 0, then

$$P(E_i / A) = \frac{P(E_i)P(A/E_i)}{\sum_{i=1}^{n} P(E_i)P(A/E_i)} \quad (1 \le i \le n)$$

Proof: Let *S* be the sample space of the random experiment, then

$$S = E_1 \cup E_2 \cup \ldots \cup E_n$$

We have $\quad A = S \cap A = [E_1 \cup E_2 \cup \ldots \cup E_n] \cap A$

where $E_1 \cap A$, $E_2 \cap A$, ..., $E_n \cap A$ are mutually exclusive

$$\therefore \quad P(A) = (E_1 \cap A) + P(E_2 \cap A) + \ldots + P(E_n \cap A)$$

(by addition theorem)

$$= P(E_1)P(A/E_1) + P(E_2)P(A/E_2) + \ldots + P(E_n)P(A/E_n)$$

$$= \sum_{i=1}^{n} P(E_i)P(A/E_i) \qquad (1)$$

Now $\quad P(E_i / A) = \dfrac{P(A \cap E_i)}{P(A)}$

$$= \frac{P(E_i \cap A)}{P(A)}$$

$$\therefore \quad P(E_i / A) = \frac{P(E_i)P(A/E_i)}{\sum_{i=1}^{n} P(E_i)P(A/E_i)} \qquad \text{[from (1)]}$$

Note: The probabilities $P(E_1)$, $P(E_2)$, …$P(E_n)$ are called a priori, or prior probabilities and the probabilities $P(E_1/A)$, $P(E_2/A)$, ..., $P(E_n/A)$ are called a posterior or inverse probabilities. Posterior probabilities are also called revised probabilities and are always conditional probabilities.

By using Bayes's rule, we can convert a priori (unconditional) probability with a posterior (conditional) probability. The notions of "priori" and "posterior" in Bayes's theorem are relative to a sample outcome.

***Example* 1:** Assume that a factory has two machines. Past records show that machine I produces 20% of the items of output and machine II produces 80% the items. Further 6% the items produced by machine I are defective and only 1% produced by machine II are defective. If a defective item is drawn at random, what is the probability that it was produced by machine I or machine II.

Solution: Let E_1 and E_2 be the events of drawing an item produced by machines I and II, respectively,

Let A be the event of drawing a defective item.

$$\therefore \quad P(E_1) = \frac{20}{100} = \frac{1}{5}, \; P(E_2) = \frac{80}{100} = \frac{4}{5}$$

and we have
$$P(A/E_1) = \frac{6}{100}, \; P(A/E_2) = \frac{1}{100}$$

The events E_1 and E_2 are mutually exclusive and exhaustive.

by *Bayes's theorem*:

P(machine I produced the defective item)

$$= P(E_1/A) = \frac{P(E_1).P(A/E_1)}{P(E_1)P(A/E_1) + P(E_2)P(A/E_2)}$$

$$= \frac{\left(\frac{1}{5}\right).\left(\frac{6}{100}\right)}{\left(\frac{1}{5}\right)\left(\frac{6}{100}\right) + \left(\frac{4}{5}\right)\left(\frac{1}{100}\right)} = \frac{6}{100} = \frac{3}{5}$$

P(machine II produced the defective item)

$$= P(E_2/A) = \frac{P(E_2)P(A/E_2)}{P(E_1)P(A/E_1)+P(E_2)P(A/E_2)}$$

$$= \frac{\left(\frac{4}{5}\right).\left(\frac{1}{100}\right)}{\left(\frac{1}{5}\right)\left(\frac{6}{100}\right)+\left(\frac{4}{5}\right)\left(\frac{1}{100}\right)} = \frac{4}{10} = \frac{2}{5}$$

***Example* 2:** Two groups are competing for the positions on the Boards of Directors of a corporation. The probabilities that the first and second groups will win are 0.6 and 0.4, respectively. Further, if the first group wins, then probability of introducing a new product is 0.7 and the corresponding probability is 0.3, if the second group wins. Find the probability that the new product was introduced by the second group,

Solution: Let E_1 and E_2 be the events of coining by the first and second groups winnings, respectively.

$\therefore$ $P(E_1) = 0.6$, $P(E_2) = 0,4$ (given)

Let A denote the event in which the new product is introduced

$\therefore$ $P(A/E_1) = 0.7$ and $P(A/E_2) = 0.3$

Required probability

= probability that the new product was introduced by the second group = $P(E_2/A)$

By Baye's theorem, we get

$$P(E_2/A) = \frac{P(E_2)P(A/E_2)}{P(E_1)P(A/E_1)+P(E_2)P(A/E_2)}$$

$$= \frac{(0.4)(0.3)}{(0.6)(0.7)+(0.4)(0.3)} = \frac{0.12}{0.42+0.12}$$

$$= \frac{0.12}{0.54} = \frac{2}{9}$$

***Example* 3:** Three machines A, B and C produce respectively 60%, 30%, 10% of the total number of items in the factory. The percentages of defective output of these machines are 2%, 3% and 4%. An item selected at random is found defective. Find the probability that the item was produced by machine C.

Solution: Let E_1, E_2, E_3 stand for the events of selection of an item from the machines A, B, C respectively,

$\therefore P(E_1) = \frac{60}{100} = 0.6,\ P(E_2) = \frac{30}{100} = 0.3,\ P(E_3) = \frac{10}{100} = 0.1$ (given)

Let E be the event in which a defective item is selected. Then

$$P(E/E_1)=\frac{2}{100}=0.02,\ P(E/E_2)=\frac{3}{100}=0.03,\ P(E/E_3)=\frac{4}{100}0.04\ \text{(given)}$$

By Bayes's theorem

$$P(E_3/E)=\frac{P(E_3).P(E/E_3)}{P(E_1)P(E/E_1)+P(E_2)P(E/E_2)+P(E_3)P(E/E_3)}$$

$$=\frac{(0.1)(0.004)}{(0.6)P(0.02)+(0.3)(0.003)+(0.1)(0.04)}$$

$$=0.16$$

∴ The probability that the defective item was produced by machine C is 0.16.

***Example* 4:** Two urns contain 1 white, 6 red and 4 white, 3 red balls and a ball is drawn from it. Find the probability of drawing a white ball.

Solution: Let E_1, E_2 be the events of drawing first urn and second urn, respectively.

$$\therefore \quad P(E_1)=\frac{1}{2},\ P(E_2)=\frac{1}{2}$$

Let A be the event of drawing a white ball

∴ $P(A/E_1)$ probability of drawing a white ball from the first urn

$$=\frac{1}{6+1}=\frac{1}{7}$$

$P(A/E_2)$ = probability of drawing a white ball from the second urn

$$=\frac{4}{4+3}=\frac{4}{7}$$

Probability of drawing a white ball

$$=P(A)=P\left[(E_1\cap A)\ \text{or}\ (E_2\cap A)\right]$$

$$=P(E_1\cap A)+P(E_2\cap A)$$

$$=P(E_1)P(A/E_1)+P(E_2)P(A/E_2)$$

***Example* 5:** A car manufacturing factory has two plants. Plant P manufactures 70% cars and plant Q manufactures 30% of cars. At plant P 80% of cars are rated to be of standard quality and at plant Q. 95% of the cars are rated to be of standard quality. A car is picked up at random and is found to be standard quality. What is the probability that it has come from plant P?

Solution: Let E_1 and E_2 be the events in which car is manufactured at plants P and Q, respectively.

$$\therefore \qquad P(E_1) = \frac{70}{100} = 07 \text{ and } P(E_2) = \frac{30}{100} = 0.3$$

Let A be the event of picking up a car of standard quality

$$\therefore \qquad P(A/E_1) = \frac{80}{100} = 0.8 \text{ and } P(A/E_2) = \frac{90}{100} = 0.9$$

Probability of picking up a car of standard quality from plant P = $P(E_1/A)$

$$\therefore \qquad P(E_1/A) = \frac{P(E_1)P(A/E_1)}{P(E_1)P(A/E_1) + P(E_2)P(A/E_2)}$$

$$= \frac{(0.7)(0.8)}{(0.7)(0.8) + (0.3)(0.9)} = \frac{0.56}{0.83}$$

$$= 56/83$$

***Example* 6:** A card from a pack of 52 cards is lost. From the remaining cards of the pack, two cards are drawn and are found to be hearts. Find the probability of the missing card to be a heart.

Solution: Let E_1, E_2, E_3, E_4 be the events of losing a card from hearts, spades, clubs and diamonds, respectively. And, let A be the event of drawing 2 hearts from the remaining cards.

We have

$$P(E_1) = \frac{13}{52} = \frac{1}{4},\ P(E_2) = \frac{13}{52} = \frac{1}{4},\ P(E_3) = \frac{13}{52} = \frac{1}{4},\ P(E_4) = \frac{13}{52} = \frac{1}{4}$$

$P(A/E_1)$ = Probability of drawing 2 cards which are hearts, given that one card of hearts is missing

$$= \frac{12_{C_2}}{51_{C_2}} = \frac{\left(\frac{12.11}{1.2}\right)}{\left(\frac{51.50}{1.2}\right)} = \frac{66}{51_{C_2}}$$

$P(A/E_2)$ = Probability of drawing two hearts, given that one spade missing

$$= \frac{13_{C_2}}{51_{C_2}} = \frac{\left(\frac{13.12}{1.2}\right)}{51_{C_2}} = \frac{78}{51_{C_2}}$$

$P(A/E_3)$ = Probability of drawing two hearts given that one club is missing

$$= \frac{13_{C_2}}{51_{C_2}} = \frac{78}{51_{C_2}}$$

P(A/E4) = Probability of drawing two hearts given that one diamond is missing

$$= \frac{13_{C_2}}{51_{C_2}} = \frac{78}{51_{C_2}}$$

∴ Probability of the missing card to be a card of hearts, given that two cards drawn from the remaining cards are hearts

$$P(E_1/A) = \frac{P(E_1)P(A/E_1)}{P(E_1)P(A/E_1)+P(E_2)P(A/E_2)+P(E_3)P(A/E_3)+P(E_4)P(A/E_4)}$$

$$= \frac{\frac{66}{51_{C_2}}.\frac{1}{4}}{\frac{66}{51_{C_2}}.\frac{1}{4}+\frac{78}{51_{C_2}}.\frac{1}{4}+\frac{78}{51_{C_2}}.\frac{1}{4}+\frac{78}{51_{C_2}}.\frac{1}{4}}$$

$$= \frac{66}{(66+78+78+78)} = \frac{66}{300} = \frac{11}{50}$$

***Example* 7:** An insurance company insured 2000 scooter drivers, 4000 car drivers and 6000 truck drivers. The probabilities of an accident involving a scooter, a car and a truck are 0.01, 0.03 and 0.15, respectively. One of the insured person meets with an accident. What is the probability that he is a scooter driver?

Solution: Total number of drivers insured = 2,000 + 4,000 + 6,000 = 12,000

Let E_1, E_2, E_3 be the events that the insured person met with an accident is a scooter driver, a car driver, a truck driver, respectively

∴ $$P(E_1) = \frac{2000}{12,000} = \frac{1}{6}$$

$$P(E_2) = \frac{4000}{12,000} = \frac{1}{3}$$

and $$P(E_3) = \frac{6000}{12,000} = \frac{1}{2}$$

Let A be the event in which an insured person meets with an accident. Then

$P(A/E_1) = 0.01,\ P(A/E_2) = 0.03,\ P(A/E_3) = 0.15$ (given)

Probability that insured person who met with an accident was a scooter driver

$$P(E_1/A)=\frac{P(E_1)P(A/E_1)}{P(E_1)P(A/E_1)+P(E_2)P(A/E_2)+P(E_3)P(A/E_3)}$$

$$=\frac{\left(\frac{1}{6}\right)(0.01)}{\left(\frac{1}{6}\right)(0.01)+\left(\frac{1}{3}\right)(0.03)+\left(\frac{1}{2}\right)(0.15)}$$

$$=\frac{\frac{1}{600}}{\left(\frac{1}{6}+\frac{3}{3}+\frac{15}{2}\right)\frac{1}{100}}$$

$$=\frac{\left(\frac{1}{6}\right)}{\left(\frac{52}{6}\right)}=\frac{1}{52}$$

$\therefore$ Required probability = 1/52

***Example* 8:** In a certain college, 4% of the men and 1% of the women are taller than 1.8 m. Furthermore, 60% of the students are women. If a student selected, at random is taller than 1.8 m, what is the probability that the student is a women.

Solution: Let E_1 be the event in which a student selected is a man

E_2 be the event in which a student selected is woman

A be the event of selecting a student taller than 1.8 m

$\therefore$ We have $P(E_1) = \frac{40}{100} = 0.40$

($\because$ 60% of the students are woman $\Rightarrow$ 40% are men)

$$P(E_2)=\frac{60}{100}=0.60$$

and, $$P(A/E_1)=\frac{40}{100}=0.04 \quad P(A/E_2)=\frac{1}{100}=0.01$$

From Bayes's theorem

$$P(E_2/A)=\frac{P(E_2)P(A/E_2)}{P(E_1)P(A/E_1)+P(E_2)P(A/E_2)}$$

$$=\frac{(0.6)(0.01)}{(0.4)(0.04)+(0.6)(0.01)}$$

$$=\frac{0.006}{0.022}=\frac{3}{11}$$

Exercise 1.4

1. Suppose that one of three men, a politician, a businessman, an educator, will be appointed as the chancellor of a university. The respective probabilities of their appointments are 0.50, 0.30, 0.20. The probabilities that research activities will be promoted by these people if they are appointed as 0.30, 0.70, 0.80 respectively, what is the probability that the research will be promoted by the new chancellor.

Ans. 0.52

2. A restaurant serves two special dishes, A and B to the customers consisting of 60% men and 40% woman. 80% of men order dish A and rest B. 70% of women order B and the rest A. In what ratio of A to B should the restaurant prepare the two dishes.

Ans. 3/2

3. Urn I has 2 white and 3 black balls. Urn II has 4 white and 1 black and urn III has 3 white and 4 black. An urn is selected at random and a ball is drawn at random is found to be white. Find the probability that urn I was selected.

Ans. 14/57

4. In a bolt factory, there are four machines A, B, C and D manufacturing 20%, 15%, 25% and 40% of the total output respectively. Of their outputs 5%, 4%, 3% and 2% in the same order are defective bolts. A bolt is chosen at random from the factory's production and is found to be defective. What is the probability that the bolt was manufactured by machine A or machine D.

Ans. 0.571 5

5. In a bolt factory, machine A, B and C manufacture 60%, 25% and 15% respectively. Of the total of their output 1%, 2% and 1% are defective bolts. A bolt is drawn at random from the total production and found to be defective. From which machine; the defective bolt is expected to have been manufactured.

Ans. Machine A

6. In a bolt factory machines A, B and C manufacture 25%, 35% and 40% respectively. Of the total of their output, 5%, 4% and 2% are defective bolts. A bolt is drawn at random from the total production and found to be defective. What are the probabilities that it was manufactured by machine A, B and C?

Ans. 25/69, 28/69, 16/69

7. Box I contains 3 red and 2 blue marbles, while Box II contains 2 red and 8 blue marbles. A fair coin is tossed. If the coin turns up heads a marble is chosen from Box I. If it turns up a tail a marble is chosen from Box II. Find the probability that a red marble is chosen.

8. A doctor is to visit a patient. From the past experience, it is known that he will come by train, bus, scooter or by other means of transport are respectively 3/10, 1/5, 1/10 and 2/5. The probabilities that he will be late are 1/4, 1/3 and 1/12. If he comes by train, bus and scooter respectively, but if he comes by any other means of transport, then he will not be late. When he is late, what is the probability that he comes by a train.

Ans. 1/2

9. Companies B_1, B_2, B_3 produce 30%, 40%, and 40% of the cars respectively. It is known that 2%, 3% and 2% of these cars produced form B_1, B_2, B_3 are defective

(i) What is the probability that a car purchased is defective

(ii) If a car purchased is found to be defective what is the probability that thus car is produced by the company B_1

[JNTU 2005]

Ans. (i) 0.0245 (ii) $\frac{12}{49}$

10. Box A contains 5 red and 3 white marbles and box B contains 2 red and 6 white marbles. If a marble is drawn from each box, what is the probability that they are both of the same colour. [JNTU 2007]

Ans. 7/16, 9/16

11. In a certain college 25% of boys and 10% of girls are studying mathematics. The girls constitute 60% of ten students. If a student is selected at random and is found to be studying mathematics find the probability that the student is (i) a girl (ii) a boy.

Ans. 3/8, 5/8

12. Box I contains eleven cards numbered 1 to 11, box II contain seven cards numbered 1 to 7. A box is selected at random and a card is drawn. If the number is even, find probability that the card is from I.

Ans. 38/68

Random Variables 2

2.1 Introduction

In this chapter we introduce random variables. The term random variable is more meaningful than the term variable and it is one of the basic concepts of the theory of probability. A real variable whose value is determined by the outcome of a random experiment is called a random variable.

***Definition* 2.1:** Let S be a sample space corresponding random experiment. A function X : S→R is called a random variable.

***Example* 1:** Let two coins be tossed simultaneously. Let S denote the sample space of the experiment. Then

$$S = \{H H, H T, TH, TT\}$$

if X denotes the number of heads obtained.

then X is a random variable

here X takes the following values 0, 1, 2

we have X(TT) = 0, X (H T) = 1, X(T H) = 1, X(H H) = 2

Random variables are denoted by capital letters X, Y, Z, etc., where as the values taken by them and denoted by corresponding small letters x, y, z,…

***Example* 2:** A fair die is tossed once. If the random variable X is "the number of even numbers" then X can take the values 0 and 1.

2.2 Types of Random Variables

There are two types of random variables:

(i) Discrete random variable

(ii) Continuous random Variable

(i) ***Discrete Random Variable:*** If a random variable takes finite or countably infinite number of values then it is called a discrete random variable.

Following are some examples of discrete random variables:

***Example* 1:** Number of accidents on a high way.

Example 2: Suppose three coins are tossed simultaneously. Let X denote the number of heads obtained. Then we have

$$S = \{ HHH, HHT, HTH, THH, HTT, THT, TTH, TTT \}$$

The random variable takes four distinct values 0, 1, 2, 3.

X is a discrete random variable

(ii) ***Continuous Random variable:*** If a random variable takes non-countable infinite number of values then it is called a continuous random variable.

***Example*:** Heights and weights of students in a class are continuous random variables.

2.3 Probability Distribution Function

Let X be a random variable. Then the function F(x) defined by $F(x) = P(X \leq x)$ where $P(X \leq x) = P\{t: X(t) \leq x\ 3\}, -\infty < t < \infty$ is called the distribution function of x

2.3.1 Properties of Distribution Function

The distribution function F(x) possesses the following properties: If x is a random variable and a, b, are real numbers such that a < b, then

(i) $P(a < X \leq b) = F(b) - F(a)$

(ii) $P(a \leq X \leq b) = F(b) - F(a) + P(X = a)$

(iii) $P(a < X < b) = F(b) - F(a) - P(X = b)$

(iv) $P(a \leq X < b) = F(b) - F(a) - P(X = b) + P(x = a)$

(v) $0 \leq F(x) \leq 1$

(vi) $F(a) \leq F(b)$; (if a < b)

(vii) $\underset{x \to -\infty}{Lt} F(x) = 0$ and $\underset{x \to +\infty}{Lt} F(x) = 1$

i.e. $F(-\infty) = 0$ and $F(\alpha) = 1$

2.4 Discrete Probability Distribution

Let x be a discrete random variable taking the values $x_1, x_2, x_3, \dots, x_n$

Let the corresponding Probabilities be denoted by

$$P(X = x_1) = p_1, P(X = x_2) = p_2, \dots, P(X = x_n) = p_n$$

such that $\sum_{i=1}^{n} b_i = 1$

Then the probability distribution of the random variable X is given by the following table:

$X = x_i$	x_1	x_2	...	x_i	...	x_n
$P(X = x_i)$	p_1	P_2	...	p_i	...	p_n

2.5 Probability Mass Function

Let x be a discrete random variable and the possible values which it can assume be $x_1, x_2, x_3, \ldots,$

It for each x_i we assign a real number $p_i = P\ (x = xi)$

such that

(i) $p_i = P\ (x = xi) \geq 0$

(ii) $\sum_{i=1}^{n} p_i = 1$

then $P_{(x = xi)} = P(x)$ is called a probability function or probability mass function

2.6 Mean, Variance and Standard Deviation of a Discrete Random Variable

Let X be a discrete random variable assuming the values $x_1, x_2, \ldots, x_n$. and let $P\ (X = x_1) =$ an p_1, $P\ (x = x_2) = P_2, \ldots, P_{(x = xn)} = p_n$ denote the corresponding frequencies

where $\sum_{i=1}^{n} P_i = 1.$

Then the mean of the random variable X is

$$\mu = \frac{\sum_{i=1}^{n} x_i\ p_i}{\sum_{i=1}^{n} p_i} = \sum_{i=1}^{n} x_i\ p_i \qquad \left(\text{since } \sum_{i=1}^{n} = p_i = 1\right)$$

The variance of X is

$$\text{Variance} = \text{Var}\ [X] = \sigma^2 = \sum_{i=1}^{n} (x_i - \mu)^2\ p_i$$

$$= \sum_{i=1}^{n} (x_i^2 - 2x_i\ \mu + \mu^2)\ p_i$$

$$= \sum_{i=1}^{n} x_i^2 p_i - 2\mu \sum x_i p_i + \mu^2 \sum p_i$$

$$= \sum_{i=1}^{n} x_i^2 p_i - 2\mu . \mu + \mu^2 . 1$$

$$= \sum_{i=1}^{n} x_i^2 . p_i - \mu^2$$

where σ is the standard deviation of X.

we have $\sigma = \sqrt{\sum_{i=1}^{n} x_i^2 p_i - \mu^2}$

Example **1:** The probability distribution of a random variable X is given below

X	**0**	**1**	**2**
P(x)	$3x^3$	$4k - 10k^2$	$5k - 1, k > 0$

Find (i) k (ii) $P(x \leq 1)$ (iii) $P(x > o)$

Solution: we have $\sum_{i=0}^{n} p_i = 1$

i.e., $P(X = 0) + P(X = 1) + P(X = 2) = 1$

or $3k^3 + 4k - 10k^2 + 5k - 1 = 1$

or $3k^3 - 10k^2 + 9k - 2 = 0$

or $(k - 1)(3k^2 - 7k + 2) = 0$

or k = 1, $k = \dfrac{7 \pm \sqrt{49 - 24}}{6} = \dfrac{7 \pm 5}{6}$

or k = 1, $\dfrac{12}{6}, \dfrac{2}{6}$

i.e., $k = 1, 2, \dfrac{1}{3}$

when k = 1, $P(X = 0) = 3(1)^3 = 3$

$P(X = 0) = 3 > 1$ is not possible

$\therefore k \neq 1$

when k = 2 $P(X = 0) = 3(2)^3 = 24 > 1$ is not possible

Hence $k \neq 2$

taking k = 1/3, we get

$$P(X = 0) = 3\left(\frac{1}{3}\right)^3 = \frac{1}{9}$$

$$P(X = 1) = 4\left(\frac{1}{3}\right) - 10\left(\frac{1}{3}\right)^3 = \frac{2}{9}$$

$$P(X = 2) = 5\left(\frac{1}{3}\right) - 1 = \frac{2}{3}$$

and $$P(X = 0) + P(X = 1) + P(X = 2) = \frac{1}{9} + \frac{2}{9} + \frac{2}{3} = 1$$

Hence we consider $k = \frac{1}{3}$

(ii) $P(x \le 1) = P(x = 0) + P(x = 1) = \frac{1}{9} + \frac{2}{9} = \frac{1}{3}$

(iii) $P(x > 0) = P(x = 1) + P(x = 2) = \frac{2}{9} + \frac{2}{3} = \frac{8}{9}$

***Example* 2:** A random variable x has the following probability distribution

x :	0	1	2	3	4	5	6	7
P(x) :	0	k	2k	2k	3k	K^2	$2k^2$	$7k^2 + k$

Determine

(i) k

(ii) $P(X < 6)$

(iii) $P(X \ge 6)$

(iv) if $P(X \le k) > \frac{1}{2}$ find the minimum value of k

(v) determine the distribution of X

(vi) Mean [JNTU 2005, 2008 s]

Solution:

(i) Since $\sum_{x=0}^{7} p_i = 1$, we have

$$0 + k + 2k + 2k + 3k + k^2 + 2k^2 + 7k^2 + k = 1$$

or $10k^2 + 9k - 1 = 0$

i.e $(10k - 1)(k + 1) = 0$

or $\quad k = \frac{1}{10}, k = -1$

but $\quad k = -1$ gives $P(X = 1) = k = -1 < 0$

Hence $k = -1$ is not considered

Hence $k = \frac{1}{10}$

(ii) $P(X < 6) = P(X = 0) + P(X = 1) + P(X = 2) + P(X = 3) + P(X = 4) + P(X = 5)$

$$= 0 + k + 2k + 2k + 3k + k^2$$

$$= 8k + k^2 = 8\left(\frac{1}{10}\right) + \left(\frac{1}{10}\right)^2 = 0.8 + 0.01$$

$$= 0.81$$

(iii) $P(X \geq 6) = 1 - P(X < 6) = 1 - 0.81 = 0.19$

(iv) We have $P(X \leq 1) = P(X = 0) + P(X = 1) = 0 + k = k = \frac{1}{10} = 0.1$

$P(X \leq 2) = P(X \leq 1) + P(X = 2) = 0.1 + 2k$

$$= 0.1 + \frac{2}{10} = 0.3$$

$P(X \leq 3) = P(X \leq 2) + P(X = 3) = 0.3 + 2K = 0.3 + \frac{2}{10} = 0.5$

$P(X \leq 4) = P(X \leq 3) + P(X = 4) = 0.5 + 3k = 0.5 = 3\left(\frac{1}{10}\right) = 0.8 > \frac{1}{2}$

Hence the minimum value of k such that $P(x \leq k) > \frac{1}{2}$ is $k = 4$

(v) The distribution of x is given in the following table

x	0	1	2	3	4	5	6	7
$F(x) = P(X \leq x)$	0	0.1	0.3	0.5	0.8	0.81	0.83	1

(vi) Mean $= \sum_{i=0}^{n} x_i^2 p_i$

$$= 0 + 1(k) + 2(2k) + 3(2k) + 4(3k) + 5(k^2) + 6(2k^2) + 7(7k^2 + k)$$

$$= k + 4k + 6k + 12k + 5K^2 + 12k^2 + 49k^2 + 7k$$

$$= 66k^2 + 30k = 66\left(\frac{1}{10}\right)^2 + 30\left(\frac{1}{10}\right) = 0.66 + 3.0$$

$$= 3.66$$

(vi) Variance of X = $\sum_{i=0}^{n} x_i^2 \, p_i - \mu^2$

$$= 0 + 1(k) + 4(2k) + 9(2k) + 16(3k) + 25k^2 + 36(2k^2) + 49(7k^2 + k) - (3.66)^2$$

$$= 440 + \left(\frac{1}{100}\right) + 124\left(\frac{1}{10}\right) - 13.3956$$

$$= 4.4 + 12.4 - 13.3956 = 3.4044$$

***Example* 3:** A discrete random variable has the following probability distribution obtain the cumulative distribution function of X.

X	0	2	3	4	5
P(X = x)	0.1	0.2	0.3	0.2	0.2

Solution: we have

$$F(x) = P(X \leq x)$$

Therefore we get

F (1) = 0.1

F (2) = 0.1 + 0.2 = 0.3

F (3) = 0.1 + 0.2 + 0.3 = 0.6

F (4) = 0.1 + 0.2 + 0.3 + 0.2 = 0.8

F (5) = 0.1 + 0.2 + 0.3 + 0.2 + 0.2 = 1

The required cumulative distribution function is

$$F(x) = \begin{cases} 0. & x < 1 \\ 0.1 \, , & 1 \leq x < 2 \\ 0.3 \, , & 2 \leq x < 3 \\ 0.6 \, , & 3 \leq x < 4 \\ 0.8 \, , & 4 \leq x < 5 \\ 1 \, , & x \geq 5 \end{cases}$$

***Example* 4:** Two cards are drawn successively without replacement from a well shuffled pack of 52 cards. Find the probability distribution of the number of aces.

Solution: Let E_1 be the event getting an ace in the first drawn and E_2 be the event in which the second drawn card (without replacement) is also an ace.

Let x be the random variable of "Number of aces" X can take the values 0, 1 and 2. we have

P(X = 0) = (Probability of getting no ace)

$$= P(\overline{E}_1) + P\left(\frac{\overline{E}_2}{\overline{E}_1}\right) = \frac{48}{52} \cdot \frac{47}{51} = \frac{188}{221}$$

P(x = 1) = (Probability of getting one ace)

$$= P(E_1 \overline{E}_2) + P(\overline{E}_1 E_2)$$

$$= P(E_1)\ P\left(\frac{\overline{E_2}}{E_1}\right) + P\left(\overline{E_1}\right) P\left(\frac{E_2}{\overline{E_1}}\right)$$

$$= \frac{4}{52} \cdot \frac{48}{51} + \frac{48}{52} \cdot \frac{4}{51} = \frac{32}{221}$$

P(X = 2) = (Probability of getting both aces) = P (E_1 E_2)

$$= P(E_1)\ P\left(\frac{E_2}{E_1}\right) = \frac{4}{52} \cdot \frac{3}{51} = \frac{1}{221}$$

The required probability distribution is

X	0	1	2
P(X)	$\frac{188}{221}$	$\frac{32}{221}$	$\frac{1}{221}$

Example 5: Find the mean and variance of the uniform probability distribution given by $f(x) = \frac{1}{n}$ for x = 1, 2, 3, …, n (JNTU 2001)

Solution: The uniform Probability distribution is

X	1	2	3	…	n
P(X = n)	$\frac{1}{n}$	$\frac{1}{n}$	$\frac{1}{n}$	…	$\frac{1}{n}$

Mean of the distribution is

$$\mu = \Sigma x_i p_i = 1 - \frac{1}{n}. + 2.\frac{1}{n} + 3.\frac{1}{n} + \ldots n.\frac{1}{n}$$

$$= \frac{1}{n}(1 + 2 + \ldots + n) = \frac{1}{n}\frac{n(n+1)}{2} = \frac{n+1}{2}$$

$$\text{Variance} = \sigma^2 = \Sigma x_i^2 p_i - \mu^2$$

$$= 1^2.\frac{1}{n} + 2^2.\frac{1}{n} + 3^2.\frac{1}{n} + \ldots + n^2.\frac{1}{n} - \left(\frac{n+1}{2}\right)^2$$

$$= \frac{1}{n}(1^2 + 2^2 + \ldots\ldots\ldots\ldots + n^2) - \frac{(n+1)^2}{4}$$

$$= \frac{1}{n}.\frac{n(n+1)(2n+1)}{6} - \frac{(n+1)^2}{4}$$

$$= \frac{(n+1)(2n+1)}{6} - \left(\frac{n+1}{4}\right)^2$$

$$= \frac{n+1}{2}\left[\frac{2n+1}{3} - \frac{n+1}{2}\right]$$

$$= \frac{(n+1)(n-1)}{2.6} = \frac{n^2-1}{12}$$

***Example* 6:** Three balls are drawn with replacement from a bag containing 5 white and 4 red balls. Find the probability distribution of the number of red balls drawn

***Solution*:** Number of balls in the bag = 5 white + 4 red = 9 balls

Let X be the random variable

then we have P(x = 0) = Probability of drawing 3 white balls (i.e., Probability of getting no red ball) "Number of red balls".

$$= \frac{5_{c_3}}{9_{c_3}} = \frac{5}{42}$$

P(x = 1) = Probability of getting two white and one red ball

$$= \frac{5_{c2}.4_{c1}}{9_{c3}} = \frac{10}{21}$$

P (x = 2) = Probability of setting one white and two red balls

$$= \frac{5_{c1} . 4_{c2}}{9_{c3}} = \frac{5}{14}$$

P(x = 3) = Probability of getting 3 red balls

$$= \frac{4_{c3}}{9_{c3}} = \frac{1}{21}$$

The required Probability distribution is

X	0	1	2	3
P(x = x)	$\frac{5}{42}$	$\frac{10}{21}$	$\frac{5}{14}$	$\frac{1}{21}$

Example 7: A die is tossed once. If the random variable X is defined as

$$x = \begin{cases} 1, \text{if the die results in an even number} \\ 0, \text{if the die results in an odd number} \end{cases}$$

Find the probability distribution of X

Solution: From the definition, X takes the values 1 or 0 with probabilities

P(x = 1) = P (2, 4, or 6)

= P(2) + P(4) + P(6)

$$= \frac{1}{6} + \frac{1}{6} + \frac{1}{6} = \frac{3}{6} = \frac{1}{2}$$

and P(X = 0) = (Probability of getting 1, 3 or 5)

= (Probability of getting 1) + (Probability of getting 3) + (Probability of getting 5)

$$= \frac{1}{6} + \frac{1}{6} + \frac{1}{6} = \frac{3}{6} = \frac{1}{2}$$

The required probability distribution is

X	0	1
P(x)	$\frac{1}{2}$	$\frac{1}{2}$

Exercise 2.1

1. Define the terms:
   (a) Random Variable
   (b) Discrete random variable
   (c) Continuous random variable
   (d) distribution function
   (e) Probability distribution

2. For the following distribution find (i) k (ii) $P(x \geq 2)$

x	0	1	2	3	4
P(X = x)	k	3k	5k	2k	k

3. A random variable x has the following probability function

X = x	**0**	**1**	**2**	**3**	**4**	**5**	**6**	**7**	**8**
P(X = x)	a	3a	5a	7a	9a	11a	13a	15a	17a

   (i) Find the value of a
   (ii) Find $P(x < 3)$, $P(x \geq 3)$, $P(0 < x < 5)$

4. A Symmetric die is rolled and the number on upper most face is noted. Find the Probability distribution

5. Suppose a random variable takes the values 3, 4, 5 with Probabilities $\frac{1}{2}, \frac{1}{6}$ and $\frac{1}{3}$ respectively. Obtain the distribution function function of the random variable

6. Let x denote the number of heads in a single toss of 4 fair coins. Determine (i) $P(x < 2)$, (ii) $P(1 < x \leq 3)$ [JNTU 2006]

7. Let x denote the minimum of the two numbers that appear when a pair of fair dice is thrown once. Determine the
   (i) Discrete probability distribution (ii) Mean (iii) variation [JNTU 2006]

8 A player wins if he gets 5 on a single throw of a dice, he loses if he gets 2 or 4. If he wins he gets Rs. 50, if he loses he gets Rs. 10, otherwise he has to pay Rs. 15. Find the value of the game.

9. Calculate the mean (expectation) and variance of x. if the Probability distribution of the random varable of x is given by

x :	– 1	0	1	2	4
f :	0.3	0.1	0.1	0.3	0.2

[JNTU 2006]

10. If 3 cars are selected from a lot of 6 cars containing 2 defective cars. Find the Probability distribution of the number of defective cars [JNTU 2008]

11. Find the mean and variance of the following discrete distribution

x	–3	–2	–1	0	1	2	3
P(X = x)	k	0.1	K	0.2	2k	0.4	2k

12. Find the mean and variance of the following probability distribution

$$x : \quad 8 \quad 12 \quad 16 \quad 20 \quad 24$$

$$P(x) : \quad \frac{1}{8} \quad \frac{1}{6} \quad \frac{3}{8} \quad \frac{1}{4} \quad \frac{1}{12}$$

13. In four tosses of a coin let x be the number of heads. Calculate the mean of the distribution obtained.

Answers 2.1

2. $k = \frac{1}{12}, P(x \geq 2) = \frac{2}{3}$

3. $a = \frac{1}{81}, P(x < 3) = \frac{9}{81} = \frac{1}{9}, P(x \geq 3) = \frac{8}{9}, P(0 < x < 5) = \frac{8}{27}$

4. $x : \quad 1 \quad 2 \quad 3 \quad 4 \quad 5 \quad 6$

$$P(x) : \quad \frac{1}{6} \quad \frac{1}{6} \quad \frac{1}{6} \quad \frac{1}{6} \quad \frac{1}{6} \quad \frac{1}{6}$$

5. $x : \quad 3 \quad 4 \quad 5$

$$F(x) : \quad \frac{1}{8^2} \quad \frac{2}{3} \quad 1$$

6. $P(x < 2) = \frac{5}{16}, P(1 < x \leq 3) = \frac{5}{8}$

7. $x : \quad 1 \quad 2 \quad 3 \quad 4 \quad 5 \quad 6$

$$P(x) : \quad \frac{11}{36} \quad \frac{9}{36} \quad \frac{7}{36} \quad \frac{5}{36} \quad \frac{3}{36} \quad \frac{1}{36}$$

8. $\frac{25}{6}$

9. 1, 2, 4.

10.

x	0	1	2
P(x)	$\frac{1}{5}$	$\frac{3}{5}$	$\frac{1}{5}$

11. 0.8 2.86

12. 16, 20

13. 2

2.7 Continuous Distribution

2.7.1 Probability Density Function

Let X be a continuous random variable. The probability density function for X in the interval (a, b) is defined as follows

$$f(x) = \begin{cases} 0 & , x < a \\ \phi(x) & , a \le x \le b \\ 0 & , x > b \end{cases}$$

The density function f(x) possesses the following properties

(i) $f(x) \ge 0$ for every x

(ii) $\int_{-\infty}^{\infty} f(x)\, dx = 1$

Example: The function f(x) defined as follows is a probability density function

$$f(x) = \begin{cases} |x| & |x| \le 1 \\ 0, & \text{otherwise} \end{cases}$$

we have $f(x) \ge 0$ for all x

and
$$\int_{-\infty}^{\infty} f(x)dx = \int_{\infty}^{\infty} |x|\, dx$$
$$= \int_{-1}^{1} f(x)\, dx = \int_{-1}^{0} |x|\, dx + \int_{0}^{1} |x|\, dx$$
$$= -\int_{1}^{0} x\, dx + \int_{0}^{1} x\, dx$$

$$= -\left(\frac{x^2}{2}\right)_{-1}^{0} + \left(\frac{x^2}{2}\right)_{0}^{1}$$

$$= -\left(0 - \frac{1}{2}\right) + \left(\frac{1}{2} - 0\right) = 1$$

Thus f(x) is a probability density function

2.7.2 Cumulative Distribution Function

Let X be continuous random variable

If $F(x) = P(X \leq x) = \int_{-\infty}^{\infty} f(x)dx$, then the function F(x) is defined as cumulative distribution function (or distribution function) of the continuous random variable X.

The cumulative distribution function has the following properties:

(i) $F'(x) = f(x) \geq 0$

(ii) $F(-\infty) = 0$

(iii) $F(\alpha) = 1$

(iv) $P(a \leq x \leq b) = \int_{a}^{b} f(x)dx$

$$= F(b) - F(a)$$

Example **1:** If f(x) has the probability density $k\,x^2$, $0 < x < 1$, determine k and find the probability that $P\left(\frac{1}{3} < x < \frac{1}{2}\right)$

Solution: Since $\int_{-\infty}^{\infty} f(x)dx = 1$, we have

$$\int_{-\infty}^{\infty} f(x)dx = \int_{0}^{1} kx^2\,dx = 1$$

or $k\left(\frac{x^3}{3}\right)_0^1 = 1$ i.e., $\frac{k}{3} = 1$ or $k = 3$

$$P\left(\frac{1}{3} < x < \frac{1}{2}\right) = \int_{1/3}^{1/2} 3\,x^2dx = 3\left(\frac{x^3}{3}\right)_{1/3}^{1/2} = \left(x^3\right)_{1/3}^{1/2} = \frac{1}{8} - \frac{1}{27}$$

$$= \frac{27-8}{216} = \frac{19}{216}$$

***Example* 2:**

Find the value k such that

$$f(x) = \begin{cases} \dfrac{x}{6} + k, & 0 \le x \le 3, \ (k > 0) \\ 0, & \text{elsewhere} \end{cases}$$

is a probability density function. Also find $P(1 \le x \le 2)$

***Solution*:**

Clearly $f(x) \ge 0$ for $k \ge 0$

We have $$\int_{-\infty}^{\infty} f(x)dx = 1$$

$$\int_{0}^{3} f(x)dx = 1$$

i.e., $$\int_{0}^{3} \left(\frac{x}{6} + k\right)dx = 1$$

i.e., $$\left[\frac{x^2}{12} + kx\right]_0^3 = 1$$

or $$\frac{3^2}{12} + 3k = 1$$

or $$3k = 1 - \frac{3}{4} = \frac{1}{4}$$

we get $$k = \frac{1}{12}$$

$$P(1 \le x \le 2) = \int_{1}^{2} \left(\frac{x}{6} + \frac{1}{12}\right)dx = \left(\frac{x^2}{12} + \frac{x}{12}\right)_1^2$$

$$= \left(\frac{2^2}{12} + \frac{2}{12}\right) - \left(\frac{1}{12} + \frac{1}{12}\right)$$

$$= \frac{1}{3} + \frac{1}{6} - \frac{2}{12} = \frac{1}{3}$$

***Example* 3:** For the following density function $f(x) = ke^{-|x|}, -\infty < x < \infty$, find the value of k.

Solution: Since $\int_{-\infty}^{\infty} f(x)\,dx = 1$

we have $\int_{-\infty}^{\infty} f(x)\,dx = \int_{-\infty}^{\infty} ke^{-|x|}\,dx = 1$

or $k\int_{-\infty}^{0} e^{-|x|}\,dx + k\int_{0}^{\infty} e^{-|x|}\,dx = 1$

or $k\int_{-\infty}^{0} e^{x}\,dx + k\int_{0}^{\infty} e^{-x}\,dx = 1$

or $k\,|e^{x}|_{-\infty}^{0} - k\,|e^{-x}|_{0}^{\infty} = 1$

or $k(1-0) - k(0-1) = 1$

or $k + k = 1$

$\therefore k = \dfrac{1}{2}$

***Example* 4:** The probability distribution function of a random variable X is

$$F(x) = \begin{cases} x & , 0 < x < 1 \\ 2 - x & , 1 \le x < 2 \\ 0 & , x \ge 2 \end{cases}$$

Find the cumulative distribution function of X

Solution: Let F(x) denote the cumulative distribution of X. Then

$$F(x) = \int_{-\infty}^{x} f(x)\,dx$$

when $0 < x < 1$

$$F(x) = \int_{-\infty}^{0} f(x)\,dx + \int_{0}^{x} F(x)\,dx$$

$$= 0 + \int_{0}^{x} x\,dx = \left(\frac{x^2}{2}\right)_0^x = \frac{x^2}{2}$$

when $1 < x \le 2$

we have
$$F(x) = \int_{-\infty}^{x} f(x)\,dx$$
$$= \int_{-\infty}^{0} f(x)\,dx + \int_{0}^{1} f(x)\,dx + \int_{1}^{x} f(x)\,dx$$
$$= 0 + \int_{0}^{1} x\,dx + \int_{1}^{x} f(2-x)\,dx$$
$$= \left(\frac{x^2}{2}\right)_0^1 + \left(2x - \frac{x^2}{2}\right)_1^x$$
$$= \left(\frac{1^2}{2} - 0\right) + \left(2x - \frac{x^2}{2}\right) - \left(2 - \frac{1^2}{2}\right)$$
$$= \frac{1}{2} + 2x - \frac{x^2}{2} - \frac{3}{2}$$
$$= 2x - \frac{x^2}{2} - 1$$

When $x \geq 2$
$$f(x) = \int_{-\infty}^{\infty} f(x)\,dx$$
$$= \int_{\infty}^{0} f(x)\,dx + \int_{0}^{1} f(x)\,dx + \int_{0}^{2} f(x)\,dx + \int_{2}^{\infty} f(x)\,dx$$
$$= 0 + \int_{0}^{1} x\,dx + \int_{1}^{2} (2-x)\,dx + \int_{2}^{\infty} 0\,dx$$
$$= \left(\frac{x^2}{2}\right)_0^1 + \left(2x - \frac{x^2}{2}\right)_1^2 + 0$$
$$= \left(\frac{1}{2} - 0\right) + \left(4 - \frac{4}{2}\right) - \left(2 - \frac{1}{2}\right)$$
$$= \frac{1}{2} + 2 - \frac{3}{2} = \frac{2}{2} = 1$$

Hence $$F(x) = \begin{cases} \dfrac{x^2}{2} &, 0 < x < 1 \\ 2x - \dfrac{x^2}{2} - 1 &, 1 < x \le 2 \\ 1 &, x \ge 2 \end{cases}$$

is the required cumulative distribution.

2.8 Joint Distribution

Let S denote a sample space of an experiment. Let X and Y be two random variables defined on S. Then the ordered pair (X, Y) defined by (X, Y) (t) = (X(t), Y(t)) is called a bivariate or two dimensional random variable on S. If the number of possible values of (X,Y) is finite then (X, Y) is called as a bivariate discrete random variable. Similarly we can define bivariate continuous random variable.

Definition: (Joint Probability mass function of (X, Y): Let (X, Y) be a discrete bivariate random variable defined on the sample space S of an experiment. Then the joint Probability mass function of (X, Y) is P(X = x, Y = y) satisfying the following conditions

(i) $P(x_i, y_j) = p_{ij} \ge 0$ for all i, j

(ii) $\sum_{i=1}^{m} \sum_{i=1}^{n} pij = 1$

where $p_{ij} = iP(x = x_i, Y = y_j)$

The set $\{(x_i, y_j, p_{ij}) ; i = 1, 2,\ldots, m, j = 1, 2 \ldots n\}$

is called joint Probability distribution of (X, Y). It can be represented as follows

X \ Y	y_1	y_2	...	y_j	...	y_n	P(x) Total
x_1	p_{11}	p_{12}	...	p_{ij}	...	p_{1n}	p_1
x_2	p_{21}	p_{22}	...	p_{2j}	...	p_{2n}	p_2
.							.
.							.
.							.
x_i	p_{i1}	p_{i2}	...	p_{ij}	...	p_{in}	$P_{i.1}$

Table *contd...*

.	:	:		:		:	
x_m	p_{m1}	p_{m2}	...	p_{mj}	...	p_{mn}	p_m
Total P(Y)	$P_{\cdot 1}$	$p_{\cdot 2}$	...	$p_{\cdot j}$	...	$p_{\cdot n}$	1

The row totals $P_1, P_2, .., P_m.$ are called the marginal Probabilities of X. Similarly the column totals $P._1, P._2, .., P._n.$ are called the marginal Probabilities of Y.

The marginal Probability distribution of X is the univariate Probability distribution of X and the marginal Probability distribution of Y is the univariate Probability distribution of Y.

The marginal Probability distribution of X can be represented as follows.

X	:	x_1	x_2	...	x_i	...	x_m	Total
$P(X = x_i)$	:	P_1	P_2	...	P_i	...	P_n	1

Similarly the marginal Probability distribution of Y can be represented as follows:

Y	:	y_1	y_2	...	y_j	...	y_n	Total
$P(Y = y_j)$	:	$P_{.1}$	$P_{.2}$	...	$P_{.j}$	...	$P_{.n}$	1

If X and Y are two continuous random variables then the joint Probability function f(x, y) for the for the random variables X and Y satisfies the following conditions.

(i) $f(x,y) \geq 0$

(ii) $\int_{-\infty}^{\infty} \int_{-\infty}^{\infty} f(x, y)\, dx\, dy = 1$

Definition: Joint (cumulative) distribution function

Let (X, Y) be a bivariate discrete random variable defined on s. The joint cumulative distribution function F(x, y) is defined as

$$F(x, y) = P(X \leq x, Y \leq y)$$

The distribution function F(x, y) satisfies the following properties:

(i) $0 \leq F(x, y) \leq 1$

(ii) (a) $F(x, y) \leq F(x', y)$ if $x \leq x'$

(b) $F(x, y) \leq F(x, y')$ if $y \leq y'$

If (x, y) is a bivariate continuous random variable then

$$F(x, y) = P(-\infty < X \leq x, \quad -\infty < Y \leq y)$$

$$= \int_{-\infty}^{x} \int_{-\infty}^{y} f(x, y)\, dx\, dy$$

where

(i) $f(x, y) \geq 0$

(ii) $\int_{-\infty}^{\infty} \int_{-\infty}^{\infty} f(x, y)\, dx\, dy = 1$

Remarks: If f(x, y) is the joint probability function of two random variables X and Y, then we can find individual marginal Probability distribution functions $f_1(x)$ and $f_2(y)$.

But the converse is not true.

Also, if $f(x, y) = f_1(x)\, f_2(y)$ then X and Y said to be independent random variables.

2.8.1 Marginal Distribution Functions

If X and Y discrete random variables, then the Marginal distribution function of x is given by

$$F(x) = P(X \leq x) = P(x \leq x, y < \infty)$$

$$= \underset{y \to \infty}{\text{Lt}} F(x, y)$$

and the marginal distribution function y is defined as

$$F(y) = P(Y \leq y) = P(X < \infty, Y \leq y)$$

$$= \underset{n \to \infty}{\text{Lt}} F(x, y)$$

If x and y are continuous random variables, then the marginal distribution functions are defined as follows

$$F(x) = \int_{-\infty}^{x} \left[\int_{-\infty}^{\infty} f(x, y)\, dy \right] dx$$

$$F(y) = \int_{-\infty}^{y} \left[\int_{-\infty}^{\infty} f(x, y)\, dx \right] dy$$

Example: Obtain (i) Marginal distribution of X

(ii) Marginal distribution of Y

for the following bivariate probability distribution

X \ Y	–1	0	1
0	$\frac{1}{15}$	$\frac{2}{15}$	$\frac{1}{15}$
1	$\frac{3}{15}$	$\frac{2}{15}$	$\frac{1}{15}$
2	$\frac{2}{15}$	$\frac{1}{15}$	$\frac{2}{15}$

Solution: we have

$$P(x = 0) = P(x = 0, y = -1) + P(x = 0, y = 0) + P(x = 0, y = 1)$$

$$= \frac{1}{15} + \frac{2}{15} + \frac{1}{15} = \frac{4}{15}$$

$$P(x = 1) = P(x = 1, y = -1) + P(x = 1, y = 0) + P(x = 1, y = 1)$$

$$= \frac{3}{15} + \frac{2}{15} + \frac{1}{15} = \frac{2}{15}$$

$$P(x = 2) = P(x = 2, y = -1) + P(x = 2, y = 0) + P(x = 2, y = 1)$$

$$= \frac{2}{15} + \frac{1}{15} + \frac{2}{15} = \frac{1}{3}$$

Hence, the Marginal distribution of X is

X	:	0	1	2
P(x)	:	$\frac{4}{15}$	$\frac{2}{5}$	$\frac{1}{3}$

Since $P(y = -1) = P(x = 0, y = -1) + P(x = 1, y = -1) + P(x = 2, y = -1)$

$$= \frac{1}{15} + \frac{3}{15} + \frac{2}{15} = \frac{2}{5}$$

$$P(y = 0) = P(x = 0, y = 0) + P(x = 1, y = 0) + P(x = 2, y = 0)$$

$$= \frac{2}{15} + \frac{2}{15} + \frac{1}{15} = \frac{1}{3}$$

$$P(y = 1) = P(x = 0, y = 1) + P(x = 1, y = 1) + P(x = 2, y = 1)$$

$$= \frac{1}{15} + \frac{1}{15} + \frac{2}{15} = \frac{4}{15}$$

The marginal distribution of Y is

Y :	–1	0	1
P(y) :	$\frac{2}{5}$	$\frac{1}{3}$	$\frac{4}{15}$

2.9 Conditional Distribution

Let x and y be two discrete random variables associated with an experiment. Let P(X = x, Y = y) be the joint probability function and let $P_1(x)$, $P_2(y)$ respectively be the marginal probability functions. Then the conditional probability function of y given x is defined as $P\left(y/x\right) = \frac{P(X = x, Y = y)}{P_1(x)}$ ($P_1(x) \neq 0$) and the conditional probability function of x given y is defined as $P\left(x/y\right) = \frac{P(X = x, Y = y)}{P_2(y)}, (P_2(y) \neq 0)$

If X and Y are continuous random variables and f(x, y) is the joint probability density function then the conditional probability density function

$$f\left(x/y\right) = \frac{f(x, y)}{f(y)}$$

where f(y) is the marginal probability density function of Y and

$$f\left(y/x\right) = \frac{f(x, y)}{f(x)}$$

where f(x) is the marginal probability density function of x.

2.10 Mathematical Expectation

In this section we introduce mathematical expectation and variance. Mathematical expectation is also called the mean of the distribution.

2.10.1 Mathematical Expectation of a Discrete Random Variable

Let X be a discrete random variable assuming the values $x_1, x_2 \ldots\ldots x_n$. Let $p_1, p_2 \ldots\ldots p_n$ denote the corresponding probabilities. Then the mathematical expectation of x, denoted by E(x) is defined as

$$E(x) = \sum_{i=1}^{n} x_i p_i$$

Mathematical expectation of X is also known as expectation or mean (average) and is denoted by μ.

2.10.2 Mathematical Expectation of a Continuous Random Variable

If X is continuous random variable having probability density function f(x), then the expectation of X is defined as

$$E(x) = \int_{-\infty}^{\infty} x\, f(x)\, dx$$

2.10.3 Variance

If X is a discrete random variable having probability function P(x) then the variance of X is defined as

$$\text{Variance }(X) = E[(x-\mu)^2]$$

where μ is the arithmetic mean of the distribution. Variance of X is denoted by Var [x] or σ^2

from the definition

$$\text{var }[x] = \sigma^2 = \sum_{i=1}^{n} (x_i - \mu)^2\, p_i$$

where x_i (i = 1, 2, ... n) are values assumed by x and p_i, (i = 1, 2..., n) are the corresponding probabilities.

If X is a continuous random variable having probability density function f(x), the variance of X is defined as

$$\text{Var }[x] = \sigma^2 = \int_{-\infty}^{\infty} (x-\mu)^2 f(x) dx$$

2.10.4 Expectation of Joint Distributions

If X and Y are two discrete random variables, and P(X, Y) = P(X = x, Y = y) is the joint probability function then the expectations of X and Y are defined as

$$\mu_x = \sum_x \sum_y x \; P(x, y)$$

and
$$\mu_y = \sum_x \sum_y y \; P(x, y)$$

If X and Y are two continuous random variables having f(x, y) as the joint density function, the expectations of X and Y are defined as follows.

$$\mu_x = E(x) = \int_{-\infty}^{\infty} \int_{-\infty}^{\infty} x \, f(x, y) \, dx \, dy$$

$$\mu_y = E(y) = \int_{-\infty}^{\infty} \int_{-\infty}^{\infty} y \, f(x, y) \, dx \, dy$$

Variance

If X and Y are two continuous random variables, then the variance of X is defined as

$$\sigma_x^2 = V(x) = \text{var}[x] = \int_{-\infty}^{\infty} \int_{-\infty}^{\infty} (x - \mu_x)^2 f(x, y) \, dx \, dy$$

and the variance of y is defined as

$$\sigma_y^2 = V(y) = \text{var}[y] = \int_{-\infty}^{\infty} \int_{-\infty}^{\infty} (y - \mu_y)^2 f(x, y) \, dx \, dy$$

2.10.5 Median, Mode and Moments of Continuous Distributions

Median: Let x be a continuous random variable defined from a to b. If M denotes the median of the distribution then it is obtained by solving

$$\int_a^M f(x) dx = \frac{1}{2}$$

and
$$\int_M^b f(x) dx = \frac{1}{2}$$

Mode: The Mode of x is given by $f'(x) = 0$, $f''(x) < 0$ for $a < x < b$

Moment about mean: If μ_r denotes the mean about the mean μ is given by

$$\mu_r = \int_a^b (x - \mu)^r f(x) dx$$

$\mu_r = r^{th}$ moment about mean

***Moment about an arbitrary number A*:**

The rth moment about an arbitrary number A is

$$\mu_r{}^1 = \int_a^b (x-A)^r f(x)dx$$

***Moment about Origin*:** The moment about origin denoted by ν_r is defined as

$$\nu_r = \int_a^b x^r f(x)dx$$

If A = 0, then $\mu_r' = \nu_r$

2.11 Properties of Expectation

1. Let x be discrete random variable and k be a real number, then

(i) E(kX) = k E(X)

(ii) E(X + k) = E(X) + k

Proof: (i) $E(k\,X) = \sum_{i=1}^{n}(kx_i)p_i$

$$= k\sum_{i=1}^{n} x_i\, p_i = kE(x)$$

(ii) $E(x + k) = \sum_{i=1}^{n}(x_i + k)p_i$

$$= \sum_{i=1}^{n} x_i p_i + k\sum P_i$$

$$= E(x) + k.1$$

$$= E(x) + k$$

2. If X and Y are discrete random variables, then E(X + Y) = E(X) + E(Y)

***Proof*:** $E(x + y) = \sum_x\sum_y (x + y)\, p\,(x, y)$

$$= \sum_x\sum_y x\,P(x,y) + \sum_x\sum_y y\,P(x,y)$$

$$= E(x) + E(y)$$

3. If P(X = x, Y = y) is the joint probability function of X and Y where X and Y are discrete and independent then we have

$$P(X = x, y = y) = P_1(x)\,P_2(y)$$

then $E(X, Y) = E(X)\,E(Y)$

***Proof*:** we have $E(X\,Y) = \sum_x \sum_y x\,y\,P(X = x, Y = y)$

$$= \sum_x \sum_y x\,y\,P_1(x)P_2(y)$$

$$= \sum_x x P_1(x) \sum y P_2(y)$$

$$= E(X)\,E(Y)$$

***Remark*:** The above properties of mathematical expectation also hold good for continuous random variable. For example consider E(k X) when X is continuous random variable. We have

$$E(k\,X) = \int_{-\infty}^{\infty} (kx) f(x)\,dx$$

$$= k \int_{-\infty}^{\infty} x f(x)\,dx$$

$$= k\,E(x)$$

***Example* 1:** The density function of a random variable X is

$$F(x) = \begin{cases} e^{-x}, & x \geq 0 \\ 0, & \text{otherwise} \end{cases}$$

Find (i) E(X) (ii) $E(X^2)$ (iii) var (X) (iv) $E(X - 1)^2$

***Solution*:**

(i)
$$E(X) = \int_{-\infty}^{\infty} x f(x)$$

$$= \int_0^{\infty} x e^{-x}\,dx$$

$$= \left[x \frac{\overline{e}^{x}}{(-1)} \right]_0^{\infty} - \left[1 . \frac{e^{-x}}{(-1)^2} \right]_0^{\infty}$$

$$= (0 - 0) - (0 - 1) = 1$$

$\therefore$ E(X) = 1

(ii) $E(X^2) = \int_{-\infty}^{\infty} x^2 f(x)dx = \int_0^{\infty} x^2 e^{-x} dx$

$$= \left[-x^2 e^{-x}\right]_0^{\infty} - \left[2xe^{-x}\right]_0^{\infty} + \left[2 - e^{-x}\right]_0^{\infty}$$

$$= (0 - 0) - (0 - 0) - 2(0 - 1) = 2$$

(iii) $\text{var}(X) = E(x^2) - [E(x)]^2$

$$= 2 - 1^2 = 2 - 1 = 1$$

(iv) $E(x - 1)^2 = \int_{-\infty}^{\infty} (x-1)^2 f(x)dx = \int_0^{\infty} (x^2 - 2x + 1)e^{-x} dx$

$$= \int_0^{\infty} x^2 e^{-x} dx - 2\int_0^{\infty} xe^{-x} dx + \int_0^{\infty} 1.e^{-x} dx$$

$$= E(X^2) - 2E(X) + E(1)$$

$$= 2 - 2.1 + 1 \qquad [\because E(1) = 1)]$$

$$= 1$$

***Example* 2:** If X is a random variable and a, b are constants, then show that $V(a\,x + b) = a^2\, V(X)$

Where V(X) denotes the variance of x. [JNTU 2003]

***Solution*:** we know that $V(x) = \text{variance of } x = E(x^2) - (E(x))^2$

Therefore

$$V(ax + b) = E(ax + b)^2 - (E(ax + b))^2$$

$$= E(a^2\, x^2 + 2ab\, x + b^2) - (E(a\, x) + E(b)]^2$$

$$= a^2\, E(x^2) + 2ab\, E(x) + E(b^2) - [aE(x) + b]^2 \quad (\because E(b) = b]$$

$$= a^2\, E(x^2) + 2ab\, E(x) + b^2 - a^2(E(x))^2 - 2ab\, E(x) - b^2$$

$$(\because E(b^2) = b^2)$$

$$= a^2\, [E(x^2) - (E(x)^2] = a^2\, V(x)$$

***Example* 3:** The distribution function of a random variable is given by

$$F(x) = \begin{cases} 1 - (1 + x)e^{-x} & \text{for} \quad x \geq 0 \\ 0, & \text{for} \quad x < 0 \end{cases}$$

Find the corresponding density function of random variable x

***Solution*:** we have

$$F(x) = \frac{d}{dx}F(x) = \frac{d}{dx}\,(1-(1+x)\,e^{-x}), \qquad x \geq 0$$

$$= 0 + [-(-1)\,(1+x)\,e^{-x} - e^{-x}]$$

$$= (1+x)\,e^{-x} - e^{x} = x\,e^{-x}$$

Hence
$$F(x) = \begin{cases} xe^{-x}, & x \geq 0 \\ 0, & x < 0 \end{cases}$$

***Example* 4:** If X and Y are random variable each having the density function

$$f(t) = \begin{cases} 2e^{-2t}, & t \geq 0 \\ 0, & \text{otherwise} \end{cases}$$

Compute the following

(i) $E(x+y)$ (ii) $E(x^2+y^2)$ (iii) $E(x\,y)$

***Solution*:**

(i)
$$E\,(x) = \int_{-\infty}^{\infty} x\,f(x)\,dx = \int_{0}^{\infty} x\left(2e^{-2x}\right)dx$$

$$= 2\int_{0}^{\infty} x\,e^{-2x}\,dx$$

$$= 2\left[x.\frac{e^{-2x}}{(-2)} - 1.\frac{e^{-2x}}{(-2)^2}\right]_0^{\infty}$$

$$= 2\left[0-\left(0-\frac{1}{4}\right)\right] = \frac{2}{4} = \frac{1}{2}$$

similarly
$$E(y) = \frac{1}{2}$$

$\therefore$
$$E(x+y) = E(x) + E(y) = \frac{1}{2} + \frac{1}{2} = 1$$

(ii) $$E(x^2 + y^2) = E(x^2) + E(y^2)$$

Now, $$E(x^2) = \int_{-\infty}^{\infty} x^2 f(x)\,dx = \int_{0}^{\infty} x^2\left(2e^{-2x}\right)dx$$

$$= 2\int_{0}^{\infty} x^2 e^{-2x}\,dx$$

$$= 2\left[x^2\frac{e^{-2x}}{(-2)} - 2x\frac{e^{-2x}}{(-2)^2} + 2\frac{e^{-2x}}{(-2)^3}\right]_0^{\infty}$$

$$= 2\left[0 - 0 + \frac{2}{(-8)}(0-1)\right]$$

$\therefore$ $$E(x^2) = \frac{2.2}{8} = \frac{1}{2}$$

Similarly $E(y^2) = \frac{1}{2}$

Hence $$E(x^2 + y^2) = E(x^2) + E(y^2)$$

$$= \frac{1}{2} + \frac{1}{2} = 1$$

Also, $$E(x\,y) = E(x)\,E(y)$$

$$= \frac{1}{2}.\frac{1}{2} = \frac{1}{4}$$

***Example* 5:** A continuous random variable x has the distribution function

$$F(x) = \begin{cases} 0\,, & x \le 1 \\ k(x-1)^4, & 1 \le x \le 3 \\ 1, & x > 3 \end{cases}$$

Determine (i) f(x) (ii) k (iii) Mean [JNTU, 2007 s]

***Solution*:** since $f(x) = \frac{d}{dx}(F(x))$

we get $$F(x) = \begin{cases} 0, & \text{if } x \le 1 \\ 4k(x-1)^3, & \text{if } 1 \le x \le 3 \\ 1 & \text{if } x > 3 \end{cases}$$

we have $\int_{-\infty}^{\infty} f(x)dx = 1$

therefore we get $\int_{-\infty}^{\infty} f(x)dx = \int_{1}^{3} 4k(x-1)^3 dx = 1$

or $= 4k\left[\frac{(x-1)^4}{4}\right]_1^3 = 1$

or $k((3-1)^4 - (1-1)^4) = 1$

or $k(16 - 0) = 1$

i.e., $k = \frac{1}{16}$

Hence $$f(x) = \begin{cases} 0, & \text{if } x \le 1 \\ \frac{1}{4}(x-1)^3, & \text{if } 1 < x \le 3 \\ 0 & \text{if } x > 3 \end{cases}$$

Mean of $x = \mu = \int_{-\infty}^{\infty} x\, f(x)dx = \int_{-\infty}^{\infty} x\frac{1}{4}(x-1)^3 dx$

$$= \frac{1}{4}\int_{-\infty}^{1} x(x-1)^3 dx + \frac{1}{4}\int_{1}^{3} x(x-1)^3 dx + \frac{1}{4}\int_{3}^{\infty} x(x-1)^3 dx$$

$$= 0 + \frac{1}{4}\int_{0}^{2}(t+1)t^3 dt + 0 \qquad \text{(substituting } x - 1 = t\text{)}$$

$$= \frac{1}{4}\int_{0}^{2}\left(t^4 + t^3\right)dt$$

$$= \frac{1}{4}\left(\frac{t^5}{5} + \frac{t4}{4}\right)_0^2 = \frac{1}{4}\left(\frac{32}{5} + \frac{16}{4}\right)$$

$$= \frac{52}{20} = \frac{13}{5}.$$

***Example* 6:** The probability density f(x) of a continuous random variable is given by

$$f(x) = k\, e^{-|x|}, \qquad -\infty < x < \infty$$

Find k, mean and variance of the distribution and also find the probability that the variate lies between 0 and 4.

Solution: we have $\int_{-\infty}^{\infty} f(x)dx = 1$

Therefore, we get $\int_{-\infty}^{\infty} k e^{-|x|} dx = 1$

$$k\left[\int_{-\infty}^{0} e^{-(-x)}dx + \int_{0}^{\infty} e^{-|x|}dx\right] = 1$$

or $$k\left[\int_{-\infty}^{0} e^{-|x|}dx + \int_{0}^{\infty} e^{-x}dx\right] = 1$$

or $$k\left[\int_{-\infty}^{0} e^{x}dx + \int_{0}^{\infty} e^{-x}dx\right] = 1$$

or $$k\left[\left|e^{x}\right|_{-\infty}^{0} + \left|\frac{e^{-x}}{-1}\right|_{0}^{\infty}\right] = 1$$

or $k(1 - 0) - (0 - 1) = 1$

i.e., $2k = 1$

or $k = \frac{1}{2}$

$\therefore$ $f(x) = \frac{1}{2}\ e^{-|x|}, \qquad -\infty < x < \infty$

Mean $$= \int_{-\infty}^{\infty} x f(x) dx = \frac{1}{2}\int_{-\infty}^{\infty} x e^{-|x|} dx = 0$$

($\because$ the integrand is an odd function of x)

Variance $$= \int_{-\infty}^{\infty} x^2 f(x) dx - \mu^2$$

$$= \int_{-\infty}^{\infty} x^2 \frac{1}{2} e^{-|x|} dx - 0 = \int_{-\infty}^{\infty} x^2 e^{-|x|} dx = \int_{0}^{\infty} x^2 e^{|-x|} dx$$

$$= 2 \cdot \frac{1}{2}\int_{0}^{\infty} x^2 e^{-|x|} dx$$

(since integrand is an even functions of x)

$$= \int_0^{\infty} x^2 e^{-x} dx$$

$$= \left[x^2 \frac{e^{-x}}{-1} - 2x \frac{e^{-x}}{(-1)^2} + 2.\frac{e^{-x}}{(-1)^3} \right]_0^{\infty}$$

$$= (0 - 0) - (0 - 0) -2(0 - 1) = 2$$

$$P(0 \leq x \leq 4) \qquad = \frac{1}{2} \int_0^4 e^{-|x|} dx = \frac{1}{2} \int_0^4 e^{-x} dx$$

$$= \frac{1}{2} \left| \frac{e^{-x}}{(-1)} \right|_0^4$$

$$= -\frac{1}{2}\left(e^{-4} - e^0\right) = \frac{1}{2}\left(1 - e^{-4}\right)$$

Example **7:** For the continuous probability function $f(x) = k\,x^2\,e^{-x}$ when $x \geq 0$, find

(i) k (ii) Mean (iii) variance [JNTU 2007]

***Solution*:**

(i) we have $\int_{-\infty}^{\infty} f(x) = 1$

or $\int_{-\infty}^{\infty} k x^2 e^{-x} dx = 1$

i.e., $\int_0^{\infty} k x^2 e^{-x} dx = 1$ (since $x \geq 0$)

i.e., $k\left[x\left(-e^{-x}\right) - 2x\,e^{-x} + (-1)\,2\,e^{-x} \right]_0^{\infty} = 1$

i.e., $k\,[0 - 0 - 2(0 - 1] = 1$

i.e., $2k = 1$

$\therefore$ $k = 1/2$

(ii) Mean $= \mu = \int_{-\infty}^{\infty} x\,f(x)\,dx = \frac{1}{2}\int_{-\infty}^{\infty} x.x^2e^{-x}dx$

$$= \frac{1}{2}\int_{-\infty}^{\infty} x^3e^{-x}dx$$

$$= \frac{1}{2}\left[x^3\left(-e^{-x}\right) - 3x^2\left(e^{-x}\right) + 6x\left(-e^{-x}\right) - 6\,e^{-x}\right]_0^{\infty}$$

$$= \frac{1}{2}\,[(0-0) - 3(0-0) + 6(0-0) - 6(0-1)]$$

$$= \frac{1}{2}\,(6) = 3$$

$\therefore\ \mu = 2$

(iii) variance $= \sigma^2 = \int_{-\infty}^{\infty} x^2 f(x)\,dx - \mu^2$

$$= \frac{1}{2}\int_0^{\infty} x^2\,x^2e^{-x}\,dx - (3)^2$$

$$= \frac{1}{2}\int_0^{\infty} x^4\,e^{-x}\,dx - 9$$

$$= \frac{1}{2}\left[x^4\left(-e^{-x}\right) - 4x^3\left(e^{-x}\right) + 12x^2\left(-e^{-x}\right) - 24x\left(e^{-x}\right) + 24\left(-e^{-x}\right)\right]_0^{\infty} - 9$$

$$= \frac{1}{2}\left[24(0-1)\right] - 9$$

$$= 12 - 9 = 3$$

Hence $k = \frac{1}{2}$, $\mu = 3$, $\sigma^2 = 3$

***Example* 8:** A continuous random variable has the probability density function given by

$$f(x) = a + bx, \qquad 0 \le x \le 1$$

If the mean of the distribution is $\frac{1}{2}$, find a and b.

***Solution*:** Since f(x) is a probability distribution function, we have

$$\int_{-\infty}^{\infty} f(x)dx = 1$$

or $$\int_{-\infty}^{0} f(x)dx + \int_{0}^{1} f(x)dx + \int_{1}^{\infty} f(x)dx = 1$$

or $$0 + \int_{0}^{1} f(x)dx + 0 = 1$$

or $$\int_{0}^{1} (a + bx)dx = 1$$

or $$\left| ax + \frac{bx^2}{2} \right|_0^1 = 1$$

i.e., $$a + \frac{b}{2} = 1$$

or $$2a + b = 2 \qquad .....(1)$$

it is given that the mean of x is 1/2 . Therefore we have

we have $$\int_{0}^{1} x\, f(x)\, dx = \frac{1}{2}$$

or $$\int_{0}^{1} x\,(a + bx)dx = \frac{1}{2} \qquad \text{or} \qquad \int_{0}^{1} (ax + bx^2)dx = \frac{1}{2}$$

or $$\left| a\frac{x^2}{2} + \frac{bx^3}{3} \right|_0^1 = \frac{1}{2} \qquad \text{or} \qquad \frac{a}{2} + \frac{b}{3} = \frac{1}{2}$$

or $$3a + 2b = \frac{6}{2} = 3 \qquad .....(2)$$

solving (1) and (2) we get a = 1, b = 0

***Example* 9:** The joint probability function of the random variables is defined by

$$f(x,y) = 2 - x - y; \quad 0 \le x \le 1, 0 \le y \le 1$$
$$= 0, \qquad \text{otherwise}$$

Find the marginal density functions of X and Y

Solution: The marginal probability density function of X is

$$f(x) = \int_0^1 f(x, y) = \int_0^1 (2 - x - y)\, dy$$

$$= \left[2y - xy - \frac{y^2}{2}\right]_0^1 = 2 - x - \frac{1}{2}$$

$$= \frac{3}{2} - x$$

The marginal probability density function of y is

$$f(Y) = \int_0^1 f(x,y)\, dx = \int_0^1 (2 - x - y)\, dx$$

$$= \left| 2x - \frac{x^2}{2} - xy \right|_0^1 = 2 - \frac{1}{2} - y$$

$$= \frac{3}{2} - y$$

***Example* 10:** Probability density function of a random variable X is

$$f(x) = \begin{cases} \frac{1}{2} \sin x, & 0 \le x \le \pi \\ 0, & \text{else where} \end{cases}$$

Find mean, mode and median

Solution:

(i) *Mean*: $= \int_{-\infty}^{\infty} xf(x)\, dx = \int_{-\infty}^{\infty} x\left(\frac{1}{2} \sin x\right) dx$

$$= \int_{-\infty}^{0} x.0\, dx + \int_0^{\pi} x\left(\frac{1}{2} \sin x\right) dx + \int_{\pi}^{\infty} x\,(0)\, dx$$

$$= \frac{1}{2} \int_0^{\pi} x \sin x\, dx = \frac{1}{2} \left| - x \cos x + \sin x \right|_0^{\pi} = \frac{1}{2} (- \pi \cos \pi - 0)$$

$$= \frac{1}{2} (- \pi)(- 1) = \frac{\pi}{2}$$

(ii) *Median*: Let M denote the median, then we have

$$\int_a^M f(x)\,dx = \int_M^b f(x)\,dx = \frac{1}{2}$$

i.e $\quad \frac{1}{2}\int_0^M \sin x\,dx = \frac{1}{2} \quad$ and $\quad \frac{1}{2}\int_M^\pi \sin x\,dx = \frac{1}{2}$

i.e. $\quad (-\cos x)_0^M = 1$ and $-(\cos \pi - \cos M) = 1$

or $\quad -(\cos M - 1) = 1$ and $-(\cos x \int_M^\pi = 1$

or $\quad \cos M = 0.$

or $\quad M = \frac{\pi}{2}$

Hence, the median is $\frac{\pi}{2}$

(iii) *Mode*: we have $\quad f(x) = \frac{1}{2}\sin x$

$\therefore \quad f'(x) = \frac{1}{2}\cos x \quad$ and $\quad f''(x) = -\frac{1}{2}\operatorname{Sin} x$

$f'(x) = 0 \Rightarrow x = \frac{\pi}{2}$

at $\quad x = \frac{\pi}{2}, \; f''(x) = -\frac{1}{2} \quad \sin\frac{\pi}{2} = -\frac{1}{2} < 0$

Hence $f(x)$ is maximum at $x = \frac{\pi}{2}$

Mode $= \frac{\pi}{2}$

Exercise 2.2

1. A continuous random variable has Probability density function

$$f(x) = \begin{cases} k\,x\,e^{-\lambda x} & \text{for}, x \geq 0, \lambda > 0 \\ 0 & , \text{otherwise} \end{cases}$$

Determine (i) k, (ii) Mean (iii) Median

2. A random variable gives measurements X between 0 and 1 with probability function

$$f(x) = \begin{cases} 12x^3 - 21x^2 + 10x, & 0 \le x \le 1 \\ 0, & \text{elsewhere} \end{cases}$$

(i) Find $P(x \le \frac{1}{2})$, $P(X > \frac{1}{2})$

(ii) Find a number k such that $P(x \le k) = \frac{1}{2}$ (JNTU, 2003)

3. A continuous random variable X has a probability density function

$$f(x) = 3x^2, \qquad 0 \le x \le 1$$

Find a and b such that

(i) $P(x \le a) = P(x > a)$

(ii) $P(x > b) = 0.05$

4. Is the function defined as follows is a probability density function

$$F(x) = \begin{cases} 0 & , \text{ if } x < 2 \\ \frac{1}{18}(3+2x) & , \text{ if } 2 \le x \le 4 \\ 0 & , \text{ if } x > 4 \end{cases}$$

If so find $P(2 \le x \le 3)$

5. A continuous random variable X is distributed over the interval [0, 1] with p.d.f. $ax^2 + bx$, where a and b are constants. If the arithmetic mean of X is 0.5, find arithmatic values of a and b.

6. If the probability density function of a random variable X is $f(x) = c\,e^{-ax}, 0 \le x < \infty$, $a > 0$, find

(i) the value of c (ii) Mean (iii) variance

7. A random variable X has the density function

$$f(x) = k.\ \frac{1}{1+x^2}, \qquad -\infty < x < \infty$$

find k and the distribution function F(x).

8. If X and Y are random variables having joint density function.

$$f(x, y) = \begin{cases} 4\,xy & , 0 \le x \le 1, 0 \le y \le 1 \\ 0 & , \text{otherwise} \end{cases}$$

verify that

(i) E(X + Y) = E (X) +E(Y) (ii) E(x y) = E(X), E(Y)

9. Find the constant k so that the function f(x) defined by

$$f(x) = \begin{cases} \frac{1}{k} & , \text{if } a \le x \le b \\ 0 & , \text{elsewhere} \end{cases}$$

is a density function

10. X is a continuous random variable with probability density function given by

$$f(x) = \begin{cases} kx & , \quad 0 \le x < 2 \\ 2k & , \quad 2 \le x < 4 \\ k(6-x) & , \quad 4 \le x < 6 \end{cases}$$

find k and mean [JNTU 2004]

11. If the probability density function of a random variable X is given by

$$f(x) = \begin{cases} 2k\,xe^{-x^2} & , x > 0 \\ 0 & \text{for} .\ x \le 0 \end{cases}$$

Determine (i) k (ii) distribution function for X

12. The probability density function of a continuous random variable is defined by

$$f(x) = \begin{cases} \frac{1}{4} e^{-x/4} & , \text{ for } x > 0 \\ 0 & , \text{ elsewhere} \end{cases}$$

find the mean and variance.

13. A continuous random variable X has the following density function

$$f(x) = \begin{cases} \frac{1}{2} & , \quad -1 \leq x < 0 \\ \frac{1}{4}(2-x), & 0 < x < 2 \\ 0 & , \quad \text{elsewhere} \end{cases}$$

obtain the distribution function of X

14. Find the value of the constant k such that

$$f(x) = \begin{cases} k x^2 (1 - x^3), & 0 < x < 1 \\ 0 & , \quad \text{otherwise} \end{cases}$$

is a probability density function of a continuous random variable X

15 Given the probability density function $f(x) = \begin{cases} 1 - x^2, & 0 < x < 1 \\ 0 & , \text{elsewhere} \end{cases}$

find the kth moment about the origin

Answers 2.2

1. $k = \lambda^2$, Mean $= \frac{2}{\lambda}$, variance $\frac{2}{\lambda^2}$

2. $\frac{9}{16}, \frac{7}{16}, 0.452$

3. $a = \left(\frac{1}{2}\right)^{\frac{1}{3}}$, $b = \left(\frac{19}{20}\right)^{\frac{1}{3}}$

4. $\frac{4}{9}$

5. – 6, 6

6. (i) C = 9, (ii) $\mu = \frac{1}{a^2}$, (iii) variance = $\frac{2}{a^3}$

7. $k = \frac{1}{\pi}$,

8. $f(x) = \frac{1}{\pi}\left[\tan^{-1} x + \frac{\pi}{2}\right]$

9. $\frac{1}{b-a}$

10. $\frac{1}{8}, \frac{1}{3}$

11. k = 1, $F(x) = \begin{cases} 1 - e^{-x^2}, & x > 0 \\ = 0, & \text{otherwise} \end{cases}$

12. 4, 80

13. $F(x) = \begin{cases} \frac{x+1}{2}, & -1 \leq x < 0 \\ \frac{4 + 4x - x^2}{8}, & 0 < x < 2 \\ 1, & \text{if } x \geq 2 \end{cases}$

14. k = 6

15. $\frac{2}{(k+1)(k+3)}$

Distributions 3

3.1 Introduction

In this chapter we shall introduce theoretical distributions. The distributions which are based on expectations on the basis of past experiences are known as theoretical distributions. We shall study both discrete and continuous distributions. We begin our study with discrete distributions. The important discrete distributions are:

1. Binomial distribution
2. Poisson distribution
3. Geometric distribution

3.1.1 Binomial Distribution

A random experiment with only two possible outcomes success or failure is called a Bernoulli trial. The corresponding distribution is called Bernoulli distribution. The probability of success in a Bernoulli trial is denoted by p and the probability of failure is denoted by q. If n denotes the number of trials, then the probability of x successes is $n_{c_x} p^x q^{n-x}$. The associated probability distribution is known as Bernoulli distribution or Binomial distribution.

Binomial distribution was discovered by James Bernoulli (1654–1705). The distribution can be used under the following assumptions:

(i) There are only two possible outcomes for each trial known as success and failure.

(ii) The probability of success in each trial is the same for each trial.

(iii) The number of trials is finite.

(iv) The trials are independent.

Bernoulli's theorem states that the probability of obtaining x successes in n trials is $n_{c_x} p^x q^{n-x}$.

It is denoted by f(x) or b(n, p, x)

Hence $b(n, p, x) = f(x) = n_{c_x} p^x q^{n-x}$

$$= n_{c_x} p^x (1-p)^{n-x}$$

The table showing the values of f(x) corresponding to the values x = 0, 1, 2, …, n is

X = x number of successes	0	1	2	x	…	n
f(x) probability	q^n	$n_{c_1} pq^{n-1}$	$n_{c_2} p^2 q^{n-2}$	$\ldots n_{c_x} p^x q^{n-x}$	…	p^n

The above table is in the form of a frequency distribution and it is called Binomial distribution. Different values of f(x) shown in the table are various terms in the expansion of $(q + p)^n$. f(x) = b(n, p, x) is called Binomial probability function. The random variable associated with Binomial distribution is called the Binomial variate.

The binomial function f(x) = b(n, p, x) satisfies the following

(i) $b(n, p, x) = f(x) \geq 0$ for x = 0, 1, 2, …, n

(ii) $\sum_{i=1}^{n} b(n, p, x_i) = 1$

3.1.2 Binomial Frequency Distribution

If an experiment, satisfying the requirements of a binomial distribution is repeated N times, then the expected frequency of getting x successes

where $0 \leq x \leq n$, is given by

$$N.P(X = x) = N.\ n_{c_x} p^x q^{n-x}, \qquad 0 \leq x \leq n$$

The theoretical (expected) frequencies of getting 0 success, 1 success, 2 successes, …, n successes are respectively the 1st, 2nd, 3rd, …, $(n + 1)^{th}$ terms in the expansion of $N(q + p)^n$.

3.1.3 The Mean and Variance of Binomial Distribution

Let X be the binomial random variable, n be the number of trials and p denote the probability of success in a trial. Then we have

$$f(x) = p(X = x) = n_{c_x} p^x q^{n-x} \qquad 0 \leq x \leq n$$

Mean of X is computed as follows

$$\text{Mean} = \mu = \sum_{x=0}^{n} x\,P(X = x)$$

$$= \sum_{x=0}^{n} x.n_{c_x} p^r q^{n-r}$$

$$= 0.\ n_{c_0}.p^o q^n + 1.n_{c_1} p^1 q^{n-1} + n_{c_2} p^2 q^{n-2} + \ldots + n_{c_n} p^n q^0$$

$$= np\left[q^{n-1} + \frac{2^{n(n-1)}}{1.2} pq^{n-2} + \ldots + p^{n-1}\right]$$

$$= np\left[(n-1)_{c_0}\ p^0 q^{n-1} + (n-1)_{c_1} pq^{n-2} + \ldots + n - 1_{c_{n-1}} p^{n-1} q^0\right]$$

$$= np\ [q + p]^{n-1}$$

$$= np\ .\ 1 = np$$

$$\therefore \qquad \mu = np$$

Variance of the distribution is

$$\sigma^2 = \sum_{x=0}^{n} x^2 p(X = x) - \mu^2 = \sum_{x=0}^{n} x^2\, n_{c_x} p^x q^{n-x} - \mu^2$$

$$= \left[0^2.n_{c_0} p^0 q^n + 1^2.n_{c_1} pq^{n-1} + 2^2 n_{c_2} p^2 q^{n-2} + \ldots + n^2\ \ n_{c_n} p^n q^0\right] - n^2 p^2$$

$$= np\left[q^{n-1} + \frac{2(n-1)}{1} pq^{n-2} + \frac{3(n-1)(n-2)}{1.2} p^2 q^{n-3} + \ldots + np^{n-1} - n^2 q^2\right.$$

$$= np\left[q^{n-1} + (n-1)_{c_1} pq^{n-2} + (n-1)_{c_2} p^2 q^{n-3} + \ldots + p^{n-1}\right]$$

$$+\left((n-1).pq^{n-2} + \frac{2(n-1)(n-2)}{1.2} p^2 q^{n-3}\right) + \ldots\ldots..$$

$$\left. + (n-1)p^{n-1}\right] - n^2 q^2 p$$

$$= np\left[(q+p)^{n-1} + (n-1)p\left(q^{n-2} + (n-2)pq^{n-3} + \ldots + p^{n-2}\right)\right] - n^2 q^2 p$$

$$= np\ [1 + (n-1)\ p((q + p)^{n-2})] - n^2\ q^2\ p$$

$= np + (n\,p)\,(n-1)\,p\,(1)^{n-2} - n^2\,p^2$

$= np + n^2\,p^2 - np^2 - n^2\,p^2$

$= np - np^2$

$= np\,(1-p)$

$= n\,p\,q$

3.1.4 Recurrence Formula for Binomial Distribution

Let X be a binomial random variable

we have $P(X=r) = n_{c_r} p^r q^{n-1}, \qquad 0 \le r \le n$

for $\quad 0 \le r \le n-1$, we can write

$$P(X = k) = P(k) = n_{c_k}\ p^k\ q^{n-k}$$

and $\quad P(X = k+1) = P(k+1) = n_{c_{k+1}}\ p^{k+1} q^{n-(k+1)}$

Hence, $\dfrac{P(k+1)}{P(k)} = \dfrac{n_{c_{k+1}} p^{k+1} q^{n-k-1}}{n_{c_k} p^k q^{n-k}}$

$$= \frac{n-k}{k+1} \cdot \frac{p}{q}$$

Thus, the required recurrence formula is

$$P(k+1) = \frac{n-k}{k+1} \cdot \frac{p}{q}\ p(k), \qquad 0 \le k \le n-1$$

Solved Examples

***Example* 1:** Eight coins are tossed simultaneously. Find the probability of obtaining atleast 6 heads.

***Solution*:** Let p be the probability of getting a head

we have $n = 8,\ p = \frac{1}{2},\ q = 1 - p = 1 - \frac{1}{2} = \frac{1}{2}$

Let X be the binomial variable number of successes

$\therefore\ P(X \ge 6)$ = Probability of getting atleast 6 heads

$= P(X = 6) + P(X = 7) + P(X = 8)$

$$= 8_{c_6} p^6 q^2 + 8_{c_7} p^7 q + 8_{c_8} p^8$$

$$= 8_{c_2} \left(\frac{1}{2}\right)^6 \left(\frac{1}{2}\right)^2 + 8_{c_1} \left(\frac{1}{2}\right)^7 \left(\frac{1}{2}\right) + \left(\frac{1}{2}\right)^8$$

$$= \frac{8.7}{1.2} \frac{1}{2^8} + 8\left(\frac{1}{2^8}\right) + \frac{1}{2^8}$$

$$= \frac{1}{2^8}(28 + 8 + 1)$$

$$= \frac{1}{256}(37) = \frac{37}{256}$$

***Example* 2:** In a throw of four dice, find the probability that atleast one dice shows up 4.

***Solution*:** When 4 dice are thrown the number of points in the sample space of the experiment is 6^4.

We have n = 4, p = probability of getting 4 = 1/6

$$q = 1 - \frac{1}{6} = \frac{5}{6}$$

$$P(X \geq 1) = 1 - P(X < 1) = 1 - P(X = 0)$$

Probability that atleast one die shows up 4 = $1 - 4_{c_0} p^0 q^{4-0}$

$$= 1 - 4_{c_0} \left(\frac{1}{6}\right)^0 \left(\frac{5}{6}\right)^{4-0}$$

$$= 1 - \left(\frac{5}{6}\right)^4 = \frac{671}{1296}$$

***Example* 3:** Ten coins are tossed simultaneously. Find the probability of getting atleast 7 heads. (JNTU 2008)

Solution: We have n = 10, p = probability of getting a head = $\frac{1}{2}$

q = probability of not getting a head

$$= 1 - p = 1 - \frac{1}{2} = \frac{1}{2}$$

$$p(X \geq 7) = p(X = 7) + p(X = 8) + p(X = 9) + p(X = 10)$$

$$= p(7) + p(8) + p(9) + p(10)$$

$$= 10_{c_7}\left(\frac{1}{2}\right)^7\left(\frac{1}{2}\right)^3 + 10_{c_8}\left(\frac{1}{2}\right)^8\left(\frac{1}{2}\right)^2 + 10_{c_9}\left(\frac{1}{2}\right)^9\left(\frac{1}{2}\right) + 10_{c_{10}}\left(\frac{1}{2}\right)^{10}$$

$$= \frac{1}{2^{10}}\left[10_{c_3} + 10_{c_2} + 10_{c_1} + 1\right]$$

$$= \frac{1}{2^{10}}\left[\frac{10.9.8}{1.2.3} + \frac{10.9}{1.2} + 10 + 1\right]$$

$$= \frac{1}{2^{10}}[120 + 45 + 11]$$

$$= \frac{176}{1024} = 0.172 \text{ (approx)}$$

***Example* 4:** There are 5 percent defective items in a large bulk of items. What is the probability that a sample of 10 items will include not more than one defective item.

Solution: We have n = 10

If p denotes the probability of getting a defective item, then

$$P = \frac{5}{100} = \frac{1}{20}, \text{ and } q = 1 - p = 1 - \frac{1}{20} = \frac{19}{20}$$

Using Binomial distribution we get

$$P(X \le 1) = P(X = 0) + P(X = 1)$$

$$= 10_{c_0}\left(\frac{1}{20}\right)^0\left(\frac{19}{20}\right)^{10} + 10_{c_1}\left(\frac{1}{20}\right)\left(\frac{19}{20}\right)^9$$

$$= \left(\frac{29}{20}\right)\left(\frac{19}{20}\right)^{10}$$

***Example* 5:** In a hurdle race a player has to cross 10 hurdles. The probability that he will clear each hurdle is 5/6. What is the probability that he will knock down fewer than 2 hurdles.

Solution: We have n = 7

$$p = \text{probability of hitting the target} = \frac{1}{4}$$

$$q = 1 - p = 1 - \frac{1}{4} = \frac{3}{4}$$

$P(X \geq 2)$ = probability of hitting the target atleast twice

$$= 1 - P(X < 2)$$

$$= 1 - [P(X = 0) + P(X = 1)]$$

$$= 1 - \left[7_{c0}\left(\frac{1}{4}\right)^0\left(\frac{3}{4}\right)^7 + 7_{c1}\left(\frac{1}{4}\right)^1\left(\frac{3}{4}\right)^6\right]$$

$$= 1 - \left[\frac{3^7}{4^7} + 7\left(\frac{1}{4}\right)\frac{3^6}{4^6}\right]$$

$$= 1 - \left(\frac{3}{4}\right)^6\left(\frac{3}{4} + \frac{7}{4}\right)$$

$$= 1 - \left(\frac{3}{4}\right)^6\left(\frac{10}{4}\right)$$

$$= 1 - \left(\frac{3}{4}\right)^6\left(\frac{5}{2}\right)$$

$$= \frac{4547}{8192}$$

***Example* 6:** The number of telephone lines busy at any instant of time in a binomial variable with probability 0.2. If an instant 10 lines are chosen at random what is the probability that (i) 5 lines are busy (ii) at most 2 lines are busy

Solution: The probability that a telephone line is busy = p = 0.2

We have n = 10, q = 1 – p = 0.8

(i) $P(X = 5) = 10_{c5}\,(0.2)^5\,(0.8)^5 = 0.0264$

$\therefore$ probability that 5 lines are busy = 0.0264

(ii) $P(X \leq 2)$ = probability that at most 2 lines are busy

$$= P(X = 0) + P(X = 1) + P(X = 2)$$

$$= 10_{c0}\,(0.2)^0\,(0.8)^{10} + 10_{c1}\,(0.2)^1\,(0.8)^9 + 10_{c2}\,(0.2)^2\,(0.8)^8$$

$$= 0.677$$

***Example* 7:** A bag contains 10 balls each marked with one of the digits 0 to 9. If four balls are drawn successively with replacement from the bag, what is the probability that none is marked with digit 0.

Solution: Let p be the probability of drawing a ball with digit 0.

We have $n = 4,\ p = \frac{1}{10},$

$$q = 1 - p = 1 - \frac{1}{10} = \frac{9}{10}$$

Let X denote the random variable "number of successes"

Then

$P(X = 0) =$ probability that none of the drawn balls is marked with digit 0

$$= 4_{c0}\left(\frac{1}{10}\right)^0\left(\frac{9}{10}\right)^4$$

$$= 1.1.\frac{9^4}{10^4} = \frac{6561}{10000} = 0.6561$$

***Example* 8:** Five cards are drawn successively with replacement from a well-shuffled pack of cards. What is the probability that

(i) all the five cards are spades

(ii) none is a spade

***Solution*:** Number of cards in a pack = 52, number of spades in a pack = 13

Let p be the probability of drawing a spade

We have $n = 5,\ p = \frac{13}{52} = \frac{1}{4},\ q = 1 - \frac{1}{4} = \frac{3}{4}$

(i) P(X = 5) = probability that all cards drawn are spades

$$= 5_{c5}\left(\frac{1}{4}\right)^5\left(\frac{3}{4}\right)^0 = \frac{1}{1024}$$

(ii) P(X = 0) = probability that none of the cards drawn is a spade

$$= 5_{c0}\left(\frac{1}{4}\right)^0\left(\frac{3}{4}\right)^5 = 1.1.\frac{243}{1024} = \frac{243}{1024}$$

***Example* 9:** The probability that the life of a bulb is 100 days is 0.05. Find the probability that one of 6 bulbs

(i) at least one (ii) greater than four (iii) none will have a life of 100 days. (JNTU 2007)

***Solution*:** We have n = 6

$$p = \text{probability that the life of a bulb is 100 days}$$

$$= 0.05$$

$$q = 1 - p = 1 - 0.05 = 0.95$$

Thus $$p = 0.05 = \frac{1}{20},\ q = 0.95 = \frac{19}{20}$$

We get

(i) $P(X \geq 1) = 1 - P(X = 0) = 1 - 6_{c0}\left(\frac{1}{20}\right)^0\left(\frac{19}{20}\right)^6 = 1 - \frac{19^6}{20^6} = 0.265$

(ii) $P(X > 4) = P(X = 5) + P(X = 6)$

$$= 6_{c5}\left(\frac{1}{20}\right)^5\left(\frac{19}{20}\right)^1 + 6_{c6}\left(\frac{1}{20}\right)^6\left(\frac{19}{20}\right)^0$$

$$= \frac{115}{(20)^6}$$

(iii) $P(X = 0) = 6_{c0}\left(\frac{1}{20}\right)^0\left(\frac{19}{20}\right)^6 = 0.735$

***Example* 10:** Determine the probability of getting a sum of 9 exactly twice in 3 throws with a pair of dice.

***Solution*:** Favourable cases for getting a sum of 9 are (3, 6), (4, 5), (5, 4), (6, 3)

Number of favourable cases = m = 4

We have $n = 6^2 = 36$

p = probability of getting a sum of 9 in one throw of pair of dice $= \frac{m}{n} = \frac{4}{36} = \frac{1}{9}$

$$q = 1 - p = 1 - \frac{1}{9} = \frac{8}{9}$$

Probability of getting a sum of 9 exactly twice in 3 throws $= 3_{c2}\left(\frac{1}{9}\right)^2\left(\frac{8}{9}\right)^1$

$$= 3.\frac{1}{9^2}.\frac{8}{9} = 0.033$$

***Example* 11:** A survey of 200 families each having 4 children was conducted. In how many families do you expect 3 boys and 1 girl if boys and girls are equiprobable.

***Solution*:**

Let p = probability of getting a boy

We have $n = 4$, $p = \frac{1}{2}$, $q = \frac{1}{2}$, $N = 200$

Probability of getting 3 boys and 1 girl

$$= P(X = 3) = 4_{c_3}\left(\frac{1}{2}\right)^3\left(\frac{1}{2}\right)^1 = \frac{4}{2^4} = \frac{4}{16} = \frac{1}{4}$$

Therefore,

Number of families with 3 boys and 1 girl

$$= N.\ P(X = 3) = 200.\frac{1}{4} = 50$$

***Example* 12:** The probability of a man hitting a target is $\frac{1}{3}$

(i) If he fires 5 times, what is the probability of his getting the target at least twice

(ii) How many times must he fire so that the probability of his hitting the target at least once is more than 90%.

***Solution*:** The probability of hitting a target = $p = \frac{1}{3}$

We have $q = 1 - p = 1 - \frac{1}{3} = \frac{2}{3}$; $n = 5$

$P(X \geq 2)$ = probability of hitting the target at least twice

$$= 1 - P(X < 2) = 1 - \left(P(X = 0) + P(X = 1)\right)$$

$$= 1 - 5_{c_0}\left(\frac{1}{3}\right)^0\left(\frac{2}{3}\right)^5 - 5_{c_1}\left(\frac{1}{3}\right)^1\left(\frac{2}{3}\right)^4$$

$$= 0.539$$

(ii) Probability of hitting the target at least once > 90%

i.e. $$P(X \geq 1) > \frac{90}{100}$$

or $1-p(x=0)>0.9$

or $1-n_{c_0}p^0q^n > 0.9$ where n is the number of times he fired

or $1-\left(\frac{2}{3}\right)^n > 0.9$ since the least positive integer n for which $1-\left(\frac{2}{3}\right) > 0.9$ holds is 6, we consider n = 6

∴ The least value is n = 6

***Example* 13:** A box contains 100 tickets each bearing one of the members from 1 to 100. If 5 tickets are drawn successively with replacement from the box, find the probability that all the tickets bear number divisible by 10

***Solution*:** The numbers between 1 and 100 (inclusive) divisible by 10 are 10, 20, 30, 40, 50, 60, 70, 80, 90, 100

If p denotes the probability of drawing a ticket whose number is divisible by 10, then $P = \frac{10}{100} = \frac{1}{10}$

We have $n = 5,\ p = \frac{1}{10},\ q = 1-p = 1-\frac{1}{10} = \frac{9}{10}$

∴ P(X = 5)= The probability all the tickets drawn are divisible by 10

$$= 5_{c_5}\left(\frac{1}{10}\right)^5\left(\frac{9}{10}\right)^0$$

$$= \frac{1}{10^5}$$

***Example* 14:** The mean and variance of a binomial distribution are respectively 9 and 6. Find the distribution

***Solution*:** we have

Mean = np = 9; Variance = npq = 6 (given)

Dividing we get

$$\frac{npq}{np} = \frac{6}{9}$$

i.e. $$q = \frac{2}{3}$$

$$\therefore\ p = 1 - q = 1 - \frac{2}{3} = \frac{1}{3}$$

Since np = 9, we get

$$n.\frac{1}{3} = 9$$

Hence n = 27

The required Binomial distribution is

$$P(X = x) = 27_{c_x}\left(\frac{1}{3}\right)^x\left(\frac{2}{3}\right)^{27-x}, \ 0 \le x \le 27$$

***Example* 15:** The mean and variance of a binomial variable X with parameters n and p are 16 and 8. Find $p(x \ge 1)$ and $p(x > 2)$ (JNTU 2004)

***Solution*:** It is given that np = mean = 16, and variance = npq = 8

Dividing, we get

$$q = \frac{npq}{np} = \frac{8}{16} = \frac{1}{2}$$

$$\therefore p = 1 - q = 1 - \frac{1}{2} = \frac{1}{2}$$

since np = 16, we get $n.\frac{1}{2} = 16$ or $n = 32$

we get

$$P(X \ge 1) = 1 - P(X < 1)$$

$$= 1 - P(X = 0)$$

$$= 1 - 32_{c_0}\left(\frac{1}{2}\right)^0\left(\frac{1}{2}\right)^{32}$$

$$= 1 - \frac{1}{2^{32}}$$

and

$$P(X > 2) = 1 - P(X \le 2)$$

$$= 1 - \left[P(X = 0) + P(X = 1) + P(X = 2)\right]$$

$$= 1 - 32_{c_0}\left(\frac{1}{2}\right)^0\left(\frac{1}{2}\right)^{32} - 32_{c_1}\left(\frac{1}{2}\right)^1\left(\frac{1}{2}\right)^{31}$$

$$-32_{c_2}\left(\frac{1}{2}\right)^2\left(\frac{1}{2}\right)^{30}$$

$$=1-\left(\frac{1}{2}\right)^{32}(1+32+496)$$

$$=1-\left(\frac{1}{2}\right)^{32}(529)$$

$$=1-\frac{529}{2^{32}}$$

***Example* 16:** Let X be a binomially distributed random variable with mean 2 and standard deviation $2/\sqrt{3}$. Find the corresponding probability function

***Solution*:** Here we have np = mean = 2

σ = standard deviation = $\sqrt{npq} = 2/\sqrt{3}$

i.e. $\sigma^2 = \left(2/\sqrt{3}\right)^2 = \frac{4}{3}$ or $npq = \frac{4}{3}$ s

dividing we get

$$q = \frac{npq}{np} = \frac{4}{3}.\frac{1}{2} = \frac{4}{6} = \frac{2}{3}$$

$$p = 1 - q = 1 - \frac{2}{3} = \frac{1}{3}$$

since np = 2

we get $n.\left(\frac{1}{3}\right) = 2$ or $n = 2.3 = 6$

Hence, the required probability function is

$$P(X = x) = 6_{c_x}\left(\frac{1}{3}\right)^x\left(\frac{2}{3}\right)^{6-x}$$

***Example* 17:** The probability that Ram hits a target is $\frac{1}{2}$. He fires 6 times. Find the probability that he hits the target. (i) exactly 2 times (ii) more than 4 times (iii) At least once.

Solution: p = probability that Ram hits a target = $\frac{1}{2}$ given

Therefore, $$q = 1 - p = 1 - \frac{1}{2} = \frac{1}{2}$$

n = number of times Ram fired = 6

(i) $P(X = 2) = 6_{c_2}\left(\frac{1}{2}\right)^2\left(\frac{1}{2}\right)^4 = \frac{6.5}{1.2}.\frac{1}{2^6} = \frac{15}{2^6}$

(ii) $P(X > 4) = P(X = 5) + P(X = 6)$

$$= 6_{c_5}\left(\frac{1}{2}\right)^5\left(\frac{1}{2}\right)^1 + 6_{c_6}\left(\frac{1}{2}\right)^6\left(\frac{1}{2}\right)^0$$

$$= \frac{1}{2^6}(6+1) = \frac{7}{2^6}$$

(iii) $P(X \geq 1) = 1 - P(X = 0)$

$$= 1 - 6_{c_0}\left(\frac{1}{2}\right)^0\left(\frac{1}{2}\right)^6 = 1 - \frac{1}{2^6}$$

***Example* 18:** Fit a Binomial distribution to the following data.

x	0	1	2	3	4	5
f	2	14	20	34	22	8

(JNTU 2004)

Solution: From the given table

$$\sum f_i = 2 + 14 + 20 + 34 + 22 + 8$$

i.e., N = 100

and $$\Sigma x_i f_i = (0)(2) + (1) - (14) + (2)(20) + (3)(34) + (4)(22) + (5)(8)$$

$$= 284$$

$\therefore$ $$\text{Mean} = \frac{\Sigma x_i f_i}{\Sigma f_i} = \frac{284}{100} = 2.84$$

we have n = 5

since mean = np = 2.84

we get 5 p = 2.84

or $$p = \frac{2.84}{5} = 0.568$$

$\therefore$ $$q = 1 - p = 1 - 0.568 = 0.432$$

Thus n = 5, p = 0.568, q = 0.432, N = 100

The Theoretical frequencies i.e expected frequencies are

$$N.P(X = 0) = 100 \,.\, 5_{c_0} (0.568)^0 (0.432)^5 = 1.5045 \simeq 2$$

$$N.P(X = 1) = 100 \,.\, 5_{c_1} \,.\, (0.568)^1 (0.432)^4 = 9.89 \simeq 10$$

$$N.P(X = 2) = 100 \,.\, 5_{c_2} (0.568)^2 (0.432)^3 = 26.0 = 26$$

$$N.P(X = 3) = 100 \,.\, 5_{c_3} (0.568)^3 (0.432)^2 = 34.1 \simeq 34$$

$$N.P(X = 4) = 100. \, 5_{c_4} (0.568)^4 (0.432) = 22.4 \simeq 22$$

$$N.P(X = 5) = 100 \,.\, 5_{c_5} (0.568)^5 = 5.9 \simeq 6$$

The required Binomial frequency distribution is

X = x	0	1	2	3	4	5
N.P(X = x)	2	10	26	34	22	6

i.e., the required fit is $N(q + p)^n = 100(0.432 + 0.568)^5$

***Example* 19:** 4 coins are tossed 100 times and the following results were obtained. Fit a binomial distribution for the data and calculate the theoretical frequencies.

Number of heads	0	1	2	3	4
Frequency	5	29	36	25	5

***Solution*:** Mean of the distribution $= \frac{\Sigma x_i f_i}{\Sigma f_i}$

$$= \frac{(0)(1)+(1)(29)+(2)(36)+(3)(25)+(4)(5)}{5+29+36+25+5}$$

$$= \frac{196}{100} = 1.96$$

$\therefore$ $np = 1.96$

since n = 4, we get $4\,p = 1.96$

or $p = 0.49$

and $q = 1 - p = 1 - 0.49 = 0.51$

The required Binomial fit is $N(q + p)^n$

$$= 100(0.51 + 0.49)^4$$

The theoretical frequencies of the distribution are various terms in the expansion of $100(0.5 + 0.49)^4$

Hence, the theoretical frequencies are

$$N\,p(X = 0) = 100(0.49)^0\,(0.51)^4 = 7$$

$$N\,p(X = 1) = 100(0.49)^1\,(0.51)^3 = 26$$

$$N\,p(X = 2) = 100(0.49)^2\,(0.51)^2 = 37$$

$$N\,p(X = 3) = 100(0.49)^3\,(0.51) = 24$$

$$N\,p(X = 4) = 100(0.49)^4 = 6$$

Thus the Binomial frequency distribution is

X	0	1	2	3	4
N p (X)	7	26	37	24	6

***Example* 20:** 8 coins are tossed at a time, 256 times. Find the expected frequencies successes (of getting a head) and tabulate the results obtained

***Solution*:** p = probability of getting a head = $\frac{1}{2}$

$$q = \frac{1}{2}$$

We have n = 8, N = 256

The expected frequencies are as shown in the Table given below

X = success	N P(X = x)	Expected frequencies
0	$256.\left(\frac{1}{2}\right)^8$	1
1	$(256)8_{c_1}\left(\frac{1}{2}\right)\left(\frac{1}{2}\right)^7$	8
2	$256.8_{c_2}.\left(\frac{1}{2}\right)^2\left(\frac{1}{2}\right)^6$	28
3	$256.8_{c_3}.\left(\frac{1}{2}\right)^3\left(\frac{1}{2}\right)^5$	56
4	$256.8_{c_4}.\left(\frac{1}{2}\right)^4\left(\frac{1}{2}\right)^4$	70
5	$256.8_{c_5}.\left(\frac{1}{2}\right)^5\left(\frac{1}{2}\right)^3$	56
6	$256.8_{c_6}.\left(\frac{1}{2}\right)^6\left(\frac{1}{2}\right)^2$	28
7	$256.8_{c_7}.\left(\frac{1}{2}\right)^7\left(\frac{1}{2}\right)$	8
8	$256.8_{c_8}.\left(\frac{1}{2}\right)^8$	1

Exercise 3.1

1. A dice is thrown 6 times. If getting an even number is a success, find the probability of (i) getting at least one success (ii) 4 successes
2. If 3 of 20 tyres are defective and 4 of them are randomly chosen for inspection what is the probability that only one of the defective tyre will be included (JNTU 2000)
3. A die is tossed thrice. A success is getting 1 or 6 on a toss. Find the mean and variance of number of successes

4. Find the maximum n such that the probability of getting no head in tossing a coin n times is greater than 0.1. (JNTU 2007)

5. In eight throws of a die 5 or 6 is considered to be a success. Find the mean number of successes and the standard deviation. (JNTU 2004)

6. Find the probability that at most 5 defective components will be found in a lot of 200. Experience shows that 2% of such components are defective. Also find the probability of more than five defective components. (JNTU 2005)

7. 20% of items produced from a factory are defective. Find the probability that in a sample of 5 chosen at random

   (i) none is defective (ii) one is defective (iii) $p(1 < x < 4)$

8. A fair coin is tossed 6 times. Find the probability of getting four heads.

9. A pair of dice is thrown. Find the probability of getting a sum eleven

   (i) once (ii) twice.

10. In tossing 10 coins, what is the probability of getting exactly 5 heads.

11. Assume that 50% of all engineering students are good in mathematics. Determine the probabilities that among 18 engineering students.

    (i) exactly 10 (ii) at least 10 (iii) at least 2 and at most 9 (iv) at most 8 are good in mathematics. (JNTU 2005)

12. In a Binomial distribution consisting of 5 independent trials probabilities of 1 and 2 successes are 0.4096 and 0.2048 respectively. Find the parameter p of the distribution. (JNTU 2004)

13. The mean of a Binomial distribution is 3 and the variance is $\frac{9}{4}$. Find (i) the value of n (ii) $p(X \geq 7)$ (iii) $p(1 \leq X < 6)$

14. Ten coins are thrown simultaneously. Find the probability of getting at least 7 heads

15. Six dice are thrown 729 times. How many times do you expect at least three dice to show a five or six.

16. If the chance that any one of the 10 telephone lines is busy at any instant is 0.2. What is the chance that 5 of the lines are busy. What is the probability that all the lines are busy.

17. If the probability that a man aged 60 will live to be 70 is 0.65. What is the probability that out of 10 men now 60, at least 7 will live to be 70.

18. If on the average rain falls 10 days in every 30 days, obtain the probability that (i) rain will fall on at least 3 days of a given week (ii) first three days of a given week will be fine and remaining 4 days wet

19. Four coins are tossed 160 times. The number of times x heads occur is given below

X	0	1	2	3	4
Number of times	8	34	69	143	6

(JNTU 2004)

Fit a binomial distribution on the hypothesis that coins are unbiased

20. Fit a binomial distribution to the following data

x	0	1	2	3	4	5
f	38	144	342	287	164	25

(JNTU 2004S)

21. Define the terms (i) Binomial distribution (ii) Binomial frequency distribution

22. If on the average one vessel in every 10 is wrecked. Find the probability that out of 5 vessels expected to arrive at least 4 will arrive safely.

Answers 3.1

1. (i) $\frac{63}{64}$ (ii) $\frac{15}{64}$

2. 0.3685

3. 1, 2/3

4. 3

5. 8/3, 4/3

6. 0.7867, 0.213

7. (i) 0.327 (ii) 0.4096 (iii) 0.256

8. $\frac{15}{64}$

9. (i) 0.105 (ii) 0.003

10. 0.246

11. (i) 0.1669 (ii) $\sum_{x=0}^{18} 18_{c_x}\left(\frac{1}{2}\right)^{18}$ (iii) $\sum_{x=2}^{9} 18_{c_x}\left(\frac{1}{2}\right)^{18}$ (iv) $\sum_{x=0}^{8} 18_{c_x}\left(\frac{1}{2}\right)^{18}$

12. 0.2

13. (i) 12 (ii) 0.1446 (iii) 0.82

14. 0.1718

15. 233

16. $10_{c_5}(0.2)^5$, $(0.8)^5$, $(0.2)^{10}$

17. 0.509 18, (i) 0.4294 (ii) 0.0037

19. 10, 40, 60, 40, 10

20. 33, 162, 316, 309, 151, 29

22. 0.918

3.2 Poisson Distribution

The Poisson distribution is a discrete probability distribution. It is derived as a limiting case of Binomial distribution. The conditions for the applicability are the same as those of for the applicability of the Binomial distribution. The addition requirement is that the probability of success is very small.

The conditions are:

1. The number of trials (n) is indefinitely large
2. The probability of success in a trial is indefinitely small (i.e p is very small)
3. The product np is a constant

The distribution is defined as follows.

Definition: A discrete random variable X taking the values 0, 1, 2, 3, ..., is said to follow Poisson distribution with parameter λ, if its probability mass function is given by

$$P(X=r)=\frac{e^{-\lambda}\lambda^r}{r!}, \quad r=0, 1, 2\ldots$$

$$=0 \text{ otherwise}$$

We now show that Poisson distribution is the limiting case of Binomial distribution.

By binomial distribution, we have

$$P(x=r) = n_{c_r}\, p^r q^{n-r}, \qquad 0 \le x \le n$$

Let $np = \lambda$

then $p = \dfrac{\lambda}{n}$

$$P(X=r) = n_{c_r} p^r q^{n-r} = n_{c_r} p^r (1-p)^{n-r}$$

$$=\frac{n!}{r!(n-r)!}\left(\frac{\lambda}{n}\right)^r\left(1-\frac{\lambda}{n}\right)^{n-r}$$

$$= \frac{n(n-1)(n-2)(......(n-r+1)(n-r)!)}{r!(n-r)!}\frac{\lambda^r}{n^r}\left(1-\frac{\lambda}{n}\right)^{n-r}$$

$$= \frac{n}{n}.\frac{n-1}{n}...\frac{(n-(r-1))}{n}.\frac{\lambda^r}{r!}\left(1-\frac{\lambda}{n}\right)^n\left(1-\frac{\lambda}{n}\right)^{-r}$$

$$= \frac{\lambda^r}{r!}\left(1-\frac{1}{n}\right)\left(1-\frac{2}{n}\right)...\left[\left(1-\frac{r-1}{n}\right)\left(1-\frac{\lambda}{n}\right)^{-n/\lambda}\right]^{-\lambda}\left(1-\frac{\lambda}{n}\right)^{-r}$$

applying limits, we get

$$\underset{n\to\infty}{Lt} P(X=r) = \frac{\lambda^r}{r!}\underset{n\to\infty}{Lt}\left(1-\frac{1}{n}\right)\underset{n\to\infty}{Lt}\left(1-\frac{2}{n}\right)...\underset{n\to\infty}{Lt}\left(1-\frac{r-1}{n}\right)$$

$$\underset{n\to\infty}{Lt}\left[\left(1-\frac{\lambda}{n}\right)^{-n/3}\right]^{-\lambda}\underset{n\to\infty}{Lt}\left(1-\frac{\lambda}{n}\right)^{-r}$$

$$= \frac{\lambda^r}{r!}(1-0)(1-0)...(1-0).e^{-\lambda}.(1-0)$$

$$= \frac{e^{-\lambda}\lambda^r}{r!}$$

i.e., when n is indefinitely larger, we have

$$P(X=r) = \frac{e^{-\lambda}\lambda^r}{r!}, \; r = 0, 1, 2 ....$$

where $P(X = r)$ is called poisson probability function

The corresponding poisson distribution is

x	0	1	2	...
P(X)	$\frac{e^{-\lambda}\lambda^0}{0!}$	$\frac{e^{-\lambda}\lambda}{1!}$	$\frac{e^{-\lambda}\lambda^2}{2!}$	...

λ is called the parameter of the distribution

3.2.1 Poisson Frequency Distribution

If an experiment satisfying the requirements of Poisson distribution is repeated N times, then the expected frequency of getting r successes is given by

$$N\,P(X=r) = \frac{Ne^{-\lambda}\lambda^r}{r!}, \qquad r = 0, 1, 2, ...$$

3.2.2 Mean of the Poisson Distribution

We have $$\text{Mean} = \sum_x x\ p\ (x = x)$$

$$= \sum_{x=0}^{\infty} x \frac{e^{-\lambda}\lambda^x}{x!}$$

$$= \sum_{x=1}^{\infty} \frac{e^{-\lambda}\lambda^x}{(x-1)!} = e^{-\lambda}\sum_{x=0}^{\infty}\frac{\lambda^{x+1}}{x!} \qquad \text{(replacing } x-1 \text{ by x)}$$

$$= e^{-\lambda}.\lambda.\sum_{x=0}^{\infty}\frac{\lambda^x}{x!}$$

$$= e^{-\lambda}\,.\,\lambda\,.\,e^{\lambda} = \lambda$$

3.2.3 Variance of Poisson Distribution

By definition $$v(x) = \sigma^2 = \sum_x x^2 P(X) - \left(\sum_x x\ P(X)\right)^2$$

$$= \sum_{x=0}^{\infty} x^2 \frac{e^{-\lambda}\lambda^x}{x!} - \lambda^2$$

$$= e^{-\lambda}\sum_{x=1}^{\infty}\frac{x\,\lambda^x}{(x-1)!} - \lambda^2$$

$$= e^{-\lambda}\left[\sum_{x=1}^{\infty}[(x-1)+1]\frac{\lambda^x}{(x-1)!}\right] - \lambda^2$$

$$= e^{-\lambda}\left[\sum_{x=2}\frac{\lambda^x}{(x-2)!} + \sum_{x=1}^{\infty}\frac{\lambda^x}{(x-1)!}\right] - \lambda^2$$

$$= e^{-\lambda}\left[\sum_{x=0}^{\infty}\frac{\lambda^{x+2}}{x!} + \sum_{x=0}^{\infty}\frac{\lambda^{x+1}}{x!}\right] - \lambda^2$$

$$= e^{-\lambda}\left[\lambda^2\sum_{x=0}^{\infty}\frac{\lambda^x}{x!} + \lambda\sum_{x=0}^{\infty}\frac{\lambda^x}{x!}\right] - \lambda^2$$

$$= e^{-\lambda}\lambda^2 e^{\lambda} + e^{-\lambda}\,.\,\lambda\,e^{\lambda} - \lambda^2 = \lambda^2 + \lambda - \lambda^2$$

$$= \lambda$$

3.2.4 Mode of the Poisson Distribution

The value of x at which p(X = x) is maximum is called the mode of the distribution.

If X = x is the mode then

$$P(X = x) \geq P(X = x + 1)$$

and $$P(X = x) \geq P(X = x - 1)$$

consider $$P(X = x) \geq P(X = x + 1)$$

we get $$\frac{e^{-\lambda}\lambda^{x}}{x!} \geq \frac{e^{-\lambda}\lambda^{x+1}}{(x+1)!}$$

or $$1 \geq \frac{\lambda}{x+1}$$

or $$x + 1 \geq \lambda$$

Hence $$x \geq \lambda - 1 \qquad .....(1)$$

similarly taking P(X = x) ≥ P(X = x – 1), we get

$$x \leq \lambda \qquad (2)$$

from (1) and (2) we have

$$\lambda - 1 \leq x \leq \lambda$$

hence the mode of the distribution lies between λ – 1 and λ

when λ is an integer λ – 1 is also an integer. In this case the distribution is binomial when λ is not an integer, the integral part of λ is the mode.

3.2.5 Recurrence formula for Poisson Distribution

We have $$P(X = x) = \frac{e^{-\lambda}\lambda^{x}}{x!}$$

therefore $$P(X = x + 1) = \frac{e^{-\lambda}\lambda^{x+1}}{(x+1)!}$$

$$= \frac{e^{-\lambda}\lambda^{x}.\lambda}{(x+1)\,x!}$$

$$= \frac{\lambda}{x+1}\left(\frac{e^{-\lambda}\lambda^{x}}{x!}\right) = \frac{\lambda}{x+1}P(X = x)$$

Hence $P(X + 1) = \dfrac{\lambda}{x+1} P(x)$ is the recurrence formula for poisson distribution

Solved Examples

***Example* 1:** Find the probability that at most 5 defective bolts will be found in a box of 200 bolts, if it is known that 2% such bolts are expected to be defective.

***Solution*:** We have n = 200, p = $\frac{2}{100}$ = 0.02

$\therefore \qquad \lambda = np = 200 \times 0.02 = 4$

Probability that at most 5 bolts are defective

$$= P(X \leq 5)$$

$$= P(X = 0) + P(X = 1) + P(X = 2) + P(X = 3) + P(X = 4) + P(X = 5)$$

$$= \frac{e^{-4}4^0}{0!} + \frac{e^{-4}4^1}{1!} + \frac{e^{-4}4^2}{2!} + \frac{e^{-4}4^3}{3!} + \frac{e^{-4}4^4}{4!} + \frac{e^{-4}4^5}{5!}$$

$$= e^{-4}\left[1 + 4 + \frac{16}{2} + \frac{64}{6} + \frac{256}{24} + \frac{1024}{120}\right]$$

$$= e^{-4} \ (42.866) = 0.0183 \times 42.866$$

$$= 0.785$$

***Example* 2:** Using Poisson distribution, find the probability that the ace of spades will be drawn from a pack of well shuffled cards at least once in 104 consecutive trials.

Solution: Probability that an ace of spades is drawn = $\frac{1}{52}$

We have n = 104

$\therefore \qquad \lambda = np = 104 \times \frac{1}{52} = 2$

$$P(X \geq 1) = P(X = 1) + P(X = 2) + \ldots + P(X = 104)$$

$$= 1 - P(X = 0)$$

$$= 1 - \frac{e^{-2}2^0}{0!} = 1 - e^{-2}$$

$$= 1 - 0.136 = 0.864$$

***Example* 3:** A car hire firm has two cars which it hires out day by day. The number of demands for a car on each day is distributed as Poisson variate with mean 1.5. Calculate the proportion of days on which (i) neither car is used (ii) some demand is refused

***Solution*:** We have λ = 1.5 (given)

$$P(X=0)=\frac{e^{-\lambda}\lambda^0}{0!}=\frac{e^{-1.5}(1.5)^0}{0!}=e^{-1.5}=0.2231$$

Proportion of days in which neither car is used = 0.2231

***Example* 4:** If X is a Poisson distribution such that 3 P(X = 2) = 2 P(X = 1). Find

(i) P(X = 0) (ii) P(X = 3)

***Solution*:** We have

$$3\,P(X=2)=2\,P(X=1)$$

therefore
$$3\frac{e^{-\lambda}\lambda^2}{2!}=2.\frac{e^{-\lambda}\lambda^1}{1!}$$

or
$$3\frac{\lambda^2}{2}=2\lambda$$

or
$$3\lambda^2-4\lambda=0$$

or
$$\lambda(3\lambda-4)=0$$

we get
$$\lambda=0,\ \lambda=\frac{4}{3}$$

$\lambda = 0$ is impossible. Hence $\lambda = 4/3$

(i) $$P(X=0)=\frac{e^{-\lambda}\lambda^0}{0!}=e^{\frac{-4}{3}}=0.264$$

(ii) $$P(X=3)=\frac{e^{-\lambda}\lambda^3}{3!}=\frac{e^{\frac{-4}{3}}}{6}\left(\frac{4}{3}\right)^3=0.1043$$

***Example* 5:** A manufacturer of cotter pins knows that 5% of his product is defective. If he sells in boxes of 100 and guarantees that not more than 4 pins will be defective, what is the approximate probability that a box will fail to meet the guaranteed quality.

***Solution*:** Let x be the Poisson Variable "number of defective pins per box"

We have $n = 100,\ P=\frac{5}{100}=\frac{1}{20},\ \lambda = np = 100\ .\ \frac{1}{20}=5$

$$\begin{aligned}P(X>4) &= 1-P(X\le 4)\\ &= 1-P(X=0)+P(X=1)+P(X=2)+P(X=3)+P(X=4)\\ &= 1-\left[\frac{e^{-5}5^0}{0!}+\frac{e^{-5}5^1}{1!}+\frac{e^{-5}5^2}{2!}+\frac{e^{-5}5^3}{3!}+\frac{e^{-5}5^4}{4!}+\frac{e^{-5}5^5}{5!}\right]\end{aligned}$$

$$= 1 - e^{-5}\left(1 + 5 + 12.5 + 20.8 + \frac{625}{24}\right)$$

$$= 1 - (0.0067)\,(65.375)$$

$$= 0.562$$

***Example* 6:** There are 50 telephone lines in an exchange. The probability that any one of them will be busy is 0.1. What is the probability that all the lines are busy.

***Solution*:** we have n = 50, p = 0.1 (given)

$\therefore\ \lambda = np = 50 \times 0.1 = 5$

Probability that all lines are busy $= P(X = 50) = \dfrac{e^{-5}5^{50}}{50!}$

***Example* 7:** The probability that a man aged 50 years will die within a year is 0.01125. What is the probability that out of 12 such men at least 11 will reach their fifty first birthday.

***Solution*:** It is given that n = 12, p = 0.01125

$$\therefore \qquad \lambda = np = 12 \times (0.1125) = 0.135$$

Probability that at least 11 will reach 51st first birthday

$$= P(\text{at most one will die within a year})$$

$$= P(X \le 1)$$

$$= P(X = 0) + P(X = 1)$$

$$= \frac{e^{-0.135}(0.135)^0}{0\,!} + \frac{e^{-0.135}(0.135)^1}{1!}$$

$$= 0.9917$$

***Example* 8:** Assume that the chance of an individual coal miner being killed in a mine accident during a year is $\dfrac{1}{1400}$. Use the Poisson distribution to calculate the probability that in a mine employing 350 miners there will be at least one fatal accident in a year

Solution: We have n = 350, $p = \dfrac{1}{1400}$

$$\lambda = np = 350\,.\left(\frac{1}{1400}\right) = 0.25$$

Probability that there will be at least one fatal accident in a year $= P(X \ge 1)$

$$= 1 - P(X = 0)$$

$$= 1 - \frac{e^{-0.25}(0.25)^0}{0!}$$

$$= 1 - e^{-0.25}$$

$$= 1 - 0.78 = 0.22$$

***Example* 9:** If the probability that an individual suffers a bad reaction from a certain injection is 0.001. Determine the probability that out of 2000, individuals (i) exactly 3 (ii) more than 2 individuals and (iii) none will suffer a bad reaction.

***Solution*:** It is given that n = 2000, p = 0.001

$\therefore\ \lambda = np = 2000 \times (0.001) = 2$

(i) $$P(X = 3) = \frac{e^{-\lambda}\lambda^3}{3!} = \frac{e^{-2}2^3}{6} = 0.1804$$

$\therefore$ probability that exactly 3 will suffer the bad reaction = 0.1804

(ii) $$P(X > 2) = 1 - [P(X = 0) + P(X = 1) + P(X = 2)]$$

$$= 1 - \left[\frac{e^{-2}.2^0}{0!} + \frac{e^{-2}.2}{1!} + \frac{e^{-2}.2^2}{2!}\right]$$

$$= 1 - e^{-2}(1 + 2 + 2)$$

$$= 1 - 0.6767$$

$$= 0.3233$$

$\therefore$ Probability that more than 2 will suffer bad reaction = 0.3233

(iii) probability that none will suffer bad reaction

$$P(X = 0) = \frac{e^{-\lambda}\lambda^0}{0!} = e^{-\lambda} = e^{-2}$$

***Example* 10:** A telephone exchange receives on an average 4 calls per minute. Find the probabilities, on the basis of Poisson distribution of

(i) 2 or less calls per minute

(ii) up to 4 calls per minute

(iii) more than 4 calls per minute

***Solution*:** It is given that $\lambda = 4$

(i) Probability of 2 or less calls per minute

$$= P(X \leq 2) = P(X = 0) + P(X = 1) + P(X = 2)$$

$$= \frac{e^{-4}4^0}{0!} + \frac{e^{-4}4^1}{1!} + \frac{e^{-4}4^2}{2!}$$

$$= e^{-4}(1 + 4 + 8)$$

$$= e^{-4}(13) = 0.2382$$

(ii) Probability of up to 4 calls per minute = $P(X \leq 4)$

$$= P(X = 0) + P(X = 1) + P(X = 2) + P(X = 3) + P(X = 4)$$

$$= \frac{e^{-4}4^0}{0!} + \frac{e^{-4}4^1}{1!} + \frac{e^{-4}4^2}{2!} + \frac{e^{-4}4^3}{3!} + \frac{e^{-4}4^4}{4!}$$

$$= e^{-4}(1 + 4 + 8 + 10.6 + \frac{32}{3})$$

$$= 0.6289$$

(iii) Probability of more than 4 calls per minute

$$= P(X > 4) = 1 - P(X \leq 4)$$

$$= 1 - 0.6289 = 0.3711$$

***Example* 11:** Suppose that an item produced by a particular machine is defective is 0.2. If 10 items produced by this machine are selected at random; what is the probability that not more than one are defective item is found.

Solution: It is given that $n = 10$, and $p = 0.2$

$$\therefore \lambda = np = (10)(0.2) = 2$$

Probability that not more than one item is defective

$$= P(X \leq 1) = P(X = 0) + P(X = 1)$$

$$= \frac{e^{-2}.2^0}{0!} + \frac{e^{-2}.2^1}{1!}$$

$$= e^{-2}(1 + 2) = 3 \times 0.1353$$

$$= 0.4059$$

***Example* 12:** A manufacturer knows that the condensers he makes contain on an average 1% defectives. He packs them in boxes of 100. What is the probability that a box picked at random will contain 3 or more faulty condensers.

Solution: Probability that a condenser is defective $= \frac{1}{100} = 0.01$

we have $n = 100$

Mean $\lambda = np = 100 \times 0.01 = 1$

Probability that a box contains 3 or more faulty condensers

$$= P(X \geq 3) = 1 - P(X < 3)$$

$$= 1 - [P(X = 0) + P(X = 1) + P(X = 2)]$$

$$= 1 - \left(e^{-1} + \frac{e^{-1}.1}{1!} + \frac{e^{-1}1^2}{2!}\right)$$

$$= 1 - e^{-1}(1 + 1 + 0.5)$$

$$= 1 - 0.9197 = 0.0803$$

***Example* 13:** Suppose 2% of the people on the average are left handed; find (i) the probability of finding 3 or more left handed (ii) the probability of finding none or one is left handed

Solution:

We have $\lambda = 2\% = \frac{2}{100} = 0.02$ (given)

(i) Probability that 3 or more are left handed = $P(X \geq 3)$

$$= 1 - P(X < 3)$$

$$= 1 - [P(X = 0) + P(X = 1) + P(X = 2)]$$

$$= 1 - \left[\frac{e^{-0.02}}{0!} + \frac{e^{-0.02}}{1!}(0.02) + \frac{e^{-0.02}}{2!}(0.02)^2\right]$$

$$= 1 - e^{-0.02}[1 + 0.02 + 0.0002]$$

$$= 1.307 \times 10^{-6}$$

(ii) $P(X \leq 1) = P(X = 0) + P(X = 1)$

$$= e^{-0.02} + e^{-0.02}(0.02)$$

$$= 0.9998$$

***Example* 14:** A pair of dice is thrown 200 times. If getting a sum of 9 is considered as success, using Poisson distribution find the mean and variance of the number of successes

Solution: Let p denote the probability of getting a sum of 9 in a throw of a pair of dice

The favourable cases are (3,6), (4, 5), (5, 4) and (6, 3)

$$\therefore p = \frac{4}{6 \times 6} = \frac{1}{9}$$

We have $n = 200$ $\quad \therefore \lambda = np = \frac{200}{9}$

$\therefore$ $\quad$ Mean $= \lambda = \frac{200}{9} = 22.22$

and variance $= \lambda = 22.22$

***Example* 15:** Fit a Poisson distribution to the following data and calculate the theoretical frequencies

X	0	1	2	3	4
f	122	60	15	2	1

***Solution*:** Mean of the distribution $= \frac{0 + 60 + 30 + 6 + 4}{200}$

$$= \frac{100}{200} = 0.5$$

$\therefore \lambda = 0.5$

we have $\quad P(X = x) = \frac{e^{-0.5}(0.5)^x}{x!}, x = 0, 1, 2, 3, 4$

The Poisson distribution of the fit is

$$N\,P(X = x) = 200 \,.\, \frac{e^{-0.5}(0.5)^x}{x!}, x = 0, 1, 2, 3, 4$$

$\therefore$

$$N\,P(X = 0) = 200.e^{-0.5}\frac{(0.5)^0}{0!} = 121$$

$$N\,P(X = 1) = 200.e^{-0.5}\frac{(0.5)^1}{1!} = 61$$

$$N\,P(X = 2) = 200.e^{-0.5}\frac{(0.5)^2}{2!} = 15$$

$$N\,P(X = 3) = 200.e^{-0.5}\frac{(0.5)^3}{3!} = 3$$

$$N\,P(X=4) = 200.e^{-0.5}\frac{(0.5)^4}{4!} = 0$$

The theoretical frequencies are

121, 61, 15, 3, 0

***Example* 16:** The number of accidents per day (x) as recorded in a textile industry over a period of 400 days is given below. Fit a Poisson distribution and calculate the theoretical frequencies.

X	0	1	2	3	4	5
f	173	168	37	18	3	1

***Solution*:** Mean of the given data = $\bar{x} = \dfrac{0+168+74+54+12+5}{400}$

$$= 0.7825$$

$\therefore$ $\bar{x} = \lambda = 0.7825$

we have $P(X=x) = \dfrac{(0.7825)^x e^{-0.7825}}{x!}$

The Poisson distribution of the fit is

$$NP(X=x) = 400.e^{-0.7825}\frac{(0.7825)^x}{x!}$$

Substituting x = 0, 1, 2, 3, 4, 5, the theoretical frequencies are as follows

$$NP(X=0) = 400.e^{-0.7825}\frac{(0.7825)^0}{0!} = 183$$

$$NP(X=1) = 400.e^{-0.7825}\frac{(0.7825)^1}{1!} = 143$$

$$NP(X=2) = 400.e^{-0.7825}\frac{(0.7825)^2}{2!} = 56$$

$$NP(X=3) = 400.e^{-0.7825}\frac{(0.7825)^3}{3!} = 15$$

$$NP(X=4) = 400.e^{-0.7825}\frac{(0.7825)^4}{4!} = 3$$

$$NP(X=5) = 400.e^{-0.7825}\frac{(0.7825)^5}{5!} = 0$$

Hence the theoretical frequencies are

183, 143, 56, 15, 3, 0

Exercise 3.2

1. It is given that 3% of the electric bulbs manufactured by a company are defective. Using Poisson distribution, find the probability that a sample of 100 bulbs will contain no defective bulb. Given that $e^{-3} = 0.05$

2. The average number of customers, who appear at a counter of a red cross blood bank per minute is two. Find the probability that during a given minute.

   (a) no customer arrives

   (b) Three or more customers appear

3. Find the probability that at most 5 defective fuses will be found in a box of 200 fuses it experiences show that 2% of such fuses are defective

4. If X is a poisson variate such that $P(X = 1) = \frac{3}{10}$ and $P(X = 2) = \frac{1}{5}$ find $P(X = 0)$ and $P(X = 3)$

5. A manufacturer knows that the condensers he makes contain on the average 1% of defectives. He packs them in boxes of 100. What is the probability that a box picked at random will contain 3 or more faculty condensers.

6. At a busy traffic intersection, the probability p of an individual car having an accident is very small say P = 0.0001. However during a certain part of the day, a large number of cars say 1000 pass through the intersection. Under these conditions, what is the probability that two or more accidents occurring during that period.

7. 10% of the tools produced in a certain factory turns out to be defective. Find the probability that in a sample of 10 tools chosen at random,

   (i) exactly two

   (ii) more than two will be defective by using poision approximation to binomial distribution.

8. A manufacturer of screws knows that 4% of his product is defective. If he sells the screws in boxes 100 and guarantees that not more than 5 screws will be defective, what is the probability that a box will fail to meet the guaranteed quality.

9. A box contains 200 tickets each bearing one of the numbers 1 to 200. Twenty tickets are drawn successively with replacement from the box. Find the probability that at most 4 tickets bear numbers divisible by 20.

10. The probability of getting misprint in a page of a book is e^{-1}. What is the probability that a page contains more than 2 misprints.

11. In a certain factory turning out razor blades there is a small chance of $\frac{1}{500}$ for any blade to be defective. The blades are in packets of 10. Use poisson's distribution to calculate the approximate number of packets containing (i) no defective (ii) one defective (iii) two defective blades in a consignment of 10,000 packets.

12. If X has a poisson distribution such that $P(X = 1) = P(X = 2)$ find $P(X = 4)$

13. The probability that a man aged 50 years will die within a year is 0.001125. What is the probability that out of 12 such men 11 men atleast will reach their 51st birthday.

14. In a poisson distribution the probability $P(X = 0)$ is twice the probability $P(X = 1)$. Find the mean of the distribution.

15. Out of 1000 balls 50 are red and the rest are white. If 6 balls are picked at random, what is the probability of picking up 3 red balls.

16. Probability that a bomb is dropped from an aeroplane will strike a certain target is 1/5. If 6 bombs are dropped find the probability that (i) exactly 2 will strike the target (ii) atleast two will strike the target.

17. A pair of dice is thrown 200 times. If getting a sum of 9 considered as a success, using the poisson distribution find the mean and variance of the number of successes.

18. Fit a poisson distribution to the following

X	0	1	2	3	4	5
f	142	158	69	27	5	1

Answers 3.2

1. 0.05
2. (a) 0.1353 (b) 0.3235
3. 0.785
4. $e^{\frac{-4}{3}}$, $e^{\frac{-4}{3}} \dfrac{\left(\frac{4}{3}\right)^3}{3!}$
5. 0.08025
6. 0.00472
7. (i) 0.18394 (ii) 0.0803
8. 0.2147
9. $\dfrac{65}{24e}$
10. 0.7618
11. (i) 9802 (ii) 196 (iii) 2
12. 0.090 13. 0.9917
14. $\dfrac{1}{2}$
15. 0.224
16. (i) 0.2169 (ii) 0.3374
17. 22.22
18. 147, 147, 74, 25, 6, 1

3.3 Geometric Distribution

A random variable x is said to follow geometric distribution, if it assumes only non-negative values and its probability mass function is given by

$$P(X = x) = q^r p, \; r = 0, 1, 2, 3, \ldots..$$
$$(0 < p \leq 1)$$

Where $q = 1 - p$

The terms of the geometric distribution are $q^0 p, \; q\,p, \; q^2 p, \; q^3 p, \ldots$

The mean of geometric distribution is $\dfrac{q}{p}$ and the variance is $\dfrac{q}{p^2}$

Example: A die is cast until 6 appears. What is the probability that it must be cast more than five times.

Solution: Probability of getting 6 in a single throw of the die = $\dfrac{1}{6}$

$$\therefore \qquad p = \frac{1}{6}, \; q = 1 - p = 1 - \frac{1}{6} = \frac{5}{6}$$

$\therefore\ P(\lambda > 5) = 1 - P(x \leq 5)$

$$= 1 - (P(x = 0) + P(x = 1) + P(x = 2) + P(x = 3) + P(x = 4) + P(x = 5)$$

$$= 1 - \left(\frac{5}{6}\right)^0\left(\frac{1}{6}\right) + \left(\frac{5}{6}\right)^1\left(\frac{1}{6}\right) + \left(\frac{5}{6}\right)^2\left(\frac{1}{6}\right) + \left(\frac{5}{6}\right)^4\left(\frac{1}{6}\right) + \left(\frac{5}{6}\right)^5\left(\frac{1}{6}\right)$$

$$= 1 - \frac{1}{6}\left[1 + \frac{5}{6} + \left(\frac{5}{6}\right)^2 + \left(\frac{5}{6}\right)^3 + \left(\frac{5}{6}\right)^4 + \left(\frac{5}{6}\right)^5\right]$$

3.4 Hypergeometric Distribution

A random variable x is said to be a hypergeometric distribution, if its probability mass connection is given by

$$f(x) = r_{c_x} \frac{N - r_{c_{n-x}}}{N_{c_n}}$$

where N, r and positive integers

Example: In a box of 25 casettes, 5 are defective. If 3 casettes are taken at random, what is the probability that atleast one of them is defective?

***Solution*:** we have N = 25

r = 5

n = 3

$$P(x = 0) = r_{c_0} \frac{N - 0_{c_{n-0}}}{N_{c_n}} = S_{C_0} \frac{r_{c_3}}{25_{c_3}}$$

$$= 0.496$$

$$P(x \geq 1) = 1 - P(x = 0) = 1 - 0.496 = 0.504$$

Exercise 3.3

1. An expert shooter is successful in hitting the target 80% of the time, what is the probability that he misses the first five shots.

Ans. 0.00032

2. The probability that a person can hit target is 0.8. What is the probability that he will hit successfully 10 times and fail to hit the target eleventh time.

Ans. 0.0215

3. There are number of competitors for a motor rally and each of them has 30% chance of successfully completing it. Find the probability that 20th person is the first to complete successfully.

Ans. 0.00034

4. In a strip of 10 ball pen refils 3 are defective. If 5 refils are solid, what is the probability that

(i) 3 are non defective?

(ii) atleast 3 of them are non defective?

Ans. 0.4167, 0.9167

5. A quality control inspector from ISI checks at random 3 tins of canned food out of a box of 20. If the box actually contains 5 tins of state food, find the probability that he discovers.

(i) atleast one of them

(ii) exactly two of them

(iii) More than

Ans. 0.6009, 0.1316, 0.1403

3.5 Normal Distribution

Normal distribution is a continuous distribution. It is regarded as the limiting form of a binomial distribution when the number of trials is large and neither p nor q is very small. Normal distribution is defined as follows:

Definition

A random variable X is said to have a normal distribution with mean μ and standard deviation σ if its probability function is given by

$$f(x) = \frac{1}{\sigma\sqrt{2\pi}} \; e^{\frac{-(x-\mu)^2}{2\sigma^2}}, \qquad -\infty < x < \infty$$

where $e = 2.7183, \sigma > 0, -\infty < \mu < \infty$

It is denoted by N (μ, σ^2) where μ, σ^2 are the parameters.

Normal distribution is also known a Gaussian distribution. The distribution was first discovered by De Moivre in the year 1773, as the limiting form of Binomial distribution. Simultaneously, it was discovered by Karl Friedrich Gauss as law of errors.

Standard Normal Variable: (S.N.V)

It X is a continuous random variable then

$$Z = \frac{X-\mu}{\sigma}$$

is called standard normal variable, where

μ = Mean of X

σ = Standard deviation of X

Z is a continuous random variable

3.6 Standard Normal Distribution

Definition

Let X be a continuous random variable. If $Z = \frac{X-\mu}{\sigma}$, (where μ = mean of X and σ = standard deviation of X, is the standard normal variate then, the standard normal distribution is defined as

$$f(z) = \frac{1}{\sqrt{2\pi}}\, e^{-\frac{1}{2} \geq z^2}, \qquad -\infty < z < \infty$$

It is denoted by N (0,1)

The probability density function with mean zero and standard deviation σ is given by

$$f(x) = \frac{1}{\sigma\sqrt{2\pi}}\ {}^{\frac{-x^2}{2\sigma^2}}, \qquad -\infty < x < \infty$$

3.7 Normal Curve and its Properties

The equation of normal curve is given by

$$y = \frac{1}{\sigma\sqrt{2\pi}}\, e^{-\frac{1}{2}\left(\frac{x-\mu}{\sigma}\right)^2}, \qquad -\infty < x < \infty$$

1. The curve is bell-shaped
2. The curve is symmetrical about the line $x = \mu$ and x ranges from $-\infty$ to $+\infty$
3. Means, mode and median coincide at $x = \mu$
4. X – axis is the asymptote to the curve
5. The points of inflexion of the curve are at $x = \mu + \sigma$ and $x = \mu - \sigma$

6. The total area under the normal curve is unity and the percentage of area under the normal curve is given below
   (a) the area covered between the limits $\mu - \sigma$ and $\mu + \sigma$ is 0.6826 (i.e 68.26% of the total area)
   (b) the area covered between the limits $\mu - 2\sigma$ and $\mu + 2\sigma$ is 0.9544 (i.e 95.44% of the total area)
   (c) the area covered between $\mu - 3\sigma$ and $\mu + 3\sigma$ is 0.9974 (i.e 99.74% of the total area).

If Z is the corresponding standard normal variable then the curve of Z is called standard normal curve.

The standard normal curve covers 68.26% of area between $z = -1$ and $z = 1$

$$\therefore \quad P(-1 \leq z \leq 1) = 0.6826$$

It covers 95.44% of the total area between $z = -2$ and $z = 2$

$$\therefore \quad P(-2 \leq z \leq 2) = 0.9544$$

and it covers 99.74% of area between $z = -3$ and $z = 3$

$$\therefore \quad P(-3 \leq z \leq 3) = 0.9974$$

7. The curve of a normal distribution is unimodal
8. The odd moments about the mean are zero

The shape of the curve is given in Fig. 3.1.

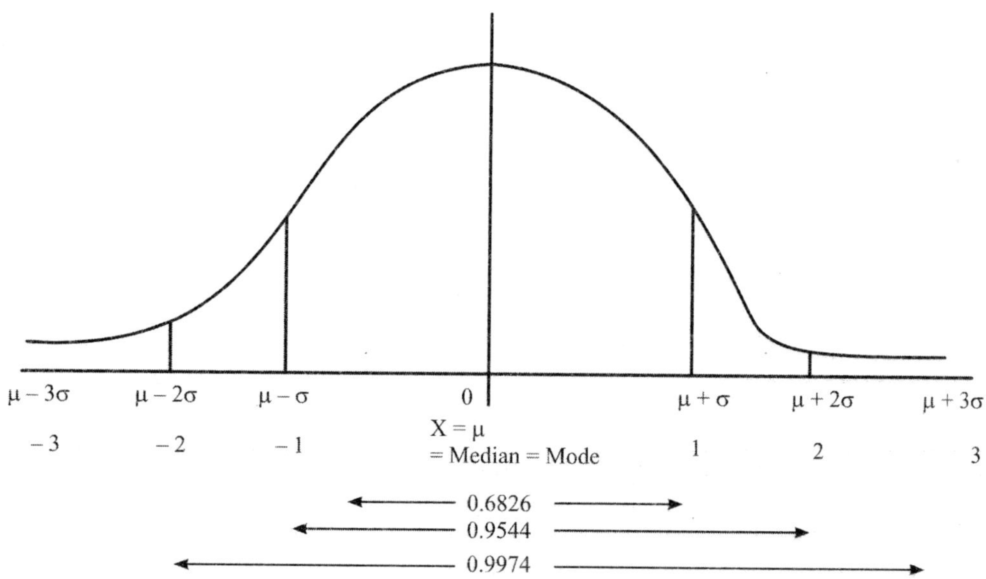

Fig. 3.1 Percentage distribution of the area under normal curve.

3.8 Mean of Normal Distribution

By definition we have

We $$f(x)=\frac{1}{\sigma\sqrt{2\pi}}\ e^{-\frac{1}{2}\left(\frac{x-\mu}{\sigma}\right)^2}, \quad -\infty < x < \infty$$

$$\text{Mean of the distribution} = \int_{-\infty}^{\infty} x f(x)\, dx$$

Putting $z=\dfrac{x-\mu}{\sigma}$, we get

$$x = \mu + \sigma z$$

and $dx = \sigma\, dz$

Mean of normal distribution

$$E(x)=\int_{-\infty}^{\infty} x f(x)\, dx$$

$$=\frac{1}{\sqrt{2\pi}}\int_{-\infty}^{\infty}(\sigma z+\mu)\ e^{\frac{-z^2}{2}}\ dz$$

$$=\frac{\sigma}{\sqrt{2\pi}}\int_{-\infty}^{\infty} z\ e^{\frac{-z^2}{2}}\ dz+\frac{\mu}{\sqrt{2\pi}}\int_{-\infty}^{\infty} e^{\frac{-z^2}{2}}\ dz$$

$$=0+\frac{\mu}{\sqrt{2\pi}}.2\int_{-\infty}^{\infty} e^{-\frac{1}{2}z^2}\ dz$$

$$=\frac{2\,\mu}{\sqrt{2\pi}}.\frac{\sqrt{\pi}}{\sqrt{2}}$$

$$=\mu$$

Hence, mean of the normal distribution = μ.

3.9 Variance of Normal Distribution

We have, variance $= E\,(x-\mu)^2$

$$= \int_{-\infty}^{\infty} (x-\mu)^2 \ f(x) \ dx$$

$$= \frac{1}{\sigma\sqrt{2\pi}} \int_{-\infty}^{\infty} (x-\mu)^2 \ e^{-\frac{1}{2}\left(\frac{x-\mu}{\sigma}\right)^2} \ dx$$

Putting $z = \frac{x-h}{\sigma}$, we get $dx = \sigma\ dz$, $x = \mu + \sigma z$

$$\text{Variance} = \frac{1}{\sqrt{2\pi}} \int_{-\infty}^{\infty} \sigma^2 z^2 \ e^{\frac{-z^2}{2}} \ (\sigma\ dz)$$

$$= \frac{\sigma^2}{\sqrt{2\pi}} \left[2 \int_0^{\infty} z^2 \ e^{\frac{-z^2}{2}} \ dz \right]$$

$$= \frac{2\sigma^2}{\sqrt{2\pi}} \int_0^{\infty} 2\ t\ e^{\theta} \ \frac{d\theta}{\sqrt{2\theta}} \qquad \left(\text{putting } \frac{z^2}{2} = \theta\right)$$

$$= \frac{2\sigma^2}{\sqrt{\pi}} \int_0^{\infty} e^{-\theta} \sqrt{\theta} \ d\theta$$

$$= \frac{2\sigma^2}{\sqrt{\pi}} \int_0^{\infty} e^{-\theta} \ \theta^{\frac{3}{2}-1} \ d\theta$$

$$= \frac{2\sigma^2}{\sqrt{\pi}} \Gamma 3/2 = \frac{2\ \sigma^2}{\sqrt{\pi}} \frac{1}{2} \Gamma 1/2_L$$

$$= \frac{\sigma^2}{\sqrt{\pi}} \sqrt{\pi} = \sigma^2$$

Hence, variance $= \sigma^2$

3.10 Median of the Normal Distribution

Let M denote the median of the distribution

we have $$\int_{-\infty}^{M} f(x) \ dx = \frac{1}{2}$$

i.e $$\frac{1}{\sigma\sqrt{2\pi}}\int_{-\infty}^{M} e^{-\frac{1}{2}\left(\frac{x-\mu}{\sigma}\right)^2} dx = \frac{1}{2}$$

or $$\frac{1}{\sigma\sqrt{2\pi}}\left[\int_{-\infty}^{\mu} e^{-\frac{1}{2}\left(\frac{x-\mu}{\sigma}\right)^2} dx + \int_{\mu}^{M} e^{-\frac{1}{2}\left(\frac{x-\mu}{\sigma}\right)^2} dx\right] = \frac{1}{2}$$

consider $$\frac{1}{\sigma\sqrt{2\pi}}\int_{-\infty}^{\mu} e^{-\frac{1}{2}\left(\frac{x-\mu}{\sigma}\right)^2} dx \qquad (1)$$

putting $\frac{x-\mu}{\sigma} = z$, we get

$$x = \mu + z\sigma, \quad dx = \sigma\, dz$$

therefore $$\frac{1}{\sigma\sqrt{2\pi}}\int_{-\infty}^{\mu} e^{-\frac{1}{2}\left(\frac{x-\mu}{\sigma}\right)^2} dx = \frac{1}{\sigma\sqrt{2\pi}}\int_{-\infty}^{0} e^{\frac{-z^2}{2}} \sigma.dz$$

$$= \frac{1}{\sqrt{2\pi}}\int_{-\infty}^{0} e^{\frac{-z^2}{2}} dz$$

$$= \frac{1}{\sqrt{2}\sqrt{\pi}}\int_{0}^{\infty} e^{\frac{-z^2}{2}} dz \qquad \text{(by symmetry)}$$

$$= \frac{1}{\sqrt{2}\sqrt{\pi}} \cdot \frac{\sqrt{\pi}}{\sqrt{2}} = \frac{1}{2} \qquad (2)$$

from (1) and (2) we get

$$\frac{1}{2} + \int_{\mu}^{M} e^{-\frac{1}{2}\left(\frac{x-\mu}{\sigma}\right)^2} dx = \frac{1}{2}$$

$$\therefore \quad \frac{1}{\sigma\sqrt{2\pi}}\int_{\mu}^{M} e^{-\frac{1}{2}\left(\frac{x-\mu}{\sigma}\right)^2} dx = 0$$

hence $\mu = M$

i.e Median of the distribution $= \mu$

3.11 Mode of the Normal Distribution

Mode of the normal distribution occurs at the point where the maximum of $f(x)$ occurs

we have $$f(x) = \frac{1}{\sigma\sqrt{2\pi}} e^{-\frac{1}{2}\left(\frac{x-\mu}{\sigma}\right)^2}, \qquad -\infty < \mathbf{x} < \infty$$

differentiating with respect to x we get

$$f'(x) = \frac{1}{\sigma\sqrt{2\pi}} e^{-\frac{1}{2}\left(\frac{x-\mu}{\sigma}\right)^2} \cdot \left[-\left(\frac{x-\mu}{\sigma}\right)\right]$$

$$= -\left(\frac{x-\mu}{\sigma}\right) f(x)$$

taking $f'(x) = 0$ we get

$$\frac{x-\mu}{\sigma} = 0 \text{ or } x-\mu = 0$$

$\therefore \qquad x = \mu$

now $$f''(x) = -\frac{1}{\sigma^2}\left[(x-\mu)f'(x) + f(x)\right]$$

$$= -\frac{f(x)}{\sigma^2}\left[1 - \frac{(x-\mu)^2}{\sigma^2}\right]$$

at the point $x = \mu$, we get

$$\left[f''(x)\right]_{x=\mu} = -\frac{f(h)}{\sigma^2}[1-0] = -\frac{1}{\sigma^3\sqrt{2\pi}} < 0$$

hence $x = \mu$ is the mode of the normal distribution.

3.12 Normal Approximation to the Binomial Distribution

We can use normal distribution to approximate the Binomial distribution. When $p = q = \frac{1}{2}$, to find the probability $\rho(X_1 < X < X_2)$ we compute the values of z_1 and z_2 by using $z_1 = \frac{x_1 - \mu}{\sigma}$ and $z_2 = \frac{x_2 - \mu}{\sigma}$

The value of $\rho(X_1 < X < X_2) = \int_{Z_1}^{z_2} \phi(z)\, dz$

which is obtained by using the normal table. When $p \neq q$, and n large, the values of z_1 and z_2 are calculated by the formulae

$$z_1 = \frac{X_1 - \frac{1}{2} - \mu}{\sigma} \text{ and } z_2 = \frac{X_2 + \frac{1}{2} - \mu}{\sigma}$$

The probability $P(X_1 < X < X_2)$ is

$$\int_{Z_1}^{Z_2} \phi(z)\, dz$$

which is obtained by using the normal table.

Solved Examples

***Example* 1:** The scores made by candidates in a certain examination are normally distributed with mean 500 and standard deviation 100. What percentage of candidates receives the score between 400 and 600?

***Solution*:** Let X be the normal variable showing the scores of the candidates

We have mean $\mu = 500$

$\sigma = 100$

$$z = \frac{X - \mu}{\sigma}$$

when $X = 400, \quad z = \frac{400 - 500}{100} = -1$

when $X = 600, \quad z = \frac{600 - 500}{100} = 1$

When X lies between 400 and 600, the value of z lies between –1 and +1

Area under the normal curve from z = –1 to z =1

= Area under the curve from z = –1 to z = 0

+ Area under the curve from z = 0 to z = 1

= 2 (Area under the curve from z = 0 to z = 1)

= 2.(0.3413)

= 0.6826

therefore percentage of candidates securing marks between 400 and 600

$= 0.6826 \times 100$

$= 68.26\ \%$

***Example* 2:** For the normal distribution with mean 2 and standard deviation 4, calculate

(i) $P[X \geq 5]$

(ii) $P[|X| < 4]$

***Solution*:** we have $\mu = 2, \sigma = 4$

therefore $$z = \frac{X-\mu}{\sigma} = \frac{X-2}{4}$$

(i) when $X = 5$, $z = \frac{5-2}{4} = \frac{3}{4} = 0.75$

$$\begin{aligned} P[X \geq 5] &= P[z \geq 0.75] \\ &= P(z \geq 0) - P(0 \leq z \leq 0.75) \\ &= 0.5 - \text{Area under the curve from } z = 0 \text{ to } z = 0.75 \\ &= 0.5 - 0.2734 \\ &= 0.2266 \end{aligned}$$

(ii) $P(|x| < 4) = 2 \times P(0 \pounds X \pounds 4)$

when $X = 4$, $z = \frac{4-2}{4} = \frac{2}{4} = 0.5$

therefore $$\begin{aligned} P(|x| < 4) &= 2.P(0 \leq X \leq 4) \\ &= 2.\, P(0 \leq Z \leq 0.5) \\ &= 2(0.1915) \\ &= 0.3830 \end{aligned}$$

***Example* 3:** The income of a group of 10,000 persons was found to be normally distributed with mean equal to Rs.750 and standard deviation equal to Rs. 50. What was the lowest income among the richest 250?

Solution: We have mean $= \mu = 750$

σ = standard deviation = 50

Let x' be the lowest income among the richest 250 persons

then $$P(X \geq x') = \frac{250}{10000} = 0.025$$

i.e $$P\left(\frac{X-\mu}{\sigma} \geq \frac{x'-750}{50}\right) = 0.025$$

or $$P\left(z \geq \frac{x' - 750}{50}\right) = 0.025$$

thus, $$\frac{x' - 750}{50} = 1.96$$

or $$x' = 750 + 50\,(1.96)$$

$$= 848$$

Hence, Rs.848 is the lowest income among the richest 250 persons.

***Example* 4:** If the masses of 300 students are normally distributed with mean 68 kgs and standard deviation 3 kgs; how many students have the masses

(i) Greater than 72 kg

(ii) less than or equal to 64 kg

(iii) Between 65 and 71 kg inclusive (JNTU 2005)

***Solution*:** The mean of the distribution = μ = 68 kg,

and standard deviation = σ =3 kg

Let X be the random variable 'masses of the students'

(i) When X = 72, $z = \frac{X - \mu}{\sigma} = \frac{72 - 68}{3} = \frac{4}{3} = 1.33$

$$P\,(X > 72) = P(z > 1.33)$$

$$= 0.5 - (\text{Area under curve from } z = 0 \text{ to } z = 1.33)$$

$$= 0.5 - 0.4082$$

$$= 0.0918$$

Hence, the number of students with mass more than

72 kg = 300 (0.0918) = 28

(ii) When X = 64, $z = \frac{64 - 68}{3} = \frac{-4}{3} = -1.33$

$$\therefore\ P\,(X \leq 64) = P\,(z \leq -1.33)$$

$$= 0.5 - A\,(1.33)$$

$$= 0.5 - 0.4082 = 0.0918$$

Number of students having masses less than or equal to 64 kg

$$= 300 \times 0.0918 = 28.$$

(iii) When X = 65, $z = \frac{65-68}{3} = \frac{-3}{3} = -1 = z_1$ (say)

when X = 71, $z = \frac{71-68}{3} = \frac{3}{3} = -1 = z_2$ (say)

therefore $P(65 \le X \le 71)$

$= P(-1 \le z \le 1)$

$= A(z_2) + A(z_1)$

$= A(1) + A(-1)$

$= 2A(1)$ by symmetry

$= 2(0.3413)$

$= 0.6826$

Hence the number of students, with masses between 65 and 71 inclusive

$= 300 \times 0.6826$

$= 205$

***Example* 5:** In a normal distribution, 7% of the items are under 35 and 89% of the items are under 63. Find the mean and standard deviation of the distribution. [JNTU 2008)

Solution: Let μ denote mean and σ denote the standard deviation of the distribution.

We have $P(X < 35) = 0.07$

and $P(X < 63) = 0.89$ (given)

therefore $P(X > 63) = 1 - P(X < 63)$

$= 1 - 0.89 = 0.11$

Where $X = 35,\ z = \frac{X-\mu}{\sigma} = \frac{35-\mu}{\sigma} = -z_1$ (say)

∴ $P(0 < z < z_1) = 0.43$ (from the table)

i.e $z_1 = 1.48$

and $P(0 < z < Z_2) = 0.39$

is $z_2 = 1.23$ (from the table)

hence $\frac{35-\mu}{\sigma} = -z_1 = -1.48$

or $35 - \mu = -1.48\,\sigma$ (1)

and $\frac{63-\mu}{\sigma} = z_2 = 1.23$

or $$63 - \mu = 1.23\sigma \tag{2}$$

solving (1) and (2) we get

$$\sigma = 10.33$$

$$\mu = 50.3$$

***Example* 6:** If X is a normal variable with mean 25 and standard deviation 5, find the probability that $15 \leq X \leq 30$

***Solution*:** We have $\mu = 25, \sigma = 5$

Let z be the standard normal variable

than $$z = \frac{X-\mu}{\sigma} = \frac{X-25}{5}$$

when $X = 15, \quad z = \frac{15-25}{5} = \frac{-10}{5} = -2$

when $X = 30, \quad z = \frac{30-25}{5} = \frac{5}{5} = 1$

Required probability

$$P(-2 \leq z \leq 1) = P(-2 \leq z \leq 0) + P(0 \leq z \leq 1)$$

$$= P(0 \leq z \leq 2) + P(0 \leq z \leq 1)$$

$$= 0.4775 + 0.3413$$

$$= 0.8185$$

$\therefore \quad P(15 \leq X \leq 30) = 0.8185$

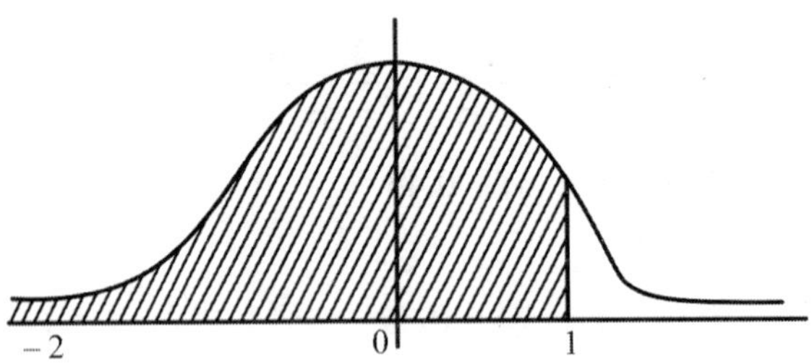

***Example* 7:** Find the area under the standard normal curve which lies

1. to the left of z = 1.73

2. between z = 1.25 and z = 1.67

***Solution*:** (i) Area to the left of z = 1.73

$= 0.5 + \text{Area between } z = 0 \text{ and } z = 1.73$

$= 0.5 + 0.4582$ (using table)

$= 0.9582$

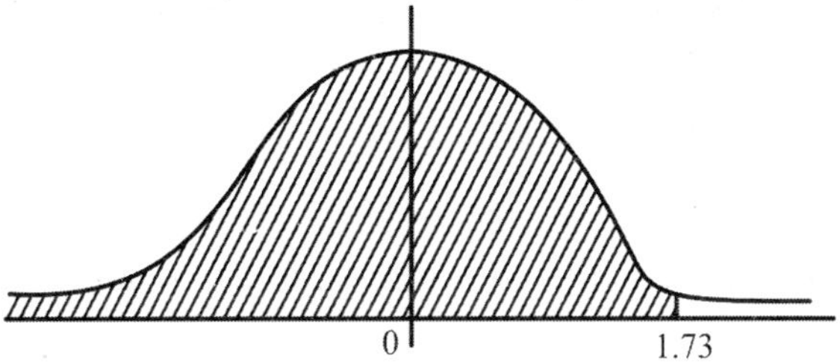

(ii) Area between z = 1.25 and z = 1.67

$= (\text{Area between } z = 0 \text{ and } z = 1.67)$

$- (\text{area between } z = 0 \text{ and } z = 1.25)$

$= 0.4525 - 0.3944$ using the table

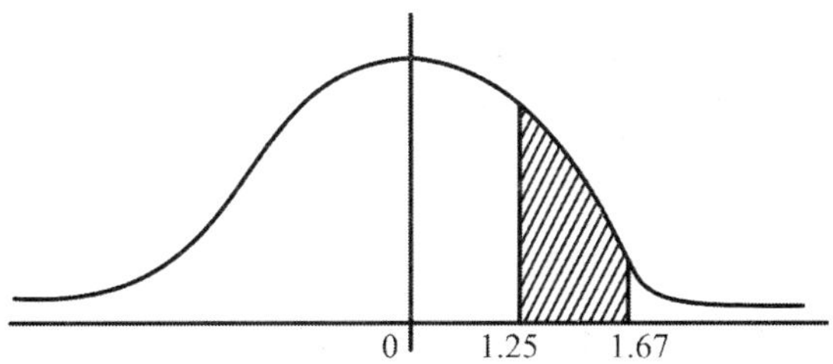

***Example* 8:** Given that the mean height of students in a class is 158 cm with standard deviation of 20 cm. Find how many students heights lie between 150 cm and 170 cm if there are 100 students in the class (JNTU 2007]

***Solution*:** We have

Mean = μ = 158 cm; Standard deviation = σ = 20 cm

$$z = \frac{X - \mu}{\sigma}$$

when $x = 150,\ z = \frac{150 - 158}{20} = \frac{-2}{5} = -0.4$

and when $x = 170,\ z = \frac{170 - 158}{20} = \frac{12}{20} = \frac{3}{5} = 0.6$

$\therefore\ P(150 \le X \le 170) = P(-0.4 \le z \le 0.6)$

$= P(-0.4 \le z \le 0) + P(0 \le z \le 0.6)$

$= P(0 \leq z \leq 0.4) + P(0 \leq z \leq 0.6)$

$= 0.1554 + 0.2257$

$= 0.3811$

Hence, Number of students whose height lie between 150 cm and 170 cm

$= 100 \times 0.3811$

$= 38.11$

$= 38$

***Example* 9:** X is a normal variable with means 30 and standard deviation 5. Find the probability that

(a) $26 \leq X \leq 40$

(b) $X \geq 45$

***Solution*:** It is given that mean $\mu = 30$ and standard deviation $\sigma = 5$

(a) Since $z = \dfrac{X - \mu}{\sigma}$

when X = 26, we get $z = \dfrac{26 - 30}{5} = \dfrac{-4}{5} = -0.8$

and when X = 40, we get $z = \dfrac{40 - 30}{5} = \dfrac{10}{5} = 2$

$\therefore \quad P(26 \leq X \leq 40) = P(-0.8 \leq X \leq 2)$

$= P(-0.8 \leq z \leq 0) + P(0 \leq z \leq 2)$

$= 0.2881 + 0.4772$

$= 0.7653$ (using the tables)

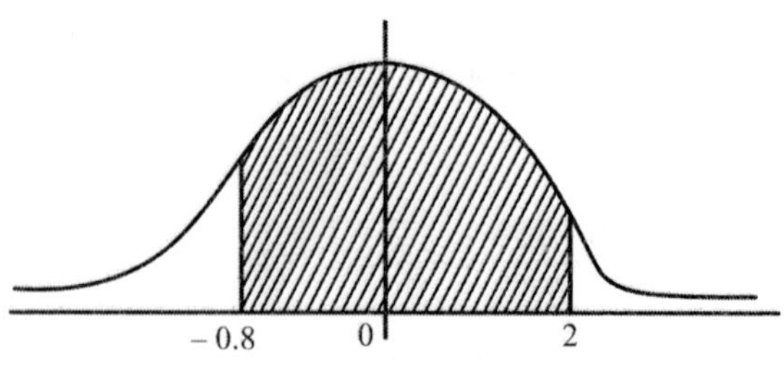

(b) When X = 45, we have

$$z = \frac{45 - 30}{5} = \frac{15}{5} = 3$$

$$P(X \geq 45) = P(z \geq 3)$$
$$= 0.5 - P(0 \leq z \leq 3)$$
$$= 0.5 - 0.4986$$
$$= 0.0014$$

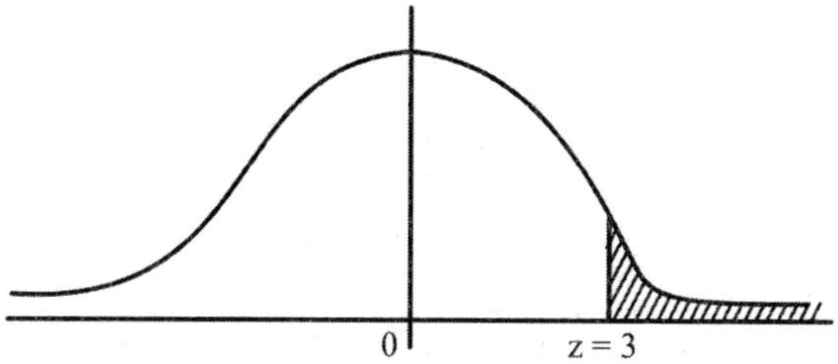

***Example* 10:** Let z be a standard normal variable. Find

(a) $P(0 \leq z \leq 1)$ (b) $P(-0.5 \leq z \leq 0)$

(c) $P(-0.6 \leq z \leq 0.42)$ (d) $P(z \geq 1.32)$

***Solution*:**

(a) From the area tables we get

$P(0 \leq z \leq 1)$ = Area bounded by the z-curve, z-axis and $z = 0$, $z = 1$, we get 0.3413

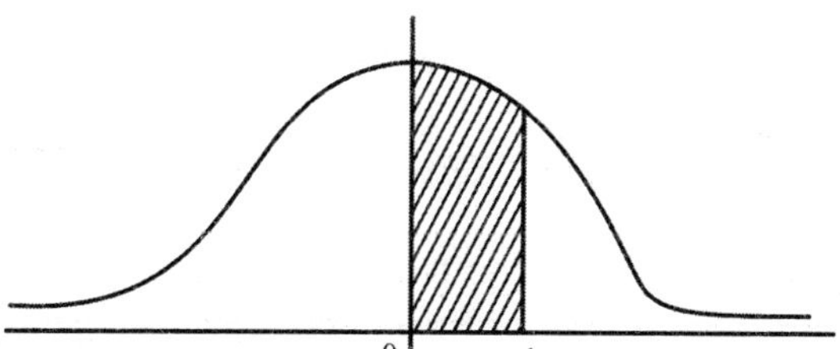

(b) $P(-0.5 \leq z \leq 0)$

$= P(0 \leq z\ 0.5)$ (by symmetry)

$= 0.1915$

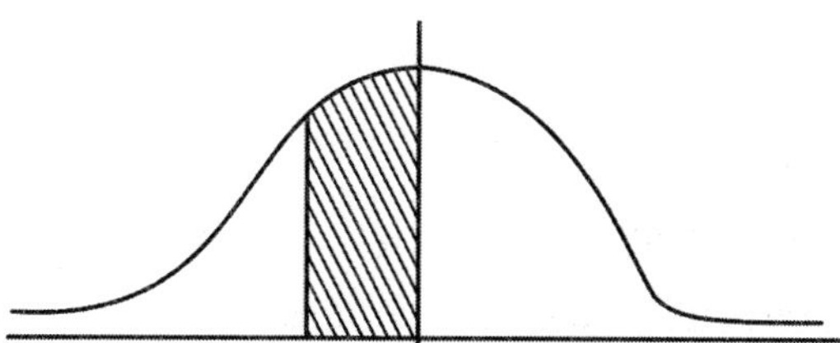

(c) $P(-0.6 \leq z \leq 0.42)$

$= P(-0.6 \leq z \leq 0) + P(0 \leq z \leq 0.42)$

$= P(0 \leq z \leq 0.6) + P(0 \leq z \leq 0.42)$

$= 0.2258 + 0.1628$

$= 0.3886$

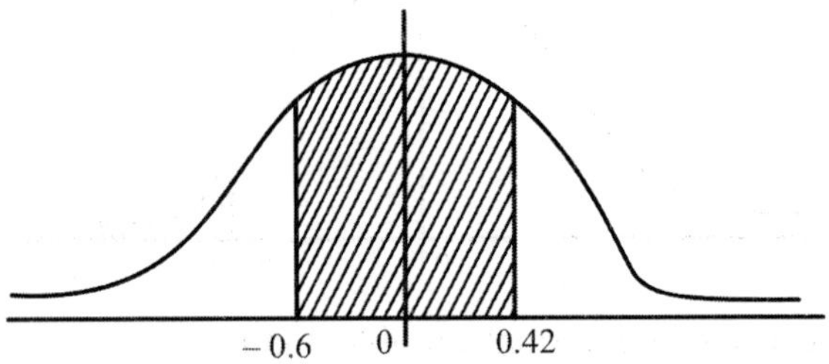

(d) $P(z \geq 1.32) = 0.5 - P(0 \leq z \leq 1.32)$

$= 0.5 - 0.4066$

$= 0.0934$

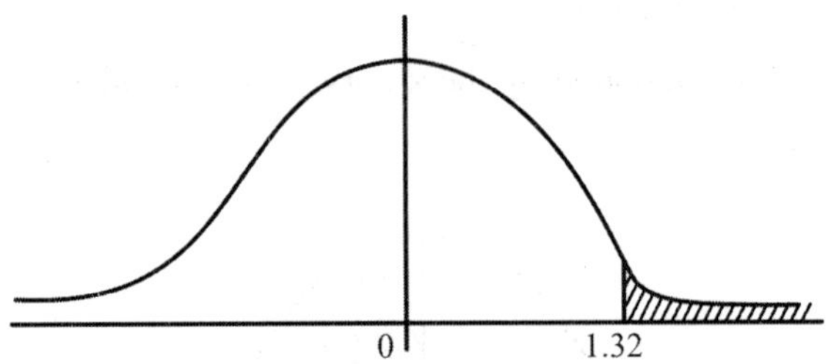

Example **11:** A sales tax officer has reported that the average sales of the 500 business that he has to deal with during a year is Rs.36,000 with a standard deviation of 10,000. Assuming that the sales in these business are normally distributed: Find

(a) the number of business as the sales of which are Rs.40,000

(b) the percentage of business the sales of which are likely to range between Rs. 30,000 and Rs. 40,000 (JNTU 2005)

***Solution*:**

Average sales of business = μ = 36,000

Standard deviation = σ = 10,000

Let X be the random variable "sales in the business"

we have $z = \frac{X - \mu}{\sigma} = \frac{X - 36000}{10000}$

when X = 40,000, $z = \frac{40000 - 36000}{10000} = \frac{4000}{10000}$

$= 0.4$

and when X = 30,000, $z = \frac{30000 - 36000}{10000} = \frac{-6000}{10000}$

$= 0.6$

(a) $P(x > 40000) = P(z > 0.4)$

$= 0.5 - P(0 \leq z \leq 0.4)$

$= 0.5 - A(0.4)$

$= 0.5 - 0.1554 = 0.3446$

Number of business made such the sales of which are

Rs.40000 = 500 × 0.3446 = 172

(b) $P(30000 < X < 40000)$

$= P(-0.6 < z < 0.4)$

$= P(-0.6 < z \leq 0) + P(0 \leq z < 0.4)$

$= P(0 \leq z < 0.6) + P(0 \leq z < 0.4)$

$= 0.2257 + 0.1554$

$= 0.3811$

Hence, the required percentage of business

$= 38.11\%$

***Example* 12:** Find the probability of getting 1 or 3 or 4 or 5 in throwing die 5 to 7 times among 9 trials, using normal distribution

***Solution*:** When a die is rolled probability of getting

$$1 \text{ or } 3 \text{ or } 4 \text{ or } 5 = 4\left(\frac{1}{6}\right) = \frac{2}{3}$$

number of trails = n = 9

we have $p = \frac{2}{3}, q = 1 - p = 1 - \frac{2}{3} = \frac{1}{3}, n = 9$

To find $P(5 \leq X \leq 7)$

$$\mu = np = 9.\frac{2}{3} = 6, \sigma = \sqrt{npq} = \sqrt{9.\frac{2}{3}.\frac{1}{3}} = \sqrt{2}$$

we have $X_1 = 5_1\ X_2 = 7$

$$\therefore \quad z_1 = \frac{X_1 - \frac{1}{2} - \mu}{\sigma} = \frac{5 - \frac{1}{2} - 6}{\sqrt{2}} = \frac{4.5 - 6}{1.414} = -1.07$$

$$z_2 = \frac{X_2 + \frac{1}{2} - \mu}{\sigma} = \frac{7 + \frac{1}{2} - 6}{\sqrt{2}} = \frac{7.5 - 6}{1.414}$$

$$= \frac{1.5}{1.414} = 1.07$$

$$P(X_1 - 0.5 < X < X_2 + 0.5)$$

$$= P(4.5 < X < 7.5)$$

$$= P(-1.07 \le z \le 1.07)$$

$$= 2.(0 < z \le 1.07) \qquad \text{(by symmetry)}$$

$$= 2\,(0.3577)$$

$$= 0.7154$$

3.13 Fitting a Normal Distribution

There are two methods

(i) Area method

(ii) Method of ordinates

These methods are explained with the help of examples given below

***Example* 13:** Fit a normal distribution to the following data by area method

Class Internal	60 –65	65 –70	70 –75	75 –80	80 –85	85 –90	90 –95	95 –100
Frequency	3	21	150	335	326	135	26	4

***Solution*:** Let μ denote the mean and σ denote the standard deviation of the distribution. Then we have

C-I	f	**x**	$f_i x_i$	$f_i x_i^2$
60-65	3	62.5	187.5	11718.75

Contd....

65-70	21	67.5	1417.5	95681.25
70-75	150	72.5	10875.0	788437.5
75-80	335	77.5	25962.5	2012093.75
80-85	326	82.5	26895.0	2218837.5
85-90	135	87.5	11812.5	1033593.75
90-95	26	92.5	2405.0	222462.5
95-100	4	97.5	390	38025.0
1000			79945	64200850.0

We have $N = \sum f_i = 1000$

$$\text{Mean of the distribution } = \mu = \bar{X} = \frac{\sum f_i x_i}{\sum f_i} = \frac{79945}{1000}$$

$$= 79.945$$

standard deviation

$$\sigma = \sqrt{\frac{1}{N}\sum f_i x_i^2 - \mu^2}$$

$$= \sqrt{\frac{6420850}{1000} - (79.945)^2}$$

$$= 5.445$$

$$\therefore \sigma = 5.445$$

Since the normal distribution takes values from $-\infty$ to $+\infty$, the given data can be modified as follows

CI	f	Lower limit of CI (X')	$z = \frac{X'-\mu}{\mu}$	Area $\phi(z)$	$\phi(z+1) - \phi(z) = \Delta\phi(z)$	Expected frequency N $\Delta\phi(z)$
$-\infty$ to 60	0	$-\infty$	$-\infty$	0	0.0001	0.1
60-65	3	60	-3.6629	0.0001	0.003	3
65-70	21	65	-2.7447	0.0031	0.0313	31.3

Contd....

70-75	150	70	– 1.8264	0.0344	0.1497	149.7
75-80	335	75	– 0.9081	0.1841	0.3199	319.9
80-85	326	80	– 0.0101	0.5040	0.3172	317.2
85-90	135	85	0.9283	0.8212	0.1459	145.9
90-95	26	90	1.8466	0.9671	0.03	30
95-100	4	95	2.7649	0.9971	0.0028	2.8
100-∞	0	100	3.6831	0.9999		

The expected frequencies are

0.1, 3, 31.3, 149.7, 319.9, 317.2, 145.9, 30, 2.8

i.e 0, 3, 31, 150, 320, 317, 146, 30, 3

***Example* 14:** Fit a normal distribution to the data and calculated the expected frequencies, by the method of ordinates

C-I	59.5 – 62.5	62.5 – 65.5	65.5 – 68.5	68.5 – 71.5	71.5 – 74.5
f	5	18	42	27	8

Given that mean of the distribution is 67.45 and standard deviation is 2.92

***Solution*:** We have mean = μ = 67.45

and $\sigma = 2.92$ given

Class internals CI	**Mid points X = x_i**	$z = \dfrac{X-\mu}{\sigma}$	**$f(z)$** $= \dfrac{1}{\sqrt{2\pi}} e^{-z^2/2}$	$y = \dfrac{N}{\sigma} f(z)$	**Expected frequencies**
59.5-62.5	61	–2.21	0.0347	1.188	3.565
62.5-65.5	64	–1.18	0.1984	6.794	20.382
65.5-68.5	67	–0.15	0.3943	13.50	40.50
68.5-71.5	70	0.87	0.2725	9.333	27.999
71.5-74.5	73	1.90	0.0656	2.247	6.741

The expected frequencies are

3.565, 20.382, 40.50, 27.999, 6.741

i.e 4, 20, 41, 28, 7

Exercise 3.3

1. If X is a normal variate, find the area A

 (i) to the left of z = – 1.78

(ii) to the right of $z = -1.45$

(iii) corresponding to $-0.8 \leq z \leq 1.53$

(iv) to the left of $z = -2.52$ and to the right of $z = 1.83$

(JNTU 2007)

3. Given that the mean height of students in a class is 158 cm with standard deviation of 20 cm. Find how many students heights lie between 150 cm and 170 cm if there are 100 students is the class (JNTU 2007 S)

4. The mean and standard deviation of a normal variate are 8 and 4 respectively. Find $\rho(0 \leq x \leq 15)$ and $\rho(X \leq 15)$ (JNTU 2004 S)

5. If the mean and standard deviation of a normal distribution are 70 and 16, find $\rho(38 < X < 46)$ (JNTU 2005)

6. If X is a normal variate with mean 30 and standard deviation 5, find the probabilities that (i) $20 \leq X \leq 40$ and (ii) $X \geq 45$

7. Find the probability that a random variable having standard normal distribution will take on a value 0.87 and 1.28 (JNTU 2007)

8. In a normal distribution 7% of items are under 35 and 89% are under 63. Find the mean and stand deviation of the distribution (JNTU 2008)

9. Suppose the weight of 800 male students are normally distributed with mean $\mu = 140$ pounds and standard deviation 10 pounds. Find the number of students whose weights are

   (i) between 138 and 148 pounds (ii) more than 152 pounds

10. In a normal distribution 31% of the items are under 45 and 8% are over 64. Find mean and standard deviation of the distribution.

11. Let X denote the number of scores on a test. If X is normally described with mean 100 and standard deviation 15, find the probability that X does not exceed 130.

12. A sample of 100 dry battery cells tested to find the length of life produced the following results. $\overline{x} = 12$ hr, $\sigma = 3$ hr

    Assuming the data to be normally distributed, what percentage of battery cells are expected to have life

    (i) more than 15 hr (ii) between 10 and 14 hr

13. Suppose the weight of 800 male students are normally distributed with mean $\mu = 140$ pounds and standard deviation 10 pounds. Find the number of students whose weights are

    (a) between 138 and 148 pounds

    (b) more than 152 pounds (JNTU 2006)

14. Find the probability of getting 1 or 4 or 5 or 6 in throwing a die 5 to 7 times among 9 trials using normal distribution

15. In a sample of 1000 cases, the mean of a common test is 14 and the standard deviation is 2.5. Assuming the distribution to be normal, find

    (i) How many students score between 12 and 15

    (ii) how many score below 18

    (iii) how many score below 8 (JNTU 2008)

16. Eight coins are tossed together. Find the probability of getting 1 to 4 heads in a single toss.

17. Fit a normal distribution to the data given below

x	8.60	8.59	8.58	8.57	8.56	8.55	8.54	8.53	8.52
f	2	3	4	9	10	8	4	1	1

18. Fit a normal curve to the data

x	4	6	8	10	12	14	16	18	20	22	24
f	1	7	15	22	35	43	38	20	13	15	1

19. Find the probability that out of 100 patients between 84 and 95 inclusive will survive a heart operation given that the chances of survival is 0.9.

20. Obtain the equation of normal probability curve that may be fitted to the following data.

x	6	7	8	9	10	11	12
F	3	6	9	13	8	5	4

21. Fit a normal distribution for the following data by the method of ordinates

CI	150 –160	160 –170	170 –180	180 –190	190 –200	200 –210	210 –210	220 –230	230 –240
f	9	24	51	66	72	48	21	6	3

Answers

1. (i) 0.0375 (ii) 0.9265 (iii) 0.725 (iv) 0.0395
2. (i) 0.0918 (ii) 0.0978 (iii) 0.6826
3. 38

4. (i) 0.6514 (ii) 0.0401

5. 0.044

6. (i) 0.7653 (ii) 0.00135

7. 0.0919

8. $\mu = 50.3, \sigma = 10.332$

9. (i) 294 (ii) 92

10. $\mu = 50, \sigma = 10$

11. 0.9772

12. 0, 15.87% (ii) 49.74%

13. 294

14. 0.7154

15. (i) 444 (ii) 55 (iii) 8

16. 0.63

17. 0.79, 2.24, 5.63, 7.5, 9.5, 7.5, 5.63, 2.24, 0.79

18. $20.83\ e^{-(x-13.85)^2/29.34}$

19. 0.9514

20. $11.916\ e^{-(x-9)^2/5.166}$

21. 7, 23, 49, 71, 71, 48, 22, 7, 2

3.14 Sampling Distribution

In this section we introduce theory of sampling, which has been developed recently. The aim of sampling studies is to obtain maximum information about the phenomena under study. The theory which helps us in studying samples is known as the theory of sampling. Sampling studies also aim at obtaining the best possible values of the parameters-Mean, Median, Standard deviation etc of the population. We begin our study by defining the terms, population and sample.

***Definition*: (Population)**

A large collection of individuals or numerical data is called a population or universe.

A population may be finite or infinite. A population containing a finite number of individuals or members is called a finite population.

A population which contains an infinite number of members is called an infinite population.

A universe (population) of concrete objects is called an existent universe, while a hypothetical universe may be defined as the collection of all possible ways in which a specified event can happen.

***Definition*: (Sample)**

A part or small section selected from a population is called a sample.

Thus a sample is a finite subset of a population. The size of a sample is denoted by n. If $n < 30$, then the sample is called a small sample. If ≥ 30, the sample is said to be a large sample. The process of selecting a sample is called sampling. A study of relationship existing between a population and samples drawn from the population is called sampling theory.

An object of sampling is to determine the reliability of the estimates when they are obtained. A sample should be selected so as to be representative of the universe.

3.15 Types of Sampling

There are many methods of sampling. In this section, we discuss few methods.

(a) *Random Sampling*:

A random sample is a sample selected in such a way that every item in the population has an equal chance of being selected.

(b) *Simple sampling*:

A simple sampling is a random sampling in which each unit of population has an equal chance of being included in the sample and that this probability is independent of the pervious drawings.

Several methods have been adopted for random selection of the sample. They are:

(i) Lottery method

(ii) Table of Random numbers

This method is a scientific method and there is less chance for personal bias.

(c) *Stratified Sampling*:

The method is a restricted random sampling. When the population is heterogeneous or different segments of strata with respect to the variable or characteristic under study, then it is stratified. First the population is divided into a number of sub groups or strata. A sample is drawn from each stratum at random. The stratified sampling is of two types, namely proportional and non-proportional. In the proportional sampling equal and proportionate representation is given to strata. In non-proportionate sampling equal representation is given to all the sub-strata regardless of their existence in the population.

***Sampling with Replacement*:**

Sampling where a number of the population may be selected more than once is called sampling with replacement.

Example: Consider all the samples of size two that can be drawn with replacement from the population consisting of the numbers 1, 5, 7, 9, 11

The samples are:

(1, 1), (1, 5), (1, 7), (1, 9), (1, 11)

(5, 1), (5, 5), (5, 7), (5, 9), (5, 11)

(7, 1), (7, 5), (7, 7), (7, 9), (7, 11)

(9, 1), (9, 5), (9, 7), (9, 9), (9, 11)

(11, 11), (11, 5), (11, 7), (11, 9), (11, 11)

If N is the size of the population and n is the size of a sample drawn from it. The number of samples with replacement that can be drawn from the population is N^n.

***Sampling without Replacement*:**

Sampling in which a member of the population cannot be chosen more than once is called sampling without replacement.

The number of samples in this case is N_{c_n}

Example: Consider all the samples of size two that can be drawn without replacement from the population consisting of the numbers 2, 4, 6, 8, 10

The samples are:

(2, 4), (2, 6), (2, 8), (2, 10)

(4, 6), (4, 8), (4, 10)

(6, 8), (6, 10)

(8, 10)

Sampling Distribution

Let us suppose that we have different samples of size n which are drawn from a population. For each and every sample of size n we can compute quantities like mean, standard deviation etc.

Suppose we group these characteristics according to their frequencies. The frequency distributions so generated are called sampling distributions.

Sampling distribution of means (σ known)

The probability distribution of $\bar{x}$ is called the sampling distribution of the mean. The sampling distribution of $\bar{x}$ will approximately be normal with mean μ and variance σ^2/n provided that the sample size is large.

The statistical measure computed from a sample of observations is called a statistic.

Example: Mean, variance etc.

The statistical constants of a population are known as parameters.

Example: Mean (μ), variance, etc

Sample Variance

If $x_1, x_2, \ldots, x_n$ are n observations of a sample then the mean of the sample denoted by $\bar{x}$

is given by $$\bar{x} = \frac{\sum_{1}^{n} x_i}{n}$$

and the variance of the sample is given by

$$\text{Variance} = S^2 = \frac{\sum_{1}^{n}(x_i - \bar{x})^2}{n-1}$$

Standard Error of Means

The standard deviation of sampling distribution of a statistic is known as its standard error.

The standard error of means is denoted by $\sigma_{\bar{x}}$ and is given by

$$\sigma_{\bar{x}} = \frac{\sigma}{\sqrt{n}}$$

Finite Population Correction Factor

Consider a finite population of size N; with mean μ and standard deviation σ.

Consider all possible samples of size n, without replacement from this population. The mean of the sampling distribution of means be denoted by $\mu_{\bar{x}}$. Then we have

$$\mu_{\bar{x}} = \mu$$

The variance of the sampling distribution of mean is given by

$$\sigma_{\bar{x}}^2 = \frac{\sigma^2}{n}\left(\frac{N-n}{N-1}\right)$$

and the standard deviation is given by

$$\sigma_{\bar{x}} = \frac{\sigma}{\sqrt{n}}\sqrt{\frac{N-n}{N-1}}$$

The factor $\frac{N-n}{N-1}$ is called the finite population correction factor.

***Example* 1:** A population consists of five numbers 2, 4, 6, 8, 10. Write all the samples of size 2 that can be drawn from the population, without replacement.

***Solution*:** The following is the list of samples of size 2 that can be drawn without replacement

(2, 4), (2, 6), (2, 8), (2, 10)

(4, 6), (4, 8), (4, 10)

(6, 8), (6, 10)

(8, 10)

Number of samples that can be drawn without replacement = $N_{c_n} = 5_{c_2} = 10$.

***Example* 2:** A population consists of 6 numbers 1, 3, 5, 7, 9, 11. Find all the samples of size 2, that can be drawn from the population with replacement.

***Solution*:**

The samples are:

(1, 1), (1, 3), (1, 5), (1, 7), (1, 9), (1, 11)
(3, 1), (3, 3), (3, 5), (3, 7), (3, 9), (3, 11)
(5, 1), (5, 3), (5, 5), (5, 7), (5, 9), (5, 11)
(7, 1), (7, 3), (7, 5), (7, 7), (7, 9), (7, 11)
(9, 1), (9, 3), (9, 5), (9, 7), (9, 9), (9, 11)
(11, 1), (11, 3), (11, 5), (11, 7), (11, 9), (11, 11)

***Example* 3:** A population consists of five numbers 1, 3, 5, 7 and 9. Find all the samples of size 2, that can be drawn with replacement from the population. Also find

(i) Mean of the population

(ii) Standard deviation of the population

(iii) The mean of the sampling distribution of means

(iv) The standard deviation of the sampling distribution of means

***Solution*:**

(i) Mean of distribution $= \sum \frac{x_i}{n}$

i.e., $\mu = \frac{1+3+5+7+9}{5} = \frac{25}{5} = 5$

(ii) Variance of the population $= \sigma^2 = \frac{\sum (x-\mu)^2}{n}$

$$= \frac{(1-5)^2 + (3-5)^2 + (5-5)^2 + (7-5)^2 + (9-5)^2}{5}$$

$$= \frac{16+4+0+4+16}{5} = \frac{40}{5} = 8$$

$\therefore$ Standard deviation $= \sqrt{\sigma^2} = \sqrt{8}$

$\therefore \quad \sigma = \sqrt{8} = 2.82$

(iii) *The sample of size 2 with replacement are*:

(1, 1), (1, 3), (1, 5), (1, 7), (1, 9)
(3, 1), (3, 3), (3, 5), (3, 7), (3, 9)
(5, 1), (5, 3), (5, 5), (5, 7), (5, 9)
(7, 1), (7, 3), (7, 5), (7, 7), (7, 9)
(9, 1), (9, 3), (9, 5), (9, 7), (9, 9)

Number of samples $= N^n = 5^2 = 25$

The sample means are:

1, 2, 3, 4, 5
2, 3, 4, 5, 6
3, 4, 5, 6, 7
4, 5, 6, 7, 8
5, 6, 7, 8, 9

$\therefore$ Mean of the sampling distribution of means

i.e $\mu_{\bar{x}} = \frac{\text{Sum of all sample means}}{N^n}$

$$\mu_{\bar{x}} = \frac{1+2+3+4+5+......+5+6+7+8+9}{25}$$

$$\therefore \quad \mu_{\bar{x}} = \frac{125}{25} = 5$$

(iv) Variance of the sampling distribution of means = $\sigma_{\bar{x}}^2$

$$\text{i.e., } \sigma_{\bar{x}}^2 = \frac{(1-5)^2 + (2-5)^2 + (3-5)^2 + (4-5)^2 + (5-5)^2 + \ldots..(7-5)^2 + (8-5)^2 + (9-5)^2}{25}$$

$$= \frac{100}{25} = 4$$

$$\sigma_{\bar{x}} = \sqrt{4} = 2$$

***Example* 4:** Find the value of the correction factor is n = 10 and N = 100

Solution: we have N = 100, n = 10

$$\text{The correction factor } = \frac{N-n}{N-1}$$

$$= \frac{100-10}{100-1} = \frac{90}{99}$$

$$= 0.909$$

***Example* 5:** A population consists of five numbers 2, 4, 6, 8 and 10. List all the possible samples of size 2 without replacement from the population and find

(i) Mean of population

(ii) Standard deviation of the population

(iii) Mean of the sampling distribution of means

(iv) Standard deviation of the sampling distribution of means.

***Solution*:**

(i) Mean of the population

$$\mu = \frac{2+4+6+8+10}{5}$$

$$= \frac{30}{5} = 6$$

(ii) Standard deviation of the population

$$\sigma = \sqrt{\frac{\sum (x-\mu)^2}{n}}$$

$$= \sqrt{\frac{(2-6)^2 + (4-6)^2 + (6-6)^2 + (8-6)^2 + (10-6)^2}{5}}$$

$$= \sqrt{\frac{16+4+0+4+16}{5}} = \sqrt{8}$$

$$= 2.828$$

(iii) The samples of size without replacement are

(2, 4), (2, 6), (2, 8), (2, 10),

(4, 6), (4, 8), (4, 10),

(6, 8), (6, 10),

(8, 10)

Number of samples = $N_{c_n} = 5_{c_2} = 10$

The means of the samples are:

3, 4, 5, 6

5, 6, 7

7, 8

9

(iii) The mean of the sampling distribution of mean =

$$\mu_{\bar{x}} = \frac{3+4+5+6+5+6+7+7+8+9}{10}$$

$$= \frac{60}{10} = 6$$

(iv) The standards deviation of sampling distribution of means =

$$= \sqrt{\frac{\begin{gathered}(3-6)^2+(4-6)^2+(5-6)^2+(6-6)^2+(5-6)^2+(6-6)^2\\ +(6-5)^2+(7-6)^2+(8-6)^2+(9-6)^2\end{gathered}}{10}}$$

$$= \sqrt{\frac{9+4+1+0+1+0+1+1+4+9}{10}} = \sqrt{\frac{30}{10}}$$

$\therefore \qquad \mu_{\bar{x}} = \sqrt{3} = 1.732$

Example **6:** A random sample of size 100 is taken from an infinite population having the mean $\mu = 76$, and variable $\sigma^2 = 256$. What is the probability that $\bar{x}$ will be between 75 and 78.

***Solution*:** We have $\mu = 76$

$$\sigma^2 = 256 \quad \text{and} \quad n = 100 \quad \text{(given)}$$

Since $\qquad \sigma^2 = 256$, we get $\sigma = \sqrt{256} = 16$

$$Z = \frac{\bar{x}-\mu}{\frac{\sigma}{\sqrt{n}}}$$

where $\bar{x} = 75$, i.e $\qquad \bar{x}_1 = 75,\ Z_1 = \dfrac{75-76}{\frac{16}{\sqrt{100}}} = \dfrac{-1}{\left(\frac{16}{10}\right)}$

$$= -0.625$$

when $\bar{x} = 78$, i.e $\qquad \bar{x}_2 = 78,\ Z_2 = \dfrac{78-76}{\frac{16}{\sqrt{100}}} = \dfrac{2}{\frac{16}{10}}$

$$= 1.25$$

$\therefore \qquad P\,(75 \le \bar{x} \le 78) = P\,(Z_1 \le Z \le Z_2)$

$$= P\,(-0.625 \le Z \le 1.25)$$

$$= P\,(-0.625 \le Z \le 0) + P\,(0 \le Z \le 1.25)$$

$$= 0.2334 + 0.3944$$

$$= 0.628$$

***Example* 7:** A random sample of size 144 is taken from an infinite population having the mean 75 and variance 225. What is the probability that $\overline{x}$ will lie between 72 and 77?

(JNTU, 2006)

***Solution*:**

Size of the sample = n = 144

Variable = 228 = σ^2

Mean of the population = 75 (given)

$$\therefore \quad \sigma = \sqrt{225} = 15$$

$$Z = \frac{\overline{x} - \mu}{\frac{\sigma}{\sqrt{n}}}$$

when $\overline{x} = 72, Z = Z_1 = \frac{72-75}{\frac{15}{\sqrt{144}}} = \frac{-3}{\frac{15}{12}} = \frac{-3}{5} \times 4 = \frac{-12}{5} = -2.4$

when $\overline{x} = 77, Z = Z_2 = \frac{77-75}{\frac{15}{\sqrt{144}}} = \frac{2}{\frac{5}{12}} \times 4 = \frac{8}{5} = 1.6$

$$\begin{aligned}\therefore \quad P(72 \le \overline{x} \le 77) &= P(-2.4 \le Z \le 1.6)\\ &= P(-2.4 \le Z \le 0) + P(0 \le Z \le 1.6)\\ &= P(0 \le Z \le 2.4) + P(0 \le Z \le 1.6)\\ &= 0.4918 + 0.4452\\ &= 0.9370\end{aligned}$$

***Example* 8:** The mean of a normal population is equal to the standard error of the mean of the samples of 64 from the distribution. Find the probability that the mean of the sample size 36 will be negative.

***Solution*:** It is given that $n = 64$,

$$\text{Standard error of mean} = \frac{\sigma}{\sqrt{n}}$$

$$\therefore \quad \mu = \frac{\sigma}{\sqrt{64}} = \frac{\sigma}{8}$$

we have $$Z=\frac{\bar{x}-\mu}{\frac{\sigma}{\sqrt{n}}}$$

when n = 36

$$Z=\frac{\bar{x}-\frac{\sigma}{8}}{\frac{\sigma}{\sqrt{36}}}=\frac{\bar{x}-\frac{\sigma}{8}}{\frac{\sigma}{6}}$$

$$=\frac{6\bar{x}}{\sigma}-\frac{6}{8}=\frac{6\bar{x}}{\sigma}-\frac{3}{4}=\frac{6\bar{x}}{\sigma}-0.75$$

If $Z < 0.75$, $\bar{x}$ is negative

$$\text{Hence } P(Z<0.75)=P(-\infty<Z<0.75)$$
$$=P(-\infty<Z<0)+P(0<Z<0.75)$$
$$=0.5+0.2734$$
$$=0.7734.$$

***Example* 9:** A normal population has a mean of 0.1 and standard deviation 2.1. Find the portability that the mean of a sample of size 900 will be negative.

***Solution*:** Here we have $\mu=0.1,\ \sigma=2.1,\ n=900$

$$Z=\frac{\bar{x}-\mu}{\frac{\sigma}{\sqrt{n}}}=\frac{\bar{x}-0.1}{\frac{2.1}{\sqrt{900}}}=\frac{\bar{x}-0.1}{\frac{2.1}{30}}$$

$$=\frac{\bar{x}-0.1}{0.07}$$

or $$\bar{x}=0.1+0.07\,Z$$

Z follows normal distribution

$$P(\bar{x}<0)$$

$$\Rightarrow \quad P(0.1+0.07\,Z<0)$$

$$=P(0.07\,Z<-0.1)$$

$$=P\left(Z<-\frac{0.1}{0.07}\right)$$

$$=P\,(Z<-1.43)$$

$$= 0.50 - P\,(0 < Z < 1.43)$$

$$= 0.50 - 0.4236$$

$$= 0.0764.$$

***Example* 10:** A population consists of 5, 10, 14, 18, 13, 24 consider all possible samples of size two which can be drawn without replacement from the population. Find

(a) Mean of the population

(b) Standard deviation of the population

(c) The mean of sampling distribution of means

(d) The standard deviation of sampling distribution of means

***Solution*:**

(a) Mean of the population

$$\mu = \frac{5+10+14+18+13+24}{6}$$

$$= \frac{84}{6} = 14$$

(b) Variance of the population

$$\sigma^2 = \frac{(5-14)^2+(10-14)^2+(14-14)^2+(18-14)^2+(13-14)^2+(24-14)^2}{6}$$

$$= \frac{81+16+0+16+1+100}{6} = \frac{214}{6}$$

$$\therefore \quad \sigma^2 = 35.666$$

Standard deviation $= \sigma = \sqrt{35.666} = 5.9721$

(c) *Samples of size 2 from the population are (without replacement)*:

(5, 10), (5, 14), (5, 18), (5, 13), (5, 24)

(10, 14), (10, 18), (10, 13), (10, 24)

(14, 18), (14, 13), (14, 24)

(18, 13), (18, 24)

(13, 24)

15 samples

Means of the samples are:

7.5, 9.5, 11.5, 9, 14.5,

12, 14, 11.5, 17

16, 13.5, 19

15.5, 21

18.5

Means of the sampling distribution of means:

$$\mu_{\bar{x}} = \frac{7.5+9.5+11.5+9+14.5+12+14+11.5+17+16+13.5+19+15.5+21+18.5}{15}$$

$\therefore\ \mu_{\bar{x}} = 14$

(d) The standard deviation of sampling distribution of means

$$\sigma_{\bar{x}} = \sqrt{\frac{(7.5-14)^2+(9.5-14)^2+(11.5-14)^2+(9-14)^2+(14.5-14)^2 +........+(21-14)^2+(18.5-14)^2}{15}}$$

$= 3.726$

***Example* 11:** A research worker wishes to estimate mean of a population by using sufficiently large sample. The probability is 95% that sample mean will not differ from the true mean by more than 25 percentage of standard deviation. How large a sample should be taken?

***Solution*:** From the table of areas under normal curve, we have

$$-1.96 < \frac{\bar{x}-\mu}{\frac{\sigma}{\sqrt{n}}} < 1.96$$

$$\frac{|x-\mu|}{\frac{\sigma}{\sqrt{n}}} = 1.96$$

i.e $$|\bar{x}-\mu| = 1.96\ \frac{\sigma}{\sqrt{n}} \qquad .....(1)$$

or $$|\bar{x}-\mu| < \frac{\sigma}{4} \qquad \text{(given)} \qquad .....(2)$$

from (1) and (2) we get

$$1.96 \frac{\sigma}{\sqrt{n}} < \frac{\sigma}{4}$$

or $$1.96 < \frac{\sqrt{n}}{4}$$

or $$(1.96)^2 < \frac{n}{16}$$

or $$n > 16\,(1.96)^2$$

i.e $$n > 61.46$$

Hence $$n = 62$$

Exercise 3.4

1. A random sample of size 100 has mean 15, the population variance being 25. Find interval estimate of the population mean with confidence level of (1) 99% (ii) 95%.

Ans. [13.7, 16.29]

[14.02, 15.98]

2. The quality control manager of a tyre company has sample of 100 tyres and has found the life time to be 30.214 km. The population S.D is 860. Construct a 95% confidence interval for the mean life time for this particular brand of tyres.

Ans. [30045.44, 30382.56]

3. The sample mean of a population was recoded as 184.67 with a probable error of 0.236. Find the 99.74% confidence limits for the true (population) mean.

Ans. [183.62, 185.72]

4. The mean and standard deviation of the diameters of a sample of 250 rivet heads manufactured by a company are 7.2642 mm and 0.0058 mm respectively. Find 98% confidence limits.

Ans. [7.2642 ± 0.00086]

5. In a random selection of 64 of 600 road crossing in a town, the mean number of automobile accidents per year was formed to be 4.2 and the sample S.D was 0.8. Construct a 95% confidence interval for the mean number of automobile accidents per crossing per year.

Ans. [4.023, 4.377]

6. A population of six number 4, 8, 12, 16, 20 and 24. Consider all the samples of size two which can be drawn without replacement from this population. Find

(a) the population mean

(b) the population S.D

(c) the mean of sampling distribution of means

(d) the standard deviation of sampling distribution of means.

Ans. [(a) 14 (b) 6.83 (c) 14 (d) 4.32

7. The mean height of students is a college is 155 cm and standard deviation is 15. What is the probability that the mean height of 36 students is less than 157 cm.

Ans. [0.7881]

8. Let S = {1, 5, 6, 8}. Find the probability distribution of the sample mean for random sample size 2 drawn without replacement.

Ans. [$\mu_{\bar{x}}$ = 5, S.D = 1.612]

9. Find the value of finite population correction factor for n = 10, and N = 100.

Ans. [0.991]

10. Find the probability is that a random variable having the standard normal distribution will take on a value

Ans. (a) between 0.87 and 1.28

(b) between – 0.34 and 0.62

Ans. [0.0919, 0.3655]

Testing of Hypothesis - I

4

4.1 Introduction

In this chapter we introduce the theory of estimation which is used to estimate the population parameters by taking random samples from the population. We begin our study with definitions.

4.2 Unbiased Estimator

A statistic is called unbiased estimator of a population parameter if the mean of the statistic is equal to the parameter and the corresponding value of the statistic is called an unbiased estimate of the parameter. Unbiased estimator is defined as follows.

Definition: An estimator T, of the parameter θ is said to be an unbiased estimator of θ if $E(T) = \theta$.

Efficient Estimator:

If the sampling distributions of two statistics have the same mean, the statistic with lesser variance is called a more efficient estimator of the corresponding value of the statistic is called efficient estimator.

4.3 Types of Estimates

There are two types of estimates about a population parameter, namely,

(i) Point estimate and (ii) Interval estimate.

4.4 Point Estimate

A point estimate is a single number that is used to estimate an unknown population parameter.

4.4.1 Point Estimator

A point estimator is a statistic for estimating a population parameter.

If θ denotes the population parameter then the point estimator of θ is denoted by $\hat{\theta}$. An estimator should always be close to the true value of unknown parameter and is not expected to estimate without an error.

4.5 Interval Estimate

An estimate of a population parameter given by two magnitudes within which a parameter can lie is called interval estimate of the parameter.

Definition: Let θ denote a population parameter. An interval estimate of θ is an interval of the form $\hat{\theta}_l < \theta < \hat{\theta}_L$ where $\hat{\theta}_l$ and $\hat{\theta}_L$ depend on the value of θ for a particular sample and also on the sampling distribution of $\hat{\theta}$.

4.6 Criteria for the Best Estimator

The criteria for the best estimator are

(i) Consistency

(ii) Efficiency

(iii) Unbiasedness

(iv) Sufficiency

(i) ***Consistency***:

An estimator k_n is consistent is given two positive numbers $\in$ and η however small we can find a positive integer N depending on $\in$ and η such that

$$P\{|k_n - \theta| < \in\} > 1 - \eta \qquad \text{for all} \quad n > N$$

If t_1 and t_2 are estimators of a parameter θ such that

$$\text{Var}(t_1) < \text{Var}(t_2) \qquad \text{for all} \quad n$$

then t_1 is said to be more efficient than t_2.

(ii) Efficiency (E) of t_1 relative to t_2 is defined as:

$$E = \frac{\text{Var}(t_1)}{\text{Var}(t_2)}$$

An estimator with lesser variability is said to be more efficient than the other.

(iii) *Unbiasedness*:

A statistic $t = t(x_1, x_2 ......x_n)$ a function of the sample observations $x_1, x_2.......x_n$ is said to be an unbiased estimate of the corresponding population parameter θ, if $E(t) = \theta$

i.e., if the expected value of the sampling distribution of the statistic is equal to parameter.

(iv) *Sufficiency*:

An estimator t_n is said to be sufficient if it contains all the information in the sample regarding the population parameter θ.

4.7 Bayesian Estimation

In Bayesian estimation, the prior feelings about the possible values of μ with direct sample evidence. The posterior distribution in Bayesian estimation is approximated by normal distribution with

$$\mu_1 = \frac{n\bar{x}\,\sigma_o^2 + \mu_o\,\sigma^2}{n\,\sigma_o^2 + \sigma^2} \quad \text{and}$$

$$\sigma_1 = \sqrt{\frac{\sigma_o^2\sigma^2}{n\,\sigma_o^2 + \sigma^2}}$$

μ_1 and σ_1 are called the mean and standard deviation of the posterior distribution.

In the computation of μ_1 and σ_1, we assume that σ^2 is assumed to be known. When the value σ^2 is unknown, σ^2 is replaced by s^2 provided the sample is large

The interval

$$\mu_1 - Z_{\frac{\alpha}{2}}.\sigma_1 < \mu < \mu_1 + Z_{\frac{\alpha}{2}}\,\sigma_1$$

is a $(1 - \alpha)$ 100% Bayesian interval.

***Example* 1:** The mean and standard deviation of a population are 11,795 and 14,054 respectively. What can one assert that 95% confidence about the maximum error if $\bar{x} = 11{,}795$ and $n = 50$? [JNTU 2008]

***Solution*:** We have $n = 50$ (sample size)

Mean of the population $= \mu = 11{,}795$

Standard deviation of the population $= \sigma = 14{,}054$

$$Z_{\frac{\alpha}{2}} \text{ for 95\% confidence} = 1.96$$

$$\text{Maximum error} = E = Z_{\frac{\alpha}{2}} \cdot \frac{\sigma}{\sqrt{n}}$$

$$= 1.96 \cdot \left(\frac{14054}{\sqrt{50}}\right)$$

$$= 3895.6$$

***Example* 2:** A random sample of size 100 has a standard deviation of 5. What can you say about the maximum error with 95% confidence?

***Solution*:** We have n = 100, $\sigma = 15$

$$Z_{\frac{\alpha}{2}} \text{ for 95\% confidence} = 1.96$$

$$\text{Maximum error. } E = Z_{\frac{\alpha}{2}} \cdot \frac{\sigma}{\sqrt{n}}$$

$$= 1.96 \frac{5}{\sqrt{100}}$$

$$= 0.98$$

***Example* 3:** It is desired to estimate the mean number of hours of continous are until a certain computer with first require repairs. If it can be assumed that $\sigma = 48$ hours; how large a sample be needed so that one will be able to assert with 90% confidence that the sample mean is off by atmost 10 hours.

***Solution*:** We have $\sigma = 48$ hours

E = Maximum error = 48 hours

For 90% confidence $Z_{\frac{\alpha}{2}} = 1.645$

$$n = \frac{Z_{\frac{\alpha}{2}}^{2} \sigma^2}{E^2} = \frac{(1.645)^2 (48)^2}{(10)^2}$$

$$= 62.346$$

Hence n = 62

***Example* 4:** The dean of a college wants to use the mean of a random sample to estimate the average amount of time students take to get from one class to the next and she wants to be able to assert with 99% confidence that the error is at most 0.25 minute. If it can be presumed from experience that $\sigma = 1.40$ minutes, how large a sample will she have to take?

Solution: It is given that, the standard deviation

$$\sigma = 1.40 \text{ minutes}$$

$$\text{Maximum error} = E = 0.25 \text{ minutes}$$

$$Z_{\frac{\alpha}{2}} = 2.575$$

Hence
$$n = \frac{Z_{\frac{\alpha}{2}}^2 \sigma^2}{E^2} = \frac{(2.575)^2 (1.4)^2}{(0.25)^2}$$

$$= 208$$

***Example* 5:** Ten bearings made by a certain process have a mean diameter of 0.5060 cm with a standard deviation of 0.0040 cm. Assuming that the data may be taken as random sample from a normal distribution, construct a 95% confidence interval for the actual average diameter of the bearings [JNTU 2005]

Solution: Given that n = 10 (small sample)

$$\sigma = 0.0040 \text{ cm}, \quad \bar{x} = 0.05060$$

Since, the size of the sample is small, we consider t – distribution

we have

$$t_{\frac{\alpha}{2}} = 2.262 \text{ for } 95\% \text{ confidence}$$

$$\therefore \quad E = t_{\frac{\alpha}{2}} \frac{\sigma}{\sqrt{n}} = (2.262). \frac{0.004}{\sqrt{10}}$$

$$= 0.00286$$

The 95% confidence interval is

$$\bar{x} \pm t_{\frac{\alpha}{2}} . \frac{\sigma}{\sqrt{n}}$$

$$= 0.5060 \pm 2.262 . \frac{(0.004)}{\sqrt{10}}$$

or
$$(0.5031, 0.5089)$$

***Example* 6:** A population random variable has mean 100 and standard deviation 16. What are the values of mean and standard deviation of the sample mean for random samples of size 4 drawn with replacement? [JNTU 2004]

***Solution*:** we have

$$\mu = 100, \sigma = 16 \quad \text{and} \quad n = 4$$

Since the sampling is with replacement, the population is taken as infinite population.

$$\therefore \quad \mu_{\bar{x}} = \mu = 100$$

and

$$\sigma_{\bar{x}} = \frac{\sigma}{\sqrt{n}} = \frac{16}{\sqrt{4}} = \frac{16}{2} = 8$$

***Example* 7:** If we can assert with 95% that the maximum error is 0.05 and P = 0.2, find the sample size.

***Solution*:** since $P = 0.2$, $Q = 1 - P = 1 - 0.2 = 0.8$

95% confidence $Z_{\frac{\alpha}{2}} = 1.96$

$E = 0.05$ (given)

Hence

$$E = Z_{\frac{\alpha}{2}} \sqrt{\frac{PQ}{n}}$$

$$\Rightarrow \quad 0.05 = 1.96 \sqrt{\frac{(0.2)(0.8)}{n}}$$

or

$$(0.05)^2 = (1.96)^2 \frac{(0.16)}{n}$$

or

$$n = \frac{(1.96)^2 (0.16)}{(0.05)^2}$$

i.e

$$n = 246$$

***Example* 8:** A random sample of size 81 was taken variance is 20.25 and mean is 32. Construct 98% confidence interval. [JNTU Dec. 2005]

***Solution*:** Here we have $\bar{x} = 32$, $\sigma^2 = 81$, $n = 81$ and

$Z_{\frac{\alpha}{2}}$ (for 98% confidence) = 2.33

$$\therefore \qquad Z_{\frac{\alpha}{2}} \frac{\sigma}{\sqrt{n}} = 2.33 \left(\frac{4.5}{\sqrt{81}} \right) = 1.165$$

The confidence interval is

$$(\bar{x} - Z_{\frac{\alpha}{2}} \frac{\sigma}{\sqrt{n}},\ \bar{x} + Z_{\frac{\alpha}{2}} \frac{\sigma}{\sqrt{n}})$$

$$= (32 - 1.165, 32 + 1.65)$$

$$= (30.835, \quad 33.165)$$

***Example* 9:** The mean of a random sample is an unbiased estimate of the mean of the population 3, 6, 9, 15, 27

(a) List all possible samples of size 3 that can be drawn from the finite population

(b) Calculate the mean of each of the sample listed in (a), and assigning each sample a probability of 1/10. Verify that the mean of these $\bar{x}$ is equal to 12, which is equal to that mean of the population θ i.e E $(\bar{x})$ = 0 i.e prove that $\bar{x}$ is an unbiased estimate of θ.

***Solution*:** The samples of size 3 that can be taken from the population 3, 6, 9, 15 and 27, without replacement are:

(3, 6, 9), (3, 6, 15), (3, 6, 27), (6, 9, 15), (6, 9, 27),

(9, 15, 27), (3, 9 15), (3, 15, 27), (6, 15, 27), (3, 9 , 27)

Number of samples = 10

$$\text{Mean of the population} = \theta = \frac{3+6+9+15+27}{5}$$

$$= \frac{60}{5} = 12$$

Means of the samples are:

6, 8, 12, 10, 14, 17, 9, 15, 16, 13

The probability distribution is

$\bar{x}$:	6	8	12	10	14	17	9	15	16	13
P($\bar{x}$):	1/10	1/10	1/10	1/10	1/10	1/10	1/10	1/10	1/10	1/10

$$E(\bar{x}) = 6.\frac{1}{10} + 8.\frac{1}{10} + 12.\frac{1}{10} + 10.\frac{1}{10} + 14.\frac{1}{10} + 17.\frac{1}{10} + 9.\frac{1}{10} + 15.\frac{1}{10} + 16.\frac{1}{10} + 13.\frac{1}{10}$$

$$= \frac{1}{10}[\,6 + 8 + 12 + 10 + 14 + 17 + 9 + 15 + 16 + 13]$$

$$= \frac{120}{10} = 12$$

$\therefore\ E(\bar{x}) = 12 = \theta$

Hence, $\bar{x}$ is an unbiased estimate of θ

***Example* 10:** A random sample of 100 teachers in a metropolitan area revealed a mean weekly salary of Rs. 487 with a standard deviation Rs. 48. With what degree of confidence can we assert that the average weekly salary of all teachers in the metropolitan area is between 472 and 502

***Solution*:** Here we have

$$\mu = 487,$$

$$\sigma = 48$$

and $$n = 100$$

Hence, $$Z = \frac{\bar{x} - \mu}{\frac{\sigma}{\sqrt{n}}}$$

$$= \frac{\bar{x} - 487}{\left(\frac{48}{\sqrt{100}}\right)} = \frac{\bar{x} - 487}{4.8}$$

when $\bar{x} = 472$, $Z = Z_1$ (say) $= \dfrac{472 - 487}{4.8}$

$$= -3.125$$

When $\bar{x} = 503$, $Z = Z_2$ (say) $= = \dfrac{502 - 487}{4.8} = 3.125$

$$\therefore \quad P(4.72 < x < 502) = P(-3.125 < Z < 3.125)$$

$$= P(0 < Z < 3.125) + P(0 < Z < 3)$$

$$= 2\,P(0 < Z < 3.125)$$

$$= 2\,(0.4991) = 0.9982$$

Hence, the degree of confidence = 99.82 %

4.8 Interval Estimation

The range of values used in making estimation of a population parameter is called interval estimation.

It is defined as the estimation of a population parameter θ with the help of the interval $[t - s, t + s]$ where t is the sample statistic.

The two limits within which the estimate for the parameter lies are known as the confidence limits or fiducial limits. The probability that we associate with an interval is called the confidence level. The most commonly used confidence levels are 90%, 95%, 98% and 99%.

In general, the interval estimation is defined as P ($l_1 < \theta < l_2$; for a given statistic Z) $= 1 - \alpha$

where α is called the level of significance.

The interval is within which the unknown parameter q is expected to lie. l_1 is called the lower limit of the confidence interval and l_2 is called the upper limit of the confidence interval.

If t is the statistic used to estimate the parameter θ, then $(1 - \alpha)$ 100% confidence limits for θ are $t - SE(t).t_\alpha$ and $t + SE(t).t_\alpha$.

4.9 Central Limit Theorem

Let $X_1, X_2, \ldots\ldots X_n$ be n independent random variables all of which have the same distribution. Let the common expectation and variance be μ and σ^2 respectively. Let $\overline{x} = \frac{\Sigma x_i}{n}$, then the distribution of $\overline{x}$ with mean μ and variance $\frac{\sigma^2}{n}$ as $n \to \infty$.

i.e., variate $Z = \dfrac{\overline{x} - \mu}{\frac{\sigma}{\sqrt{n}}}$ has standard normal distribution.

As per central limit theorem, the sampling distribution of the sample statistic t will be asymptotically normal

i.e $$Z = \frac{t - E(t)}{SE(t)}$$

is a standard normal variate with mean zero and variance 1 as $n \to \infty$.

Confidence interval for large samples:

(i) When σ, the standard deviation of the normal population is known

$$SE(\overline{x}) = \frac{\sigma}{\sqrt{n}}$$

where n is the sample size

confidence interval is $\overline{x}-\frac{\sigma}{\sqrt{n}}Z_{\frac{\alpha}{2}}<\mu<\overline{x}+\frac{\sigma}{n}Z_{\frac{\alpha}{2}}$

(when α is known, and population is normal)

(ii) when σ is unknown and n is large, the confidence interval is

$$\left(\overline{x}-\frac{S}{\sqrt{n-1}}Z_{\frac{\alpha}{2}},\ \overline{x}+\frac{S}{\sqrt{n-1}}Z_{\frac{\alpha}{2}}\right)$$

$Z_{\frac{\alpha}{2}}$ is Z - value leaving an area of $\frac{\alpha}{2}$ to the right.

4.10 Maximum Error

The maximum error estimate E with $(1-\alpha)$ probability is

$$E=Z_{\frac{\alpha}{2}}\frac{\alpha}{\sqrt{n}} \qquad \text{(for large samples)}$$

For small samples the maximum error estimate is given by

$$E=t_{\frac{\alpha}{2}}\frac{s}{\sqrt{n}} \qquad \text{(S = standard deviation of the sample)}$$

***Example* 11:** An industrial engineer intends to use the mean of a random sample of size n = 150 to estimate the average mechanical aptitude of assembly line works in a large industry. If on the basis of experience the engineer can assume that $\sigma = 6.2$ for such data, What can he assert with probability 0.99 about the maximum size of his error.

***Solution*:** It is given that

σ = Standard deviation of the population = 6.2

sample size (n) = 150

$Z_{\frac{\alpha}{2}} = 2.575$

Maximum error $\quad Z_{\frac{\alpha}{2}}.\frac{\sigma}{\sqrt{n}} = 2.575.\left(\frac{6.2}{\sqrt{150}}\right) = 1.3$

Exercise 4.1

1. A random sample of 400 items is found to have mean of 82 and S.D of 18. Find the 95% confidence limits for the mean of the population form which the sample is drawn

Ans: [80.236, 83.764]

2. A random sample size of 16 values from a normal population showed a mean of 41.5 inches and the sum of squares of deviations form mean is 135 sq. inches. Find the maximum error with 95% confidence

Ans. [1.598]

3. A researcher wants to determine the average time it takes a mechanic to rotate the tyres of a car and he wants to be able to assert with 95% confidence that the mean of his sample is off by atmost 0.5 minutes. If he can presume from past experience that $\sigma = 1.6$ mts, how large a sample will he has to take

Ans. [40]

4. Suppose that we observe a random variable having the binomial distribution and get X successes in n trials. Show that $\frac{X}{n}$ is an unbiased estimate of the binomial parameter P.

5. A random sample of size 100 is taken from a population with $\sigma = 5.1$. Given that the sample mean is $\overline{X} = 21.6$. Construct a 95% confidence interval for the population mean μ.

Ans. [20.6; 22.6]

6. It is desired to estimate the mean time of continuous use until an answering machine will first require service. If it can be assumed that $\sigma = 60$ days. How large a sample is needed so that one will be able to assert with 90% confidence that the sample mean is off by at most 10 days.

Ans. [72]

7. If the mean breaking of copper wire is 505 lbs with a standard deviation of 15 lbs, the size of the sample is 49. Construct 95% confidence interval for the mean.

Ans. [(500.8, 509.2)]

8. What is the maximum error one can expect to make with probability 0.9 when using the mean of a random sample of size n = 64 to estimate the mean of a population with $\sigma^2 = 2.56$

Ans. [0.329]

4.11 Introduction

In this section we introduce the methods testing hypothesis which enables us to make probability statement about population parameters. Before we explain how hypotheses are tested through different tests, meant for the purpose, it will be appropriate to explain clearly the meaning of hypothesis and the related concepts for the better understanding of the techniques of hypothesis testing.

4.12 Hypothesis

A hypothesis is a proposition or set of propositions or a set of propositions set forth as an explanation for the occurrence of some specified group of phenomena. It is defined as follows

Definition: A hypothesis is a statement about the population parameter.

Hypothesis should be specific. It should be capable of being tested. A hypothesis should be stated as far as possible in simple terms.

4.13 Test of Hypothesis

The test of hypothesis a test which discloses the fact whether the difference between sample statistic and the corresponding hypothetical population parameters significant or not significant.

4.14 Types of Hypothesis

There are two of hypotheseis:

1. Null hypothesis
2. Alternative hypothesis

1. *Null hypothesis*:

Definition: The hypothesis which is to be tested for possible rejection under the assumption that it is true is called null hypothesis.

The null hypothesis set up for testing a statistical hypothesis to decide whether to accept or reject it i.e the hypothesis.

Null hypothesis is denoted by H_o.

2. *Alternative hypothesis*:

The negative of null hypothesis is called alternative hypothesis.

It is denoted by H_1 and is set in such a way that the rejection of null hypothesis implies the acceptance of alternative hypothesis.

For example, if we want to test the null hypothesis that the average weight of the students in a class is 45 kg i.e $\mu_o = 45$ kg (say), then the null hypothesis is

$$H_o : \mu = \mu_o = 45$$

and the alternative hypothesis would be

$H_1 : \mu \neq \mu_o$ (i.e $\mu > \mu_o$ or $\mu < \mu_o$) (two tailed test)

$H_1 : \mu_1 > \mu_o$ (one-tailed test)

$H_1 : \mu_1 < \mu_o$ (one-tailed test)

4.15 Critical Region

The region of the standard normal curve corresponding to predetermined level of significance α is known as critical region. It is also called the region of rejection.

4.16 Acceptance Region

The region under the normal curve which is not covered by the rejection region is called acceptance region.

4.17 Level of Significance

The level of significance is the maximum probability of making an error. It is denoted by α.

That is

$$P\text{ (rejecting } H_0 \text{ when } H_0 \text{ is true)} = \alpha$$

The levels of significance usually employed in testing hypothesis are 1% and 5%. It is fixed in advance.

***Types of error in hypothesis testing*:**
There are two types of errors.

(i) Types I error and (ii) type II error.

***Type I error*:**

The error of rejecting null hypothesis when H_o is true is called type II error.

The probability of making type I error is denoted by α. (i.e. the level of significance)

***Type II error*:**

The error of accepting the null hypothesis H_o, when it is false is called type II error.

The probability of making a type II error is denoted by β.

We have the following table

	H_0 is true	H_0 is false
Accept H_0	Correct decision	Wrong decision Type II error (β)
Reject H_0	Wrong decision Type I error (α)	Correct decision.

The probability of making correct decision is $1 - \alpha$.

4.18 Critical Value

The value of the statistic of the test statistic computed to test the null hypothesis is called critical value.

The initial value of a test statistic separates the rejection region from the acceptance region.

4.19 Two Tailed Test and One Tailed Test

In the test of acceptance or non-acceptance of a hypothesis, if the focus of attention lies in the two tails of the distribution, the test is called a two tailed test.

Definition:

When the test is made on the basis of rejection region represented by both sides of the standard normal curve, it is called a two tailed test.

The two tailed test is of the form:

$H_0 : \mu = \mu_0$

$H_1 : H_1 : \mu \neq \mu_0$ $\qquad (\mu > \mu_0 \text{ or } \mu < \mu_0)$

The two tailed test is applied in such cases when difference between the sample mean and the population mean is tending to reject the null hypothesis.

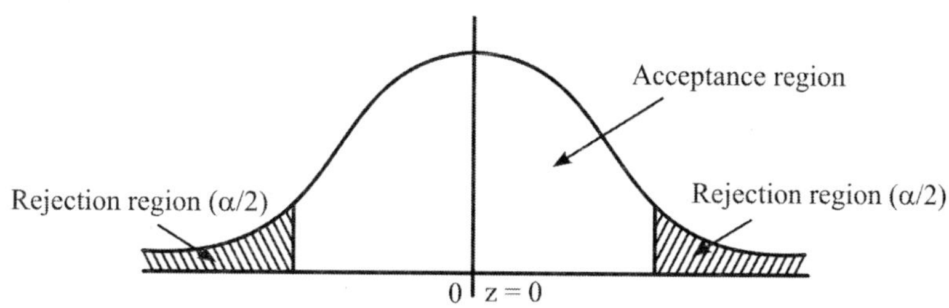

Fig. 4.1 Two tailed test.

***One-tailed test*:**

A test of hypothesis where the alternative hypothesis is one sided is called one-tailed test.

One tailed test may be left tailed or right tailed. In the case of a left tailed test the rejection region lies entirely on the left tail of the normal curve and in the case of right tailed test the rejection region lies entirely on the right tail of the normal curve.

$H_0 : \mu = \mu_0$

$H_1 : \mu > \mu_0$ (Right tailed

$H_1 : \mu < \mu_0$ (Left tailed)

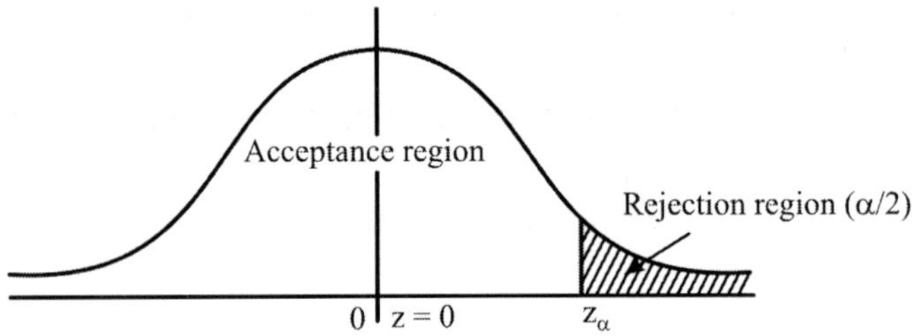

Fig. 4.2 Right tailed test.

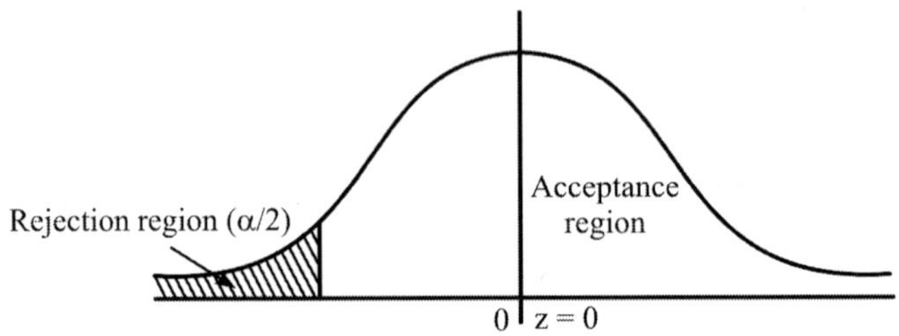

Fig. 4.3 Left tailed test.

The critical values of the tests for a large n are shown in the table given below

Critical value (significance value)	Level of Significance		
	1%	5%	10%
Two tailed test	$\lvert Z_{\alpha/2}\rvert = 2.58$	$\lvert Z_{\alpha/2}\rvert = 1.90$	$\lvert Z_{\alpha/2}\rvert = 1.645$
Right tailed test	2.33	1.645	1.28
One tailed test	– 2.33	–1.645	– 1.28

4.20 Procedure for Testing Hypothesis

The following steps are involved in hypothesis testing

1. Setting up of hypothesis
2. Computation of test statistic
3. Level of significance
4. Test statistic
5. Critical values for the test
6. Conclusion

4.21 Test of Significance for Large Value of n

For large values of n, the Binomial, and Poisson are very closely approximated by normal distribution.

If X follows normal distribution with parameters μ and σ^2 and $Z = \dfrac{\bar{X}-\mu}{\sigma^2} \sim N(0, 1)$ we compute the 5% or 1% confidence intervals for the statistic Z. The confidence limits are

$$\bar{X} - Z_{\alpha/2}\frac{\sigma}{\sqrt{n}} < \mu < \bar{X} + Z_{\alpha/2}\frac{\sigma}{\sqrt{n}}$$

The significance at 5% level for a two tailed test is 1.96 and the significance at 1% level is 2.58. If $|Z| > 1.96$ the null hypothesis is rejected at 5% level of significance and if $|Z| > 2.58$. H_o is rejected at 1% level of significance.

***If the test is one-tailed*:**

H_o is accepted at 5% level of significance when $|Z| < 1.645$

H_o is rejected at 5% level of significance where $|Z| > 1.645$

H_o is accepted at 1% level of significance when $|Z| < 2.33$ and H_o is rejected at 1% level of significance when $|Z| > 2.33$.

Test of significance for single mean

When we want to test whether the given sample of size n is drawn from a population with mean μ, we set up H_o that then is no difference between the sample mean $\bar{X}$ and μ

The test statistic is

$$Z = \frac{\bar{X} - \mu}{\sigma / \sqrt{n}}$$

where σ is the standard deviation of the population.

When the population S.D in not known, this statistic

$$Z = \frac{\bar{X} - \mu}{\sigma / \sqrt{n}} \text{ is used}$$

where S is the sample standard deviation.

***Example* 1:** It is claimed that a random sample of 100 tyres with a mean life of 15269 is drawn from a population of tyres which has a mean life of 15200 km and a standard deviation of 1248 km Test the validity of the claim

***Solution*:** we have mean life of the population = 15200 km

i.e $\mu = 15200$

$\bar{X} = 15269$ km (mean of the sample)

$\sigma = 1248$

$n = 100$

Null Hypothesis : $\mu = 15269$

i.e $H_o : \mu = 15269$ km

$H_1 : \mu \neq 15269$

when level of significance = 0.5, $Z_{\alpha/2} = 1.96$

level of significance = 0.1, $Z_{\alpha/2} = 2.58$

$$Z = \frac{\bar{X} - \mu}{\sigma / \sqrt{n}} = \frac{15269 - 15200}{\frac{1248}{\sqrt{100}}} = \frac{69 \times 10}{1248} = \frac{690}{1248}$$

$$= 0.55$$

The calculated value of Z is less than the table value. Hence we accept Null Hypothesis.

***Example* 2:** In a study of an automobile insurance a random sample of 80 body repair costs had a mean of 473.26 and standard deviation Rs. 62.35.

If $\bar{x}$ is used as a point estimate to the true average repair cost, with what confidence we assert that the maximum error does not exceed Rs. 10.

***Solution*:** Sample size = n = 80, $\sigma = 5.0 = 62.35$

Maximum error = E = 10

we have $E = Z_{\alpha/2} \dfrac{\sigma}{\sqrt{n}}$

i.e $10 = Z_{\alpha/2} \dfrac{62.35}{\sqrt{80}}$

or $Z_{\alpha/2} = \dfrac{10.4\sqrt{5}}{62.35} = 1.43$

From the tables when Z = 1.43, the probability is 0.4236

Hence the total area under the curve = 2 × 0.4236

= 0.8472

i.e Maximum error of Rs.10 when the confidence is 85%

***Example* 3:** A sample of size 400 was drawn and the sample mean was found to be 99. Test whether this sample would have come form a normal population with mean 100 and standard deviation 8 at 5% level of significance.

***Solution*:** Here we have, $n = 400$

$\bar{x} = 99$, $\mu = 100$, $S.D = \sigma = 8$

$H_0 : \mu = 100$

$H_1 : \mu \neq 100$ (Two tailed test)

Level of significance = σ = 0.05, table value of Z = 1.96

$$S.E(\bar{x}) = \frac{\sigma}{\sqrt{n}} = \frac{8}{\sqrt{400}} = \frac{8}{20} = 0.4$$

$$Z = \frac{\bar{X} - \mu}{\sigma/\sqrt{n}} = \frac{\bar{x} - \mu}{S.E(\bar{x})} = \frac{99 - 100}{0.4} = \frac{-1}{0.4} = \frac{-10}{4} = -2.5$$

we have $|Z_\alpha| = 1.96$, $|Z| = 2.5$

i.e $|Z| > |Z_\alpha|$

i.e calculated value of Z is greater than the table value, Null Hypothesis is rejected.

***Example* 4:** The mean life time of sample of 400 fluorescent light tubes produced by a company is found to be 1570 hours, with standard deviation of 150 hours. Test the hypothesis that the mean life time of the tubes produced by the company is 1600 hours against the alternative hypothesis that is greater than 1600 hours at 1% level of significance.

***Solution*:** sample size $n = 400$ (large sample)

$\bar{x} = 1570$ $S = 150$, $\sigma = 1600$, $H_o : \mu = 1600$

$H_1 : \mu > 1600,$ (one-tailed test)

Level of significance $\alpha = 0.01$

Table value of Z at 1 % level , i,e., $Z_\alpha = 2.33$

$$S.E(\bar{x}) = \frac{S}{\sqrt{n}} = \frac{150}{20} = 7.5$$

$$Z = \frac{\bar{x} - \mu}{S.E(\bar{x})} = \frac{1570 - 1600}{7.5} = \frac{-30}{7.5} = -4$$

$$\therefore \qquad |z| = 4$$

The calculated value of Z is greater than the table value of Z. Hence, the null hypothesis is rejected.

***Example* 5:** According to the norms established for a mechanical aptitude test who are 18 years old have an average height of 73.2 inches, with a standard deviation of 8.6. If 45 randomly selected persons of that age averaged 76.7 inches. Test the null hypothesis $\mu = 73.2$ against alternative hypothesis at the 0.01 level of significance.

***Solution*:** Here $\mu = 73.2$

$\bar{x} = 76.7$

$\sigma = 8.6$

$n = 45$

table value of Z at 0.01 level = 2.33

level of significance : 0.01

$$Z = \frac{\bar{X} - \mu}{\sigma / \sqrt{n}} = \frac{76.7 - 73.2}{\left(\frac{8.6}{\sqrt{45}}\right)} = \frac{3.5}{1.282} = 2.7301$$

Since the calculated value of Z is greater than the table value of Z at 0.01 level, we reject Null Hypothesis H_o.

***Example* 6:** A sample of 900 members has a mean 3.4 cm and standard deviation 2.61 cm. Can the sample be regarded as one drawn from a population with mean 3.25 cm. Using the level of significance as 0.05, is the claim acceptable.

***Solution*:** Here, we have

$n = 900 : \bar{x} = 3.4$ cm

$S = 2.61 :$ and $\mu = 3.25$

H_o : Null Hypothesis $\mu = 3.25$

H_1 : Alternative Hypothesis: $\mu \neq 3.25$

Level of significance = α = 0.05

Table value of Z at α = 0.05 = 1.96

$$\text{S.E of mean} = \text{S.E}(\overline{x}) = \frac{S}{\sqrt{n}} = \frac{2.61}{\sqrt{900}} = \frac{2.61}{30}$$

$$= 0.087$$

$$Z = \frac{\overline{x} - \mu}{\frac{S}{\sqrt{n}}} = \frac{3.4 - 3.25}{0.087} = 1.72$$

Here, the calculated value of Z is less than the table value of Z at 5% level (i.e 0.05)

Hence, the Null Hypothesis is accepted i.e the sample has been drawn from a population with mean 3.25 cm.

***Example* 7:** If a random sample of size 20 from a normal population with S.D 5.2 shows a mean of 16.9 test at 5% level of significance level that the population mean is 15.5. Also calculate 99% confidence limit for mean

***Solution*:** It is given that

$$\overline{X} = 16.9 \; ; \; n = 20$$

level of significance = 5%

$$\sigma = 5.2 \; ; \; \mu = 15.5 \; ; \; Z_\alpha = 1.96$$

$$\text{test statistic } Z = \frac{\overline{x} - \mu}{\sigma / \sqrt{n}}$$

H_o : Null hypothesis $\mu = 15.5$

H_1 : $\mu \neq 15.5$

$$Z = \frac{16.9 - 15.5}{5.2 / \sqrt{20}} = 1.20$$

Calculated value of Z is less than the table value of Z at 5% level of significance. Therefore H_o is accepted

$$\text{99\% confidence limits } \overline{n} \pm \frac{\sigma}{\sqrt{n}} Z_\alpha$$

$$= 16.9 \pm \frac{5.2}{\sqrt{20}} (2.58)$$

$$= 16.9 \pm 3$$

$$= (13.9, \; 19.9)$$

4.22 Test of Significance for Difference of Means

Consider a population with mean μ_1 and variance σ_1^2. Let $\overline{x}_1$ be the mean of sample of size n_1 drawn from this population.

Let μ_2 denote the mean of another population with variance σ_2^2 and $\overline{x}_2$ denote the mean of the sample of size n_2.

To test whether there is any significance difference between σ_2^2 and $\overline{x}_2$ denote the mean of the sample of size n_2.

To test whether there is any significance difference between $\overline{x}_1$ and $\overline{x}_2$, the statistic

$$Z = \frac{\overline{X}_1 - \overline{X}_2}{\sqrt{\frac{\sigma_1^2}{n_1} + \frac{\sigma_2^2}{n_2}}}$$

is used

If the samples of sizes n_1 and n_2 are drawn from the same population then we have $\sigma_1^2 = \sigma_2^2 = \sigma^2$.

The test statistic the this case is

$$Z = \frac{\overline{X}_1 - \overline{X}_2}{\sqrt{\frac{\sigma^2}{n_1} + \frac{\sigma^2}{n_2}}} = \frac{\overline{X}_1 - \overline{X}_2}{\sigma\sqrt{\frac{1}{n_1} + \frac{1}{n_2}}}$$

where $\overline{X}_1$ and $\overline{X}_2$ denote the means of the samples.

If σ is unknown then we find σ^2 by using the formula $\sigma^2 = \frac{n_1 s_1^2 + n_2 s_2^2}{n_1 + n_2}$.

***Example* 8:** The means of two large samples of sizes 1000 and 2000 members are 67.5 inches and 68 inches respectively. Can the samples be regarded as drawn from the same population of S.D 2.5 inches?

***Solution*:** Here we have $\overline{x}_1 = 67.5$ inches, $n_1 = 1000$

$\overline{x}_2 = 68$ inches , $n_2 = 2000$

Population $5.0 = \sigma = 2.5$ inches

H_o: Null Hypothesis: The samples are drawn from the same population with S.D 2.5 inches i.e $\mu_1 = \mu_2$

H_1 : $\mu_1 \neq \mu_2$

the test statistic $$Z = \frac{\overline{x}_1 - \overline{x}_2}{\sqrt{\frac{\sigma^2}{n_1} + \frac{\sigma^2}{n_2}}}$$

$$= \frac{67.5 - 68}{\sigma\sqrt{\frac{(2.5)^2}{1000} + \frac{(2.5)^2}{2000}}}$$

$$= \frac{-0.5}{0.0968} = -5.16$$

$$|Z| = 5.16$$

The calculated value of Z is greater than 1.96 i.e table value at 5% level of significance. Hence, Null hypothesis is rejected.

***Example* 9:** Samples of students were drawn from the universities and from their weights in kilo grams; mean and standard deviations are calculated and shown below. Make a large sample test to test the significance of the difference between the means.

[JNTU 2005]

	Mean	**S.D**	**Size of the sample**
University A	55	10	400
University B	57	15	100

***Solution*:** we have

$\overline{x}_1 = 55,$ $S_1 = 10,$ $n_1 = 400$

$\overline{x}_2 = 57,$ $S_2 = 15,$ $n_2 = 100$

Null Hypothesis: H_o : $\overline{x}_1 = \overline{x}_2$ i.e., there is no difference

alternative hypothesis : H_1 : $\overline{x}_1 \neq \overline{x}_2$

level of significance : $\alpha = 0.05$

values of $Z = 1.96$

test statistic = $$Z = \frac{\overline{x}_1 - \overline{x}_2}{\sqrt{\frac{S_1^2}{n_1} + \frac{S_2^2}{n_2}}}$$

$$= \frac{55-57}{\sqrt{\frac{100}{400}+\frac{225}{100}}} = \frac{-2}{\sqrt{\frac{1}{4}+\frac{9}{4}}}$$

$$= \frac{-2}{\sqrt{10}} \times 2 = \frac{-4}{\sqrt{10}} = -1.26$$

$$\therefore \quad |Z| = 1.26 < 1.96$$

Hence Null Hypothesis is accepted at 5% level of significance.

***Example* 10:** Intelligent test of two groups of boys and girls gives the following results.

Girls : $\bar{x}_1 = 84$, S.D (S_1) = 10, $n_1 = 121$

$\bar{x}_2 = 81$, S.D (S_2) = 12, $n_2 = 81$

(a) is the difference in means scores significant

(b) is the difference between S.D's significant

***Solution*:** Null Hypothesis: $H_o : \mu_1 = \mu_2$

level of significance = 0.05

$Z_\alpha = 1.96$

$$\text{test statistic } Z = \frac{\bar{X}_1 - \bar{X}_2}{\sqrt{\frac{S_1^2}{n_1}+\frac{S_2^2}{n_2}}}$$

$$= \frac{84-81}{\sqrt{\frac{100}{121}+\frac{144}{81}}}$$

$$= \frac{3}{\sqrt{0.826+1.777}}$$

$$= \frac{3}{\sqrt{2.6037}}$$

$$= \frac{3}{1.6133} = 1.8595$$

Since the calculated value of Z is less than the table value at 5% level of significance, the null hypothesis is accepted.

***Example* 11:** A simple random sampling survey in respect of monthly earnings of semi-skilled workers of two cities gives the following statistical information.

City	Mean monthly earnings in Rs	S.D of sample data of monthly earning (Rs)	Size of sample
A	695	40	200
B	710	60	175

Test the hypothesis 5% level that there is no difference between monthly earnings of workers in the two cities

***Solution*:** It is given that

$$\bar{x}_1 = 695 \text{ Rs} \qquad \bar{x}_2 = 710 \text{ Rs}$$

$$\sigma_1 = 40 \text{ Rs} \qquad \sigma_2 = 60 \text{ Rs}$$

$$n_1 = 200 \qquad n_2 = 175$$

$H_o : \mu_1 = \mu_2$

$H_1 : \mu_1 \neq \mu_2$ (two – tailed test)

Level of significance : 5%

Table value of Z = 1.96

Since the size of the sample is large, we apply Z –test for difference of means

$$Z = \frac{\bar{X}_1 - \bar{X}_2}{\sqrt{\frac{\sigma_1^2}{n_1} + \frac{\sigma_2^2}{n_2}}} = \frac{695 - 710}{\sqrt{\frac{40^2}{200} + \frac{60^2}{175}}}$$

$$= \frac{-15}{\sqrt{8 + 20.57}} = -2.809$$

$$|Z| = 2.809$$

Calculated value of Z is greater than the table value at 5% level of significance. Hence we reject null hypothesis.

Exercise 4.2

1. Define the terms

   (i) Hypothesis (ii) Null Hypothesis (iii) Alternative Hypothesis

2. Define:

   (a) Critical region (b) Level of significance

   (c) Type I error (d) Type II error

3. Define the terms (i) Two tailed test (ii) One tailed test

4. A sample of 100 iron bars is said to be drawn from a large number of bars, whose lengths are normally distributed with mean 4 ft and S.D 6ft. If the sample mean is 4.2 feet, can the sample be regarded as truly a random sample?

Ans. H_0 is rejected i.e., The sample cannot be regarded as a random sample

5. In air pollution study, the following amounts of suspended benzene soluble organic matter (in micro grams per cubic meter) were obtained at an experiment station for eight different samples of air 2.2, 1.8, 3.1, 2.0, 2.4, 2.0, 2.1 and 1.2 construct a 95% confidence interval for the corresponding true mean

   [JNTU 2004]

Ans. 1.683, 2.517

6. A stenographer claims that she can type at the rate of 120 words per minute. Can we reject her claim on the basis of 100 trials in which she demonstrates a mean of 116 words with S.D of 15 words. Use 5% level of significance

Ans. H_0 rejected

7. For a given sample of 200 items drawn from a large population the mean is 65 and the S.D is 8. Find 95% confidence limits.

Ans. 63.89, 66.19

8. A random sample of 50 items drawn from a particular population has a mean 30 with a S.D 28. Construct a 98% confidence interval estimate of the population mean.

Ans. 19.57, 26.43

9. A sample of 900 members has a mean 3.4 cm and S.D 2.6 cam. If this sample has been taken from a large population of mean 3.95 cm and S.D.2.61 cm, population is normal and its mean is known. Find 95% and 98% confidence limits of the true mean.

Ans. 3.23, 3.57 and 3.197, 3.603

10. Give the following information relating to two places A and B. Test whether there is any significance difference between their mean wages

	A	B
Mean Wages	47	49
S.D. (Rs)	28	40
Number of workers	1000	1500

Ans. H_0 accepted

11. A mean yield of wheat from a district A was 210 pounds with S.D. 10 pounds, per acre from a sample of 100 plots. In another district the mean yield was 220 pounds with S.D 12 pounds from the sample of 150 plots. Assuming that the S.D of yield in the entire state was 11 pounds, test whether there is any significant difference between the mean yield of crops in the two districts.

Ans. There is significant difference between the mean yield of crops in two district.

12. A random sample of 100 articles selected from a batch of 2000 articles shows that the average diameter of the articles = 0.354 with S.D = 0.048. Find 95% confidence interval for the average of this batch of 2000 articles.

Ans. 0.34, 0.36

13. A sample of 100 workers in a large plant gave a mean assembly time of 294 seconds with a S.D of 12 seconds, in a time and motion study. Find a 95% confidence interval for the mean assembly time for all the workers in the plant.

Ans. 291.64, 296.35

14. A machine produced 20 defective articles in a batch of 400. After overhauling it produced 10 defectives in a batch of 300. Has the machine improved.

Ans. Not significant

15. Sample of sales in similar shops in two towns are taken for a new product with the following results.

Town	**Means sales**	**Variance**	**Size of the sample**
A	57	5.3	5
B	61	4.8	7

Is there any evidence of difference in sales in two towns. Use 5% level of significance for testing this difference between means of two samples.

Ans. Null Hypothesis is rejected

16. The mean produce of wheat of a sample of 100 fields is 200 lbs. per acre; with standard deviation of 10 lbs. Another sample of 150 fields gives the mean of 220 lb with S.D of 12 lbs. Can the two samples be considered to have been taken from the same population whose S.D is 11 lbs. use 5percent level of significance.

Ans. H_0 rejected

Testing of Hypothesis - II

5

5.1 Introduction

Where we have qualitative phenomena, the data is based on the presence or absence of an attribute. With such data the sampling distribution may take the form of binomial distribution, whose mean is np and standard deviation is $\sqrt{npq}$, where p is the probability of success, q is the probability of failure such that $p + q = 1$ and n is the size of the sample. Instead of taking mean and standard deviation of number of successes we may record proportion of successes in each sample in which case the mean and standard deviation of the sampling distribution may be obtained as follows

Mean proportion of successes = np/n = p

Standard deviation of proportion of successes $= \sqrt{\frac{pq}{n}}$

When is large, the binomial distribution tends to become normal distribution. We use the test statistic Z

If p is the sample proportion and P is the population proportion, then

$$Z = \frac{p - P}{\sqrt{\frac{PQ}{n}}}$$

The confidence interval is

$$\left(P - Z_{\frac{\alpha}{2}}\sqrt{\frac{PQ}{n}}, \quad P + Z_{\frac{\alpha}{2}}\sqrt{\frac{PQ}{n}}\right)$$

or

$$\left(P - 3\sqrt{\frac{PQ}{n}}, \quad P + 3\sqrt{\frac{PQ}{n}}\right)$$

we have

Standard Error of $p = \sqrt{\frac{PQ}{n}}$

Variance $(p) = \frac{PQ}{n}$

Maximum Error $= Z_{\frac{\alpha}{2}} \sqrt{\frac{PQ}{n}}$

i.e $E = Z_{\frac{\alpha}{2}} \sqrt{\frac{PQ}{n}}$

size of the sample is $n = \frac{\left[Z_{\frac{\alpha}{2}}\right]^2}{E^2} . PQ$

$$= \left[\frac{Z_{\frac{\alpha}{2}}}{E}\right]^2 PQ$$

$$= \frac{Z_{\frac{\alpha}{2}}}{E} P(1-P)$$

where p is not given, we have

$$n = \frac{1}{4}\left[\frac{Z_{\frac{\alpha}{2}}}{E}\right]^2 PQ$$

5.2 Testing for Single Proportion

Let n denotes the size of a sample taken from a normal population and p denote the sample proportion. To test the significance difference between the sample proportion and population proportion, we use the test statistic

$$Z = \frac{p - P}{\sqrt{\frac{PQ}{n}}}$$

where P is the population proportion

The limits for population proportion are given by $p \pm 3\sqrt{\frac{PQ}{n}}$

where $Q = 1 - P$

Solved Examples

***Example* 1:** A manufacturer claimed that atleast 95% of the equipment which he supplied to a factory conformed to specifications. An examination of a sample of 300 pieces of equipment revealed 23 were faulty. Test his claim at 5% level of significance

(given: the value of Z for 5% level of significance = 1.645 for one-tailed test)

***Solution*:** we have

$$n = 300, \quad P = 95\% = \frac{95}{100} = 0.95$$

Number of pieces conforming to specification = 300 – 23 = 277

$$p = \text{proportion of pieces conforming to specification} = \frac{277}{300} = 0.9233$$

Null hypothesis H_o: $P < 95\%$ i.e., $P = 0.95$

Alternative hypothesis $H_1 = P < 95\ \%$ i.e., $P < 0.95$

Level of significance: 5%

Value of $Z = 1.645$ (given)

The test statistic is

$$Z = \frac{p - P}{\sqrt{\frac{PQ}{n}}}$$

$$= \frac{0.9233 - 0.95}{\sqrt{\frac{0.95 \times 0.5}{300}}} = \frac{-0.026}{0.2179} \times 17.32$$

$$= -2.066$$

$\therefore\ |Z| = 2.066$

Since the calculated value of Z is greater than the table value 1.645 of Z, we reject null hypothesis. H_o at 5% level of significance

The manufacture's claim is rejected.

***Example* 2:** Among 900 people in a state 90 are found to be chapathi eaters. Construct 99% confidence interval for true proportions. [JNTU 2005]

***Solution*:** It is given that $n = 900$, $X = 90$

$$\therefore\ P = \frac{X}{n} = \frac{90}{900} = 0.1,$$

$$Q = 1 - P = 1 - 0.1 = 0.9$$

and
$$\sqrt{\frac{PQ}{n}} = \sqrt{\frac{(0.1)(0.9)}{900}} = 0.01$$

The confidence interval is

$$\left(P - 3\sqrt{\frac{PQ}{n}}\ ,\ P + 3\sqrt{\frac{PQ}{n}}\right)$$

$$= (0.1 - 3 \times 0.01,\quad 0.1 + 3 \times 0.01)$$

$$= (0.1 - 0.03,\quad 0.1 + 0.03)$$

$$= (0.07, 0.13)$$

***Example* 3:** If 80% patients are treated with an antibiotic 59 got cured. Find a 99% confidence limits to the true population of cure [JNTU 2004S]

***Solution*:** We have $X = 59$, $n = 80$

we get
$$P = \frac{X}{n} = \frac{59}{80} = 0.7375$$

and
$$Q = 1 - P = 1 - 0.7375 = 0.2625$$

$$\sqrt{\left(\frac{PQ}{n}\right)} = \sqrt{\frac{(0.7375)(0.2625)}{80}} = 0.049$$

The required confidence interval is

$$\left(P - 3\sqrt{\frac{PQ}{n}}\ ,\ P + 3\sqrt{\left(\frac{PQ}{n}\right)}\right)$$

$$= (0.7375 - 3 \times 0.049,\quad 0.7375 + 3 \times 0.049)$$
$$= (0.59\ , 6.88)$$

***Example* 4:** In a random sample of 400 industrial accidents, it was found that 231 were due at least partially to unsafe working conditions. Construct a 99% confidence interval for the corresponding true proportion.

[JNTU 2006]

***Solution*:** We have $X = 231$, $n = 400$

therefore $P = \dfrac{X}{n} = \dfrac{231}{400} = 0.5775$

and $Q = 1 - P = 1 - 0.5775 = 0.4225$

we get $\sqrt{\dfrac{PQ}{n}} = \sqrt{\dfrac{0.5775 \times 0.4225}{400}} = 0.0247$

The required confidence interval is

$$\left(P - 3\sqrt{\frac{PQ}{n}}\ ,\ P + 3\sqrt{\frac{PQ}{n}}\right)$$

$$= (0.5775 - 3\ (0.02471,\ 0.5775 + 3\ (0.0247))$$

$$= (0.5034,\ 0.6516)$$

***Example* 5:** Experience has shown that 20% a manufactured product is of top quality. In one day's production of 400 articles only 50 are of top quality. Test the hypothesis at 0.05 level.

[JNTU 2008]

***Solution*:** It given that $X = 50,\ n = 400$

we have $P = \dfrac{X}{n} = \dfrac{50}{400} = 0.125, \quad P = 0.2$

Null hypothesis $H_o : P = 0.2$

Alternative hypothesis $H_1 : P \neq 2$ (two – tested test)

Level of significance $\alpha = 0.05$

Value of $Z = 1.96$

Test statistic is

$$Z = \frac{p - P}{\sqrt{\dfrac{PQ}{n}}}$$

$$= \frac{0.125 - 0.2}{\sqrt{\dfrac{(0.2)(0.8)}{400}}}$$

$$= \frac{-0.075}{0.02} = -3.75$$

$\therefore \quad |Z| = 3.75 > 1.96$

Calculated value of Z > table value of Z

Hence, we reject null hypothesis

i.e $P = 0.2$ is not correct

***Example* 6:** Twenty people were attacked by a disease and only 18 survived, will you reject the hypothesis that the survival rate if attacked by this disease is 85% in favour of the hypothesis that is more at 5% level.

Solution: we have $X = 18$ (number of people survived)

$n = 20$ (size of the sample)

$$\therefore \quad P = \frac{X}{n} = \frac{18}{20} = 0.9$$

$P = 0.85$ (given)

$Q = 1 - P = 1 - 0.85 = 0.15$

Null hypothesis $H_o : P = 0.85$

Alternative hypothesis $H_1 = P_1 > 0.85$ (one – tailed test Right tailed)

Level of significance $\alpha = 0.5$

Table value of $Z = 1.645$

The test statistic is

$$Z = \frac{p - P}{\sqrt{\left(\frac{PQ}{n}\right)}} = \frac{0.9 - 0.85}{\sqrt{\frac{(0.85)(0.15)}{20}}}$$

$$= 0.625$$

Since, calculated valued of Z at 5% level of significance is less than the table value of Z, we accept null hypothesis H_o.

Hence, we conclude that the proportion of survived people is 0.85

***Example* 7:** A dice was thrown 9000 times and of these 3220 yielded a 3 or 4. Is this consistent with the hypothesis that the dice was biased.

***Solution*:** Here, we have $X = 3220, \quad n = 9000$

$$\text{Sample proportion} = \frac{X}{n} = \frac{3220}{9000} = 0.3580$$

$$\text{The population proportion is } P = \frac{2}{6} = \frac{1}{3}$$

$$Q = 1 - P = 1 - 1/3 = 2/3$$

Null hypothesis $H_o : P = 1/3$ i.e the coin is unbiased.

Alternative hypothesis $H_1 : P \neq \frac{1}{3}$ (Two tailed test)

***Test Statistics*:**

$$Z = \frac{p - P}{\sqrt{\frac{PQ}{n}}}$$

$$= \frac{0.358 - 0.3333}{\sqrt{\frac{1}{3} \cdot \frac{2}{3} \frac{1}{9000}}} \qquad \text{(since } P = \frac{1}{3}\text{)}$$

$$= \frac{0.025}{0.005} = 5$$

***Example* 8:** A random sample of 400 persons from a large population 120 are females. Can it be said that males and females are in the ration 5:3 in the population? Use 10% level of significance.

***Solution*:** Here $X = 3$, $n = 5 + 3 = 8$

P = Population proportion of females

$$= \frac{3}{8} = 0.375$$

$$Q = 1 - P = 1 - 0.375 = 0.625$$

Null hypothesis $H_o : P = 0.375$

Alternative hypothesis $H_1 : P \neq 0.375$

Test statistic

$$Z = \frac{p - P}{\sqrt{\frac{PQ}{n}}} = \frac{0.30 - 0.375}{\sqrt{\frac{0.375 \times 0.625}{400}}}$$

$$= \frac{-0.075}{0.024} = -3.125$$

$$\therefore |Z| = 3.125 > 1.96$$

At 5% level of significance the calculated value of Z is more than the table value. Hence, we reject Null Hypothesis.

***Example* 9:** A sample of 600 persons selected at random form a large city shows that the percentage of male in the sample is 53%. It is believed that male to the total population ratio in the city is ½. Test whether this belief is confirmed by the observation.

***Solution*:** Here we have

$P = 50, \quad Q = 100 - 50 = 50$

$p = 53,$ critical value at 5% level of significance = 1.96

Null hypothesis $H_o : P = 50\%$

Alternative hypothesis $H_1 : P \neq 50\%$

Test statistic:

$$Z = \frac{p - P}{\sqrt{\frac{PQ}{n}}} = \frac{53 - 50}{\sqrt{\frac{50 \times 50}{600}}}$$

$$= \frac{3}{2.04} = 1.4705$$

Since the calculated value of Z is less than the table value, Null hypothesis H_o is rejected i.e male population in the city is 50%.

***Example* 10:** Experience has shown that 10% of a manufactured product is of quality. What can you say that about the maximum error of 95% confidence for 100 items.

***Solution*:** $P = \frac{x}{n} = \frac{10}{100} = \frac{1}{10} = 0.1$

we get $Q = 1 - P = 1 - 0.1 = 0.9$

we have $Z_{\frac{\alpha}{2}} = 1.96$

Maximum error of proportions $= Z_{\frac{\alpha}{2}} \sqrt{\frac{PQ}{n}}$

$$= 1.96 \sqrt{\frac{0.9 \times 0.1}{100}}$$

$$= 1.96 \times \sqrt{\frac{0.09}{100}}$$

$$= 0.588$$

***Example* 11:** What is the size of the smallest sample required to estimate an unknown proportion within a maximum error of 0.06 with at least 95% confidence

Solution: The maximum error is E = 0.06

Confidence limit is 95%

$\therefore \alpha = 1 - 0.95 = 0.05$

and $\dfrac{\alpha}{2} = 0.025$

$Z_{\frac{\alpha}{2}} = 1.96$

The sample in size is $n = \dfrac{1}{4}\left(\dfrac{Z_{\frac{\alpha}{2}}}{E}\right)^2 = \dfrac{1}{4}\dfrac{(1.96)^2}{(0.06)^2}$

$= 264$

5.3 Test of Significance for Difference of Proportions

Let n_1 and n_2 denote the sizes of two samples drawn from two different populations. Let p_1 and p_2 be the proportion of the samples. To test the significant difference between the sample proportions p_1 and p_2 the test statistic is

$$Z = \frac{p_1 - p_2}{\sqrt{pq\left(\frac{1}{n_1} + \frac{1}{n_2}\right)}}$$

Where $p = \dfrac{n_1 p_1 + n_2 p_2}{n_1 + n_2}$ and $q = 1 - p$

If the population proportions P_1 and P_2 are given and $P_1 \neq P_2$, to test the hypothesis that the difference $P_1 - P_2$ in population proportions is likely to be hidden in samples of sizes n_1 and n_2 from the two populations respectively. Then

$$Z = \frac{(p_1 - p_2) - (P_1 - P_2)}{\sqrt{\frac{P_1 Q_1}{n_1} + \frac{P_2 Q_2}{n_2}}}$$

If the sample proportions are known, we use the test statistic

$$Z = \frac{|P_1 - P_2|}{\sqrt{\frac{P_1 Q_1}{2} + \frac{P_2 Q_2}{2}}}$$

The confidence interval for the difference of two proportions, when the size of sample is large

$$= \left(p_1 - p_2 - Z_{\frac{\alpha}{2}} \sqrt{PQ\left(\frac{1}{n_1} + \frac{1}{n_2}\right)}, \quad p_1 - p_2 + Z_{\frac{\alpha}{2}} \sqrt{PQ\left(\frac{1}{n_1} + \frac{1}{n_2}\right)} \right)$$

where the standard error = SE(p_1 –p_2)

$$= \sqrt{PQ\left(\frac{1}{n_1} + \frac{1}{n_2}\right)}$$

and the maximum error is given by

$$Z_{\frac{\alpha}{2}} \sqrt{PQ\left(\frac{1}{n_1} + \frac{1}{n_2}\right)}$$

If we set up $p_1 = p_2$ as the null hypothesis, the difference in the population proportions is likely to be hidden in sampling. Then the statistic is given by

$$Z = \frac{P_1 - P}{\sqrt{\frac{P_1Q_1}{n_1} + \frac{P_2Q_2}{n_2}}}$$

The confidence interval in this case is

$$p_1 - p_2 - Z_{\frac{-\alpha}{2}} \sqrt{\frac{P_1Q_1}{n_1} + \frac{P_2Q_2}{n_2}}, \; p_1 - p_2 + Z_{\frac{+\alpha}{2}} \sqrt{\frac{P_1Q_1}{n_1} + \frac{P_2Q_2}{n_2}}$$

where, the standard error is $\sqrt{\frac{P_1Q_1}{n_1} + \frac{P_2Q_2}{n_2}}$

and the Maximum error = $Z_{\frac{\alpha}{2}} \sqrt{\frac{P_1Q_1}{n_1} + \frac{P_2Q_2}{n_2}}$.

***Example* 12:** In random samples of 600 and 1000 men from two cities 400 and 600 men are found to be literate. Do the data indicate at 5% level of significance that the populations are significantly different in the percentage literacy.

***Solution*:** We have $n_1 = 600$, $n_2 = 1000$

$$p_1 = \frac{400}{600} = \frac{2}{3}, \quad p_2 = \frac{600}{1000} = \frac{3}{5}$$

$$p = \frac{n_1p_1 + n_2p_2}{n_1 + n_2} = \frac{(600)\left(\frac{2}{3}\right) + (1000)\left(\frac{3}{5}\right)}{600 + 10000}$$

$$\therefore \qquad p = \frac{400+600}{1600} = \frac{1000}{1600} = \frac{10}{16} = \frac{5}{8}$$

and $\quad q = 1 - p = 1 - \frac{5}{8} = \frac{3}{8}$

Null hypothesis $H_o: P_1 = P_2$

Alternative hypothesis: $P_1 \neq P_2$

Level of significance = 5%

Value of z = 1.96

Test statistic is

$$Z = \frac{p_1 - p_2}{\sqrt{pq\left(\frac{1}{n_1} + \frac{1}{n_2}\right)}} = \frac{\frac{2}{3} - \frac{3}{5}}{\sqrt{\frac{5}{8} \times \frac{3}{8}\left(\frac{1}{1000} + \frac{1}{1000}\right)}}$$

$$= \frac{10-9}{15} \times \frac{8 \times \sqrt{600 \times 1000}}{\sqrt{15(1600)}}$$

$$= \frac{8 \times 774.59}{154.9} = 2.6669$$

Calculated value of z at 5% level of significance is more than the table value.

We reject H_O

Therefore populations are significantly different in the percentage of literacy

***Example* 13:** Before an increase in excise duty on tea 400 people out of a sample of 500 persons were found to be tea drinkers. After an increase in the duty, 400 persons were known to be the tea drinkers in a sample of 600 people. Do you think that there has been a significant decrease in the consumption of tea after the increase in the excise duty?

***Solution*:** Here, we have

$$n_1 = 500, \qquad x_1 = 400$$

$$n_2 = 600, \qquad x_2 = 400$$

$$\therefore \qquad p_1 = \frac{400}{500} = 0.8, \; p_2 = \frac{400}{600} = \frac{2}{3}$$

Null hypothesis $H_0 : P_1 = P_2$

Alternative hypothesis $H_1 : p_1 > p_2$ (one)

Level of significance = 5%. Value of z = 1.645.

we get $$p = \frac{n_1p_1 + n_2p_2}{n_1 + n_2} = \frac{500 \times 0.8 + 600 \times \left(\frac{2}{3}\right)}{500 + 600}$$

$$= \frac{400 + 400}{1100} = \frac{800}{1100} = \frac{8}{11}$$

$\therefore$ $$q = 1 - p = 1 - \frac{8}{11} = \frac{3}{11}$$

Test statistic $$z = \frac{p_1 - p_2}{\sqrt{pq\left(\frac{1}{n_1} + \frac{1}{n_2}\right)}}$$

$$= \frac{0.8 - \frac{2}{3}}{\sqrt{\frac{8}{11} \times \frac{3}{11}\left(\frac{1}{500} + \frac{1}{600}\right)}}$$

$$= \frac{(0.8 - 0.67)(11)\sqrt{500 \times 600}}{\sqrt{24(1100)}} = \frac{783.24}{162.48}$$

$$= 4.8205$$

$$|z| = 4.82\,05 > z_{0.05} = 1.645$$

$\therefore$ H_0 is rejected

We conclude that there is significant difference in the consumption of tea after the increase in the excise duty.

***Example* 14:** A Manufacturer of electronic equipment subjects samples of two brands of transistors to an accelerated performance test. If 45 of 180 transistors of the first kind and 34 of 120 transistors of the second kind fail the test, what can we conclude at the level of significance $\alpha = 0.05$ about the difference the corresponding sample proportions?

***Solution*:** we have $n_1 = 180$, $n_2 = 120$

$$x_1 = 45, x_2 = 34$$

$$p_1 = \frac{x_1}{n_1} = \frac{45}{180} = 0.25, \quad p_2 = \frac{x_2}{n_2} = \frac{34}{120} = 0.283$$

$\therefore$ $$p = \frac{n_1p_1 + n_2p_2}{n_1 + n_2} = \frac{45 + 34}{180 + 120} = \frac{79}{300} = 0.263$$

$$q = 1 - p = 1 - 0.263 = 0.737$$

Null hypothesis H_o : $p_1 = p_2$

Alternative hypothesis H_1 : $p_1 \neq p_2$

Level of significance $\alpha = 0.05$

$Z_\alpha = 1.96$

Test statistic

$$\therefore \qquad |Z| = \left| \frac{p_1 - p_2}{\sqrt{pq\left(\frac{1}{n_1} + \frac{1}{n_2}\right)}} \right|$$

$$= \left| \frac{0.25 - 0.283}{\sqrt{(0.263)(0.737)\left(\frac{1}{180} + \frac{1}{120}\right)}} \right|$$

$$= \left| \frac{-0.033}{(0.194)\ (0.0134)} \right| = 0.647$$

Since $|Z| = 0.647 < 1.96$, we accept H_0 at 5% level of significance

Hence, there is no difference in proportions

***Example* 15:** In a random samples of 600 and 1000 men from two cities 400 and 600 men are found to be literate. Do the data indicate at 5% level of significance that the population are significantly different in the percentage literacy.

Solution:

Here, we have $n_1 = 600$, $n_2 = 1000$,

$$p_1 = \frac{400}{600} = \frac{2}{3}, \qquad p_2 = \frac{600}{1000} = \frac{3}{5}$$

$$p = \frac{n_1\ p_1 + n_2\ p_2}{n_1 + n_2} = \frac{(600)\left(\frac{2}{3}\right) + (1000)\left(\frac{3}{5}\right)}{600 + 1000}$$

$$= \frac{5}{8}$$

Null hypothesis H_0 : $p_1 = p_2$

Alternative hypothesis H_1 : $p_1 \neq p_2$

level of significance $\alpha = 0.05$,

value of Z at 5% level of significance = 1.96

$$Z = \frac{p_1 - p_2}{\sqrt{\frac{pq}{n_1} + \frac{pq}{n_2}}} = \frac{\frac{2}{3} - \frac{3}{5}}{\sqrt{\left(\frac{5}{8}\right)\left(\frac{3}{8}\right)\left(\frac{1}{600} + \frac{1}{1000}\right)}} = 2.67$$

Calculated value of Z at 5% level is greater than the table value. Hence, H_0 is rejected

Exercise 5.1

1. A manufacturer of electric bulbs claims that the percentage of defectives in his product does not exceed 0.06. A sample of 40 bulbs is found to contain 5 defectives. Would you consider the claim justified?

(JNTU 2007)

Ans. The claim is justified

2. A die is thrown 256 times. An even digit turns up 150 times. Can we say that the die is unbiased? (*Hint* : $n = 256, 2 = \frac{x - nP}{\sqrt{nP}}$ where $P = \frac{1}{2}, Q = \frac{1}{2}$)

Ans. Die is unbiased

3. A random sample of 500 apples was taken from a large consignment of 60 were found to be bad. Obtain the 98% confidence limits for the percentage number of pad apples in the consignment

Ans. 8.5, 15.5 (JNTU 2007)

4. A random sample of size 200 is taken where variance is 12.25 and the mean is 56. Construct 90% confidence interval for mean.

Ans. 55.5929, 56.4071

5. In a random sample of 400 industrial accidents it was found that 231 were due to least partially to unsafe working conditions. Construct a 99% confidence interval for the corresponding true population using large sample confidence formula

Ans. 0.514 : 0.642

6. A coin is tossed 10,000 times and it turns up head 5195 times. Discuss whether the coin may be regarded as unbiased one

Ans. The coin is biased

7. A manufacturer claims only 4% of his products are defective. A random sample of 500 were taken among which 100 were defective. Test the hypothesis at 0.05 level

(JNTU 2005)

Ans. Null hypothesis rejected

8. A coin is tossed 512 times. Head turned up 110 times. Test whether the coin is unbiased

Ans. The coin is biased

9. A die was thrown 900 times. 1 or 2 was obtained 500 times. Can you say that the die is biased

Ans. Die is unbiased

10. Among 100 students in a class 15 are using ball pens. Construct 95% camphene interval of proportion

Ans. 0.081, 0.219

11. Random samples of 300 men and 500 women were asked whether they would like to have flyover near their residence. 150 men and 200 women were in favour of the proposal. Find the 95% confidence interval for the true difference of proportions

Ans. 0.0784, 0.1216

12. If the proportion P = 0.4 and maximum error with 95% confidence is 0.05. Find the size of the sample

Ans. 369

13. In a sample of 500 students 15 use ball pens, and among 800 of another sample 80 use ball pens. Construct large sample of 99% confidence interval for true difference of two proportions

Ans. – 0.0365, – 0.1035

14. In a hospital 475 female and 500 male babies were born in a week. Do those figure confirm the hypothesis that males and females are born in equal number.

Ans. H_0 accepted at 5% level

15. A bag contains defective article, the exact number of which is not known. A sample of 100 from the bag gives 10 defective articles. Find the limits for the proportion of defective articles in the bag

Ans. 0.1588, 0.0412

16. A sample of size of 600 persons selected at random from a large city shows that the percentage of males in the sample is 53. It is believed that the ratio of males to the total population in the city is 0.5. Test whether the believe is confirmed by observation

Ans. H_0 accepted at 5% level

17. In the large population there are 30% and 25% respectively of fair haired people. Is this difference likely to be hidden in samples of 1200 and 900 respectively from the two populations

(H_0 is accepted)

18. In a town A, there were 956 births of which 52.5% was males while in towns A and B combined, this proportion in total of 1406 births was 0.496. Is there any significant difference in proportion of male births in the two towns.

Ans. (H_0 rejected)

Small Samples 6

6.1 Introduction

In this chapter we introduce tests of significance of small samples. The following are some important tests for small samples.

(i) Student's t-test

(ii) F-test

(iii) X^2 - test

6.2 t - Distribution

The parameter t was introduced by W.S.Gosset in 1908, but t-distribution was introduced by Fisher in 1928. It is defined as

$$y = f(t) = \frac{\left(1+\frac{t^2}{v}\right)^{-\frac{1}{2}(v+1)}}{\sqrt{v}\,\beta\left(\frac{1}{2},\frac{v}{2}\right)}, \qquad -\infty < x < \infty$$

where $v = n - 1$ is called the number of degrees of freedom. The values of a sample which are freely variable without affecting the mean is know as the degree of freedom.

6.3 t - test

t is defined by the statistic

$$t = \frac{\bar{x} - \mu}{S/\sqrt{n}}$$

where $\bar{x} = \frac{1}{n}\sum xi$ (sample mean), μ = population mean

$$S^2 = \frac{1}{n-1}\sum(x_i - \bar{x})^2, \quad n = \text{size of the sample}$$

There are two types of t – test

(i) Unpaired t - test

(ii) Paired t-test

6.4 Criteria for Applying t-test

(i) The samples are drawn from normal population

(ii) size of the sample is less than 30

(iii) for testing the equality of two population means, the population variances are regarded as equal

Properties of t-distribution

(i) t-distribution is symmetrical distribution with mean zero

(ii) t-distribution is asymptotic to X-axis. The t-probability curve extends to infinity on either side.

(iii) The shape of t-distribution curve varies with degrees of freedom

(iv) If the number of degrees of freedom is large, then the t-distribution curve resembles the standard normal curve.

Applications of t-distribution: t – distribution is applied

1. To test the significance of a single mean when the population mean is unknown
2. To test the significance of difference between two sample means the population variances, being equal and unknown.
3. To test the significance of an observed correlation on coefficient.

6.5 Significant Value of t

The significant value of t at level of significance α and degrees of freedom v, for two tailed test is given by

$$P\{|t| > t_v(\alpha)\} = \alpha$$

$$P\{|t| \leq t_v(d)\} = 1 - \alpha$$

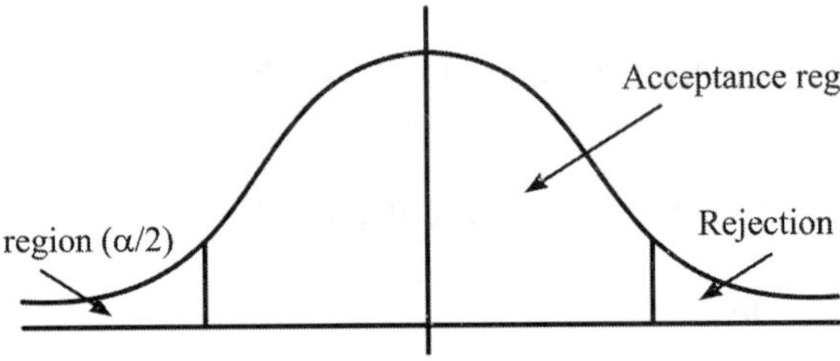

The significant value of t at level of significance α for a one-tailed test can be obtained form those of two tailed test by referring to the values at 2α. The significant values are given α in the table known as the t-table.

If the calculated value of t exceeds the table value of 5% level of significance, then the null hypothesis is rejected at 5%. Similarly for 1% level of significance we can reject the null hypothesis at 1% if the calculated value of t exceeds the table value.

6.6 t - test of Significance for Single Mean

To test the significance of a mean, the test statistic is

$$t = \frac{\bar{x} - \mu}{S.E\ \bar{x}}$$

i.e

$$t = \frac{\bar{x} - \mu}{S / \sqrt{n-1}}$$

S.E ($\bar{x}$) is also given by

$$\frac{S}{\sqrt{n}}$$

Hence, we have

$$t = \frac{\bar{x} - \mu}{S / \sqrt{n}} \quad \text{or} \quad \frac{\bar{x} - \mu}{S}.\sqrt{n}$$

Confidence interval for μ:

If $t_{0.05}$ is the table value of t for (n – 1) df at 5% level of significance then 95% confidence limits for μ is given by

$$\bar{x} \pm t_{0.05} \frac{S}{\sqrt{n}}$$

for $$P(|t| > t_{0.05}) = 0.05$$

or $$P(|t| \leq t_{0.05}) = 0.95$$

The 95% confidence interval is given by

$$\bar{x} - t_{0.05}\frac{S}{\sqrt{n}} < \mu < \bar{x} + t_{0.05}\frac{S}{\sqrt{n}}$$

***Example* 1:** A random sample of size 7 from a normal population gave a mean of 977.51 and a standard deviation of 4. 42. Find 95% confidence interval for the population mean.

***Solution*:** Here we have

$$n = 7, \ \bar{x} = 977.5, \text{ and } S = 4.72$$

degrees of freedom = $\nu = n - 1 = 7 - 1 = 6$

The 95% confidence limits for μ for 6 df are

$$\bar{x} \pm t_{0.05}\left(\frac{S}{\sqrt{n-1}}\right)$$

$$= 977.51 \pm (2.447)\frac{4.42}{\sqrt{6}}$$

$$= 977.51 \pm 4.416$$

i.e $$(977.51 - 4.416, \quad 977.51 + 4.416)$$

$$= [973.094, 981.926]$$

***Example* 2:** A sample of 20 items has mean 42 units and standard deviation 5 units. Test the hypothesis that it is a random sample from a normal population with 45 units.

***Solution*:** We have

$$n = 20, \ \bar{x} = 42, \ S.D = S = 5$$

degrees of freedom $\nu = n - 1$

$$= 20 - 1 = 19$$

***Null hypothesis H_o*:** There is no significant difference between the sample mean and population mean.

***Alternative Hypothesis H_1*:** There is significant difference between the sample mean and population mean

Level of significance $\alpha = 0.05$

Table value of $t = t_{0.05}$ for 19 df = 2.09

Since $\quad S = 5$, we get $\quad S^2 = \dfrac{n}{n-1}\ S^2$

$$= \frac{20}{20-1}\ S^2 = \frac{20 \times 25}{19} = 26.31$$

$$\therefore\ S = \sqrt{26.31} = 5.129$$

$$\therefore\ f = \frac{\bar{x} - \mu}{S/\sqrt{n}} = \frac{42 - 45}{5.129/\sqrt{20}} = \frac{-3}{5.129}\sqrt{20}$$

Since $|t| = 2.615 > 2.09$ i.e table value of t at 5% level, and 19 df

We reject null hypothesis i.e there is significant difference between sample mean and population mean.

***Example* 3:** A random sample for the test of fasting sugar of 10 boys give the following data in mg/dl

70, 120, 110, 101, 88, 83, 95, 107, 100, 98

Do these data support the assumption of population mean of 100 mg/dl. Find the reasonable range in which most of the mean fasting sugar test of samples of 10 boys lie.

***Solution*:** Null Hypothesis is $H_o : \mu = 100$

i.e The data support the assumption of a mean 100 mg/dl in the population.

Alternative hypothesis: $\mu \neq 100$ (Two tailed test)

We have $\bar{x} = \dfrac{\sum x}{n} = \dfrac{70+120+110+101+88+83+95+107+100+98}{10}$

$$= \frac{972}{10} = 97.2$$

$$\sum_i \left(x - x^2\right) = (70-97.2)^2 + (120-97.2)^2 + (110-97.2)^2 + (101-97.2)^2\ (88-97.2)^2$$

$$+ (83-97.2)^2 + (95-97.2)^2 + (107-97.2)^2 + (100-97.2)^2 + (98-97.2)^2$$

$$= 1833.60$$

$$S^2 = \frac{\sum(x_i - \bar{x})^2}{n-1} = \frac{1833.60}{10-1} = \frac{1833.60}{9} = 203.74$$

$$S = \sqrt{203.74}$$

Test statistic is

$$t = \frac{\bar{x} - \mu}{S/\sqrt{n}} = \frac{\bar{x} - \mu}{\sqrt{S^2/n}} = \frac{97.2 - 100}{\sqrt{\dfrac{203.74}{10}}}$$

$$= \frac{-2.8}{4.51} = -\ 0.621$$

$$|t| = |-0.621| = 0.621$$

we have

degrees of freedom = n – 1 = 10 – 1 = 9

level of significance = 5%

$t_{0.05} = 2.262$ for 9 df

Since, calculated value of t is less than the table value of t at 5% level for 9 df, we accept null hypothesis

The confidence limits are

$$\bar{x} \pm t_{0.05} = 97.2 \pm (2.262)\ (4.51)$$

The confidence interval is

(87.0, 107.40)

***Example* 4:** A sample of 26 bulbs gives a mean life of 990 hours with a S.D of 20 hours. The manufacturer claims that the mean life of bulbs is 1000 hours. Is the sample not up to the standard?

***Solution*:** Here the size of the sample = n = 26; S.D = 20

Sample mean $= \bar{x} = 990$ hours

Population mean $\mu = 1000$ hours

Degrees of freedom = n – 1 = 26 = – 25

Null hypothesis H_o : The sample is up to the standard i.e $\mu = 1000$ hours

Alternative hypothesis $H_1 = \mu < 1000$ (one tailed test)

Tabulated value of t at 5% level of significance for 25 df = 1.708

$$t = \frac{\bar{x} - \mu}{\left(\dfrac{S.D}{\sqrt{n}}\right)} = \frac{990 - 1000}{\dfrac{20}{\sqrt{25}}}$$

$$= \left(\frac{-10}{20}\right) 5 = -2.5$$

$$\therefore \qquad |t| = 2.5$$

Calculated value of t is greater than the table value, for 25 df at 5%. Hence we reject null hypothesis.

The sample is not upto the standard.

***Example* 5:** The average breaking strength of the steel rod is specified to be 18.5 thousand pounds. To test this a sample of 14 rods was tested. The mean and standard deviations obtained were 17.85 and 1.955 respectively. If the result of the experiment significant.

Solution: Here $n = 14, \quad \bar{x} = 17.85, \quad \mu = 18.5, \quad S = 1.955$

$$df = n - 1 = 14 - 1 = 13$$

H_o : The result of the experiment is not significant

H_1 : The result of the experiment is significant

We have

$$t = \frac{\bar{x} - \mu}{\frac{S}{\sqrt{n-1}}} = \frac{17.85 - 18.5}{\frac{1.955}{\sqrt{13}}}$$

$$= \frac{0.65}{0.542} = -1.195$$

$$\therefore |t| = 1.199$$

Level of significance = 5%, df = 13, table value of t = $t_{0.05}$ = 2.16

Since the calculated value of t is less than the table value at 5% level for 13 df, we accept H_o and conclude that the result of the experiment is not significant.

***Example* 6:** The mean weekly sales of soap bars in a departmental stores was 146. 3 bars per store. After an advertising campaign the mean weekly sales in 22 stores for a typical week increased to 153.7 and showed a S.D of 17.2. Was the advertising campaign successful.

***Solution*:** Here $n = 22$, $\bar{x} = 153.7$, $\mu = 146.3$, S.D = 17.2

$$df = n - 1 = 22 - 1 = 21$$

Null hypothesis H_o : The advertising campaign was not successful.

Alternative hypothesis: H_1 The advertising campaign was successful.

$$t_{0.05} \text{ for 21 df} = 1.72$$

$$t = \frac{\bar{x} - \mu}{\frac{S}{\sqrt{n-1}}} = \frac{153.7 - 146.3}{\frac{17.2}{\sqrt{22-1}}} = 1.97$$

The calculated value of t is greater than the table value at 5% level for 21 df.

Therefore H_o is rejected

$\therefore$ Advertising campaign was successful.

***Example* 7:** Ten objects are chosen at random form a large population and their weights are found to be gms as

63, 63, 64, 65, 66, 69, 69, 70, 70, 71

In light of the above data discuss the suggestion that the mean weight in the universe is 65 gm

***Solution*:** Here n = 10

$$df = n - 1 = 9$$

level of significance = 5%

table value of t at 5% for 9 df = 2.262

H_o : $\mu = 65$

i.e., There is no difference between the mean weight of the sample and population.

H_1 : $\mu \neq 65$

We have

$$\bar{x} = \frac{\sum x}{n} = \frac{63+63+64+65+66+69+69+70+70+71}{10}$$

$$= \frac{670}{10} = 67$$

$$S^2 = \frac{\sum (x_i - \bar{x})^2}{n-1}$$

$$= \frac{(63-67)^2 + (63-67)^2 + \ldots\ldots\ldots + (71-67)^2}{10-1}$$

$$= \frac{88}{9} = 9.78$$

$\therefore$ $$S = \sqrt{9.78} = 3.127$$

$$t = \frac{\bar{x} - \mu}{\frac{S}{\sqrt{n}}} = \frac{(67-65)}{\left(\frac{3.127}{\sqrt{10}}\right)} = \frac{2 \times \sqrt{10}}{3.127} = 2.024$$

$$t = 2.024 < 2.262$$

Calculated value of t at 5% level for 9 df is less than the table value. Hence, we reject null hypothesis.

6.7 t - Test for Difference of Means

To test the difference between two means $\overline{x}_1$ and $\overline{x}_2$ of sample of sizes n_1 and n_2, we use the statistic

$$t = \frac{\overline{x}_1 - \overline{x}_2}{S\sqrt{\frac{1}{n_1} + \frac{1}{n_2}}}$$

where $$S^2 = \frac{\sum(x_1 - \overline{x}_1)^2 + \sum(x_2 - \overline{x}_2)^2}{n_1 + n_2 - 2}$$

or $$S^2 = \frac{n_1 S_1^2 + n_2 S_2^2}{n_1 + n_2 - 2}$$

S_1, S_2 are standard and deviations of samples

degrees of freedom = $n_1 + n_2 - 2$.

***Example* 8:** Two horses A and B were tested according to the time (in seconds) to run a particular track with the following results.

Horse A	28	30	32	33	33	29	34
Horse B	29	30	30	24	27	29	–

Test weather they have same running capacity (JNTU 2006)

Solution: From the given data

$n_1 = 7, \quad n_2 = 6$

$\overline{x}_1$ = Mean of first sample

$$= \frac{\sum x_1}{n_1} = \frac{28 + 30 + 32 + 33 + 33 + 29 + 34}{7}$$

$$= \frac{219}{7} = 31.286$$

$$\bar{x}_2 = \frac{\sum x_2}{n_2} = \frac{29+30+30+24+27+29}{6}$$

$$= \frac{169}{6} = 28.16$$

x_1	$x_1-\bar{x}_1$	$(x_1-\bar{x}_1)^2$	x_2	$x_2-\bar{x}_2$	$(x_2-\bar{x}_2)^2$
28	– 3.286	10.8	29	0.84	0.7056
30	– 1.286	1.6538	30	1.84	3.3856
32	0.714	0.51	30	1.84	3.3856
33	1.714	2.94	24	– 4.16	17.3056
33	1.714	2.94	27	– 1.16	1.3456
24	– 2.286	5.226	29	0.84	0.7056
34	2.714	7.366	–	–	–
219		31.4358			26.8336

$$S^2 = \frac{\sum(x_1-\bar{x}_1)^2 + \sum(x_2-\bar{x}_2)^2}{n_1+n_2-2}$$

$$= \frac{31.4358+26.8336}{11} = 5.23$$

$$S = \sqrt{5.23} = 2.286$$

Null Hypothesis $H_o : \mu_1 = \mu_2$

Alternative hypothesis $H_1 = \mu_1 \neq \mu_2$

Level of significance = $\alpha = 0.05$

$t_{0.05}$ for 11 df = 2.2

$$t = \frac{\bar{x}_1 - \bar{x}_2}{S\sqrt{\frac{1}{n_1}+\frac{1}{n_2}}} = \frac{31.286-28.16}{2.3\sqrt{\frac{1}{7}+\frac{1}{6}}}$$

$$= \frac{3.126}{2.3\sqrt{\frac{6+7}{42}}} = \frac{3.126\sqrt{42}}{2.3\sqrt{13}}$$

$$= \frac{(3.126)(6.480)}{(2.3)(3.6055)}$$

$$= \frac{20.2564}{8.2926} = 2.4419$$

Calculated value of t > table value of t for 11 df at 5% level of significance

Hence, we reject the null hypothesis.

***Example* 9:** To compare two kinds of bum beer guards, 6 of each kind were mounted on a car and then the car was run into a concrete wall. The following are the cost of repairs.

Guard 1	107	148	123	165	102	119
Guard 2	134	115	112	151	133	129

Use the 0.01 level of significance to test the difference between two sample means is significant (JNTU 2005)

***Solution*:** Here $n_1 = 6$, $n_2 = 6$

$$\bar{x} = \frac{107 + 148 + 123 + 165 + 102 + 119}{6}$$

$$= \frac{764}{6} = 127.33$$

$$\bar{y} = \frac{134 + 115 + 112 + 151 + 133 + 129}{6}$$

$$= \frac{774}{6} = 129$$

x	$x - \bar{x}$	$(x - \bar{x})^2$	y	$y - \bar{y}$	$(y - \bar{y})^2$
107	– 20.33	413.31	134	5	25
148	20.67	427.25	115	–14	196
123	– 4.33	18.75	112	–17	289
165	37.67	1419.03	151	22	484
102	–25.33	641.61	133	4	16
119	– 8.33	69.39	129	0	0
764		2989.34	774		1010

$$S^2 = \frac{\sum(x-\bar{x})^2 + \sum(y-\bar{y})^2}{n_1+n_2-2} = \frac{2989.34+1010}{(6+6-2)}$$

$$= \frac{3999.34}{10} = 399.934$$

$$S = \sqrt{399.934} = 19.998$$

Null hypothesis H_o: $\mu_1 = \mu_2$

Alternative hypothesis $H_1 = \mu_1 \neq \mu_2$
level of significance $\alpha = 0.01$

Degrees of freedom = 10

Table value of t for 10 df at 5% level = 3.169

$$t = \frac{\bar{x}-\bar{y}}{S\sqrt{\frac{1}{n_1}+\frac{1}{n_2}}} = \frac{127.33-129}{19.998\sqrt{\frac{1}{6}+\frac{1}{6}}}$$

$$= \frac{-1.67}{11.546} = -0.1446$$

$\therefore$ $|t| = 0.1446$

Since calculated value of t is less than table value of t the null hypothesis is accepted.

The is no significant difference between means.

***Example* 10:** The body weight of 8 adult males and eight adult females in kg are presented respectively in the first and second columns of the table. Find the whether or not the mean weight of males in significantly higher than that of females.

	Weight is kg							
Males (X_1)	50	58	60	55	59	56	54	64
Females (X_2)	49	52	51	56	55	53	52	48

***Solution*:**Null hypothesis H_o : Mean weight of males is not significantly higher than that of females

Alternative Hypothesis H_1: Mean weight of males is significantly higher than that of females

Degrees of freedom: $n_1 + n_2 - 2 = 8 + 8 - 2 = 16 - 2 = 14$

Level of significance = 5% i.e 0.05

Critical value i.e table value of t for 14 dt is 2.14

$$\bar{x}_1 = \frac{\sum X_1}{n_1} = \frac{456}{8} = 57 \qquad \bar{X}_2 = \frac{\sum x_2}{n_2} = \frac{416}{8} = 52$$

S.No	Males X_1	$X_1 - \bar{X}_1$	$(X_1 - \bar{X}_1)^2$	Females X_2	$X_2 - \bar{X}_2$	$(X_2 - \bar{X}_2)^2$
1	50	− 7	49	49	− 3	9
2	58	+ 1	1	52	0	0
3	60	+ 3	9	51	−1	1
4	55	− 2	4	56	+ 4	16
5	59	+ 2	4	55	+ 3	9
6	56	− 1	1	53	+ 1	1
7	54	− 3	9	52	0	0
8	64	+ 7	49	48	− 4	16
	456		126	416		52

$$\sigma = \text{Standard deviation} = \sqrt{\frac{\sum(X_1 - \bar{X}_1)^2 + \sum(X_2 - \bar{X}_2)^2}{n_1 + n_2 - 2}}$$

$$= \sqrt{\frac{126+52}{8+8-2}} = \sqrt{\frac{178}{14}}$$

$$= \sqrt{12.714} = 3.57$$

$$\text{S.E}\,(X_1 - X_2) = \sigma\sqrt{\frac{1}{n_1} + \frac{1}{n_2}}$$

$$= 3.57\sqrt{\frac{1}{8} + \frac{1}{8}} = 3.57\sqrt{\frac{1}{4}}$$

$$= \frac{3.57}{2} = 1.785$$

$$t = \frac{\bar{X}_1 - \bar{X}_2}{\text{S.E}(X_1 - X_2)} = \frac{57.52}{1.785}$$

$= 2.80$

Table value of t for 14 df at 5% level is 2.14. The calculated value of t is greater than the table value of t at 5% level, for 14 df. Hence

Null hypothesis H_o is rejected

Mean weight of males is not significantly higher than the mean weight of females.

***Example* 11:** The average number of articles produced by two machines per day are 200 and 250 with S.D's 20 and 25 respectively on the basis of records of 25 days production. Can you regard both the machines equally efficient at 1% level of significance

***Solution*:** It is given that

$$n_1 = 25, \quad n_2 = 25$$

$$\bar{x}_1 = 200, \quad \bar{x}_2 = 250$$

$$S_1 = 20, \quad S_2 = 25$$

$$\therefore \quad S^2 = \frac{1}{n_1 - n_2 - 2} \left[n_1 S_1^2 + n_2 S_2^2\right]$$

$$= \frac{1}{(25 + 25 - 2)} \left[25 \times 20^2 + 25 \times 25^2\right]$$

$$= \frac{1}{50 - 2} \left[25 \times 400 + 25 \times 625\right]$$

$$= 533.85$$

$$\therefore \quad S = \sqrt{533.85} = 23.10$$

Null hypothesis H_o: $\mu_1 = \mu_2$

Alternative hypothesis H_1 : $\mu_1 \neq \mu_2$

$$|t| = \left|\frac{\bar{x}_1 - \bar{x}_2}{S\sqrt{\frac{1}{n_1} + \frac{1}{n_2}}}\right| = \left|\frac{200 - 250}{23.10\sqrt{\frac{1}{25} + \frac{1}{25}}}\right| = 7.65$$

Table value of t for 48 df at 1% level. = 2.58

The calculated value of t is greater than the table value at 1% level, for 48 df. Therefore we reject null hypothesis H_o.

The machines are not equally efficient.

***Example* 12:** Samples of two types of electric bulbs were tested for length of life and the following data ware obtained.

	Type I	**Type II**
Sample number	$n_1 = 8$	$n_2 = 7$
Sample means	$\overline{x}_1 = 1234$ hrs	$\overline{x}_2 = 1036$ hrs
Sample S.D	$S_1 = 36$ hrs	$S_2 = 40$ hrs

Is the difference significant to warrant that type I is superior to type II regarding the length of life.

***Solution*:** From the given data we get

$$S^2 = \frac{n_1 s_1^2 + n_2 s_2^2}{n_1 + n_2 - 2}$$

$$= \frac{(8)(36)^2 + 7(1600)}{8+7-2} = 1659.08$$

$H_o : \mu_1 = \mu_2$ i.e the two types of electric bulbs are identical

$H_1 : \mu_1 > \mu_2$ (one – tailed)

Level of significance: 5% $(\alpha = 0.05)$

Degrees of freedom: df $= n_1 + n_2 - 2$

$= 8 + 7 - 2 = 13$

$t_\alpha = t_{0.05}$ for 13 df $= 1.77$ for one tailed

Test statistic
$$t = \frac{\overline{x}_1 - \overline{x}_2}{\sqrt{S^2\left(\frac{1}{n_1} + \frac{1}{n_2}\right)}} = \frac{1234 - 1036}{\sqrt{1659.08\left(\frac{1}{8} + \frac{1}{7}\right)}}$$

Calculated value of t is greater than the table value of t at 5% level, for 13 df. Hence we reject null hypothesis H_o. The bulbs are not identical.

Exercise 6.1

1. Below are given the gain in weight (in lbs) of pigs fed on two diets A and B

Diet A	25	32	30	34	24	14	32	24	30	35	25	–	–
Diet B	44	34	22	10	47	31	40	32	35	21	35	29	22

Test if the two diets differ significantly as regards their effect on increase in weight.

Ans. H_o Accepted

2. A random blood sample for the test of fasting sugar of 10 boys give the following data in mg/dl.

70, 120, 110, 101, 88, 83, 95, 107, 100, 98. Do these data support the assumption of population mean of 100 mg/dl? Find a reasonable range in which the most of the mean fasting sugar test of samples of 10 boys lie.

Ans. 87.0, 107.40

3. Ten objects are chosen at random from a large population and their weights are found to be is gms 63, 63, 64, 65, 66, 69, 69, 70, 70, 71. In the light of above data discuss the suggestion that the mean weight in the universe is 65 gms.

Ans. The mean weight is 65 gm

4. Two types of batteries are tested for their length of life and the following data are obtained.

	No. of Samples	Mean Life 600 hrs	Variance
Type A	9	600 hr	121
Type B	8	640 hr	144

Is there significance difference in two means. ($t_{0.05}$ for 15 df = 2.131)

Ans. H_o rejected: There is no significant difference is the two means.

5. The following data shows the cost in hundred rupees per square meter of the floor area concerning randomly selected 7 schools and 5 office blocks from those completed during the period 2004 to 2005.

School	28	31	26	27	23	38	37
Office blocks	37	42	34	37	35	–	–

Do the data support the hypothesis that cost per square meter for the office blocks was greater than that for schools? Test at 5% level of significance

Ans. Cost per square meter for office block is greater than for school block

6. Below are given the gain in weights in kg of cows fed on two diets X and Y

Diet X	25	32	30	32	24	14	32	–	–	–
Diet Y	24	34	22	30	42	31	40	30	32	35

Test at 5% level whether the two diets differ as regards their effect on mean increase in weight ($t_{0.05}$ for 15 df = 2.131).

Ans. The two diets do not differ significantly as regards their effect on mean increase in weight.

7. Ten cartons are taken at random from an automatic filling machine. The mean net weight of the ten cartons is 11.8 kg and standard deviation is 0.15 kg. Does the sample mean differ significantly from intended weight of 12 kg? You are given df = 9, $t_{0.05} = 2.26$

Ans. The sample means differ significantly

8. Certain pesticide is packed into bags by a machine. A random sample of 10 bags is drawn and their contents are found to weigh (in kg) as follows

50, 49, 52, 44, 45, 48, 46, 45, 49, 45

Test if the average packing can be taken to be 50 kg.

Ans. Average packing can not be taken as 50 kg.

9. Two samples of sizes 6 and 5 give the following data

	Sample I	**Sample II**
Mean	40	50
S.D	8	10

Is the difference of the mean significant? ($t_{0.05}$ for 9 df = 2.26)

Ans. The difference in means is not significant.

10. A fertilizer mixing machine is set to give 12 kg of nitrate for every quintal bag of fertilizer. Ten 100 kg bags examined. The percentage of nitrate as follows.

11, 14, 13, 12, 13, 12, 13, 14, 11, 12

Is there reason to believe that the machine is defective?

Ans. There is no reason to believe that machine is defective.

11. Ten individuals are chosen at random from a population and their heights in inches are found to be 63, 63, 66, 67, 68, 69, 70, 70, 71, 71. Discuss the suggestion that the mean height of the population is 66 inches.

Ans. The mean height in the population is 66 inches.

12. An I.Q test was administrated to 5 persons before and after they were trained. The results are given below

I-Q before Training	110	120	123	132	125
I Q after Training	120	118	125	136	121

Test whether there is any change in I.Q after the training programme?

Ans. No change in I.Q after the training.

13. Two salesmen A and B are working in a certain district. From a sample survey conducted by the head office, the following results were obtained. State whether there is any significant difference in the average sales between the two salesmen?

	A	**B**
No of Sales	10	18
Averages sales (in Rs)	170	205
S.D (in Rs)	20	25

Ans. There is significant difference in the average sales.

14. A certain stimulus is administered to each of 12 patients resulted in the following change in Blood pressure.

5, 2, 8, –1, 3, 0, –2, 1, 5, 0, 4, 6

It can be concluded that the stimulates will in general be accompanied by an increase in blood pressure.

Ans. H_o is rejected

6.8 F – Test

F – Test is a test of hypothesis concerning two variances derived from two samples. It is defined as the ratio of two independent unbiased estimations of population variances and is given by

$$F = \frac{S_1^2}{S_2^2}$$

If n_1 is the size of the sample whose variance is S_1^2 and n_2 is the size of the sample whose variance is S_2^2 then the degrees of freedom for the numerator is $n_1 - 1$ and the

degrees of freedom for the denominator is $n_2 - 1$. Provided $S_1^2 > S_2^2$ otherwise F is defined as
$$F = \frac{S_2^2}{S_1^2}$$

If the calculated value of F for the df $(n_1 - 1, n_2 - 1)$ at a given level of significance is less than the table value of F then we accept null hypothesis otherwise we reject null hypothesis.

6.9 Assumption of F-test

1. The values in each group should be normally distributed.
2. The error should be independent of each value.
3. The variances within each group should be equal for all groups.

6.10 Uses of F – Test

F- Test is used to test whether the independent estimates of the population variances are homogeneous or not. It is used to test the equality of population variances. It is also used to test whether two independent samples have been drawn from the normal population with same variances.

***Example* 1:** In a laboratory experiment two samples gave the following results

Sample	Size	Sample Mean	Sum of Squares of Deviations from the Mean
1	10	15	90
2	12	14	108

Test the equality of sample variances at 5% level of significance.

***Solution*:** Null hypothesis $H_o : \sigma_1^2 = \sigma_2^2$

Alternative hypothesis $H_1 : \sigma_1^2 \neq \sigma_2^2$

We have $n_1 = 10,\ n_2 = 12,\ \bar{x}_1 = 15,\ \bar{x}_2 = 14$

$$\sum(x_1 - \bar{x}_1)^2 = 90,\ \sum(x_2 - \bar{x}_2)^2 = 108$$

$$S_1^2 = \frac{\sum(x_2 - \bar{x}_2)^2}{n_1 - 1} = \frac{90}{10-1} = \frac{90}{9} = 10$$

$$S_2^2 = \frac{\sum(x_2 - \bar{x}_2)^2}{n2 - 1} = \frac{108}{12 - 1} = \frac{108}{11} = 9.818$$

$S_1^2 > S_2^2$ therefore df = (n_1 – 1, n_2 – 1)

= (10 – 1, 12 – 1) = (9, 11)

Table value of F at 5% level for (9, 11) df = 2.90

Test statistic: $$F = \frac{S_1^2}{S_2^2} = \frac{10}{9.818}$$

= 1.018

Since the calculated value of F is less than the table value at 5% level and (9.11) df, we accept H_o. The two populations have the same variance.

***Example* 2:** In a sample of observations, the sum of squares of deviation of the sample values from the sample mean was 94.5 and in another sample of 10 observations it was found to be 101.7. Test whether the difference of variance is significant.

***Solution*:** We have

$$\sum(x_1 - \bar{x}_1)^2 = 94.5$$

$$\sum(x_2 - \bar{x}_2)^2 = 101.7 \qquad \text{(given)}$$

$n_1 = 8, \quad n_2 = 10$

$\therefore \quad n_1 - 1 = 7, \quad n_2 - 1 = 9,$

Null hypothesis $H_o : \sigma_1^2 = \sigma_2^2 = \sigma^2$ i.e. The difference in variances is not significant.

Alternative hypothesis H_1: The difference is significant

Level of significant = 5%

$$S_1^2 = \frac{\sum(x_1 - \bar{x}_1)^2}{n_1 - 1} = \frac{94.5}{7} = 13.5$$

$$S_2^2 = \frac{\sum(x_2 - \bar{x}_2)^2}{n_2 - 1} = \frac{101.7}{9} = 11.3$$

$\therefore \; S_1^2 > S_2^2$

Degrees of freedom = (n_1 – 1, n_2 – 1) = (7, 9)

$F_{0.05}$ for (7, 9) df = 3.29

$$F = \frac{S_1^2}{S_2} = \frac{13.5}{11.3} = 1.195$$

Since calculated value of F at 5% level of significance for (7, 9) df is less than the table value, we accept null hypothesis.

Hence, the difference is not significant at 5% level of significance

***Example* 3:** Two samples are drawn from two normal populations. From the following data test whether the two samples have the same variance at 5% level?

Sample I	60	65	71	74	76	82	85	87	–	–
Sample II	64	66	67	85	78	88	86	85	63	91

***Solution*:** Null hypothesis : $H_o : \sigma_1^2 = \sigma_2^2$ i.e two samples have the same variances

$$n_1 = 8, \qquad n_2 = 10$$

$$\bar{x} = \frac{\sum x}{n} = \frac{600}{8} = 75 \qquad \bar{y} = \frac{\sum y}{n} = \frac{770}{10} = 77$$

Alternative hypothesis $H : \sigma_1^2 \neq \sigma_2^2$

Sample I			**Sample II**		
x	$x = \bar{x}$	$(x - \bar{x})^2$	**y**	$y - \bar{y}$	$(y - \bar{y})^2$
60	60 – 75 = – 15	225	61	61 – 77 = – 16	256
65	65 – 75 = – 10	100	66	66 – 77 = –11	121
71	71 – 75 = – 4	16	67	67 –77 = – 10	100
74	74 – 75 = – 1	1	85	85 – 77 = 8	64
76	76 – 75 = 1	1	78	78 – 77 = 1	01
82	82 – 75 = 7	49	88	88 – 77 = 11	121
85	85 – 75 = 10	100	86	86 – 77 = 9	81
87	87 – 75 = 12	144	85	85 – 77 = 8	64
–	–	–	63	63 – 77 = –14	196
–	–	–	91	63 – 77 = 14	196
600		636	770		1200
$= \sum x$		$= \sum (x - \bar{x})^2$	$= \sum y$		$= \sum (y - \bar{y})^2$

$$S_1^2 = \frac{\sum(x-\bar{x})^2}{n_1 - 1} = \frac{636}{8-1} = 90.857$$

$$S_2^2 = \frac{\sum(y-\bar{y})^2}{n_1 - 1} = \frac{1200}{9} = 133.33$$

Null hypothesis $H_o : \sigma_1^2 = \sigma_2^2$

Alternative hypothesis $H_1 : \sigma_1^2 \neq \sigma_2^2$

$$F = \frac{S_1^2}{S_2^2} \qquad \left(\because S_2^2 > S_1^2\right)$$

$$= \frac{133.33}{90.857} = 1.467$$

$F_{0.05}$ for (8 – 1, 10 – 1) = (7, 9) df = 3.68

∴ Calculated value of F is less than the table value for (7, 9) df at 5% level of significance.

Hence, we accept H_o i.e two samples have the same variance.

***Example* 4:** The time taken by workers in performing a job by methods I and II is given below.

Method I	20	16	26	27	23	22	–
Method II	27	33	42	35	32	34	38

Do the data show that the variances of time distribution form population from which these samples are drawn do not differ significantly

***Solution*:** Computation of sample variances

x	$x-\bar{x}$	$(x-\bar{x})^2$	y	$y-\bar{y}$	$(y-\bar{y})^2$
20	– 2.3	5.29	27	– 7.4	54.76
16	– 6.3	39.69	33	– 1.4	1.96
26	3.7	13.69	42	7.6	57.76
			35	0.6	0.36
27	4.7	22.09	32	–2.4	5.76
23	0.7	0.49	34	– 0.4	0.16
22	– 0.3	0.09	38	3.6	12.96
134		81.34	241		133.72

Here, we have $n_1 = 6, n_2 = 7$

$$\bar{x} = \frac{\sum x}{n} = \frac{134}{6} = 22.3 \qquad \bar{y} = \frac{\sum y}{n} = \frac{241}{7} = 34.4$$

$$\sum(x-\bar{x})^2 = 81.34, \qquad \sum(y-\bar{y})^2 = 133.72$$

$$S_1^2 = \frac{\sum(x-\bar{x})^2}{n_1 - 1} = \frac{81.34}{6-1} = 16.26$$

$$S_2^2 = \frac{\sum(y-\bar{y})^2}{n_2 - 1} = \frac{133.72}{7-1} = 22.29$$

H_o : These is no significant difference between the sample variances

$H_1 : \sigma_1^2 \neq \sigma_2^2$

$$F = \frac{S_1^2}{S_2^2} = \frac{22.29}{16.26} = 1.3699$$

Table values of F for $(n_2 - 1, n_1 - 1) = (7 - 1, 6 - 1) = (6, 5)$ df at 5% is 4.95. Therefore the calculated value of F is less than the table value. Hence, we accepted null hypothesis and conclude that there is no significant difference between sample variances

***Example* 5:** The Nicotine content in mgs in two samples of tobacco were found to be as follows

Sample A	24	27	26	21	25	–
Sample B	27	30	28	31	22	36

Can it be said that the two samples come from same normal population?

Solution: Calculation of variances

$$\bar{x} = \frac{\sum x}{n_1} = \frac{123}{5} = 24.6, \qquad \bar{y} = \frac{\sum y}{n_2} = \frac{174}{6} = 29$$

x	$x-\bar{x}$	$(x-\bar{x})^2$	y	$y-\bar{y}$	$(y-\bar{y})^2$
24	06	0.36	27	– 2	4
27	2.4	5.76	30	1	1
26	1.4	1.96	28	– 1	1
21	3.6	12.96	31	2	4
25	0.4	0.16	22	– 7	49
–	–	–	36	7	49
123		21.2	174		108

$$S_1^2 = \frac{\sum(x-\bar{x})^2}{n_1-1} = \frac{21.2}{4-1} = 5.3, \quad S_2^2 = \frac{\sum(y-\bar{y})^2}{n_2-1} = \frac{108}{5} = 21.6$$

Null hypothesis $H_o : \sigma_1^2 = \sigma_2^2$

Alternative hypothesis $H_1 : \sigma_1^2 \neq \sigma_2^2$

$$F = \frac{S_2^2}{S_1^2} = \frac{21.6}{5.3} = 4.07$$

Degrees of freedom = $(n_2 - 1, n_1 - 1)$

$= (6-1, 5-1) = (5, 4)$

$F_{0.05}$ for (5, 4) df = 6.26

Since the calculated value of F is less than the value of F at 5% level of significance for (5, 4) df, we accepted H_o: and conclude that the variances are equal.

Exercise 6.2

1. Pumpkins were grown under the experimental conditions. Two random samples of 11 and 9 pumpkins show the sample standard deviations of their weights as 0.8 and 0.5 respectively. Assuming that the weight distributions are normal, test hypothesis that the true variances are equal

   ($F_{0.05}$ for (10, 8) df = 3.35)

Ans. The true variances are equal

2. In one sample of 10 observations, the sum of the squares of the deviations of the sample values from sample mean was 120 and in the other sample of 12 observations it was 3.14. Test whether the difference is significant at 5 % level?

Ans. Not significant

3. The methods of performing a certain operation are compared. The following data are obtained

   $\bar{x}_1 = 50.5$ $\quad S_1^2 = 6.5$ $\quad n_1 = 15$

   $\bar{x}_2 = 57.2$ $\quad S_2^2 = 5.7$ $\quad n_2 = 12$

   Test the hypothesis that the two variances are equal at 5% level of significance

4. Two samples were drawn independently from two normal populations. The data are

   $n_1 = 15,$ $\quad \bar{x}_1 = 62.2$ $\quad \sum(x_1 - \bar{x}_1)^2 = 56.12$

   $n_2 = 19,$ $\quad \bar{x}_2 = 61.8$ $\quad \sum(x_2 - \bar{x}_2)^2 = 83.27$

   Test whether the population variances are equal.

Ans.

5. Two samples drawn from two normal populations have the following data. Test whether the two samples have the same variance at 5% level

Sample I	60	65	71	74	82	85	87	–	–
Sample II	61	66	67	85	63	85	86	88	91

Ans. $\sigma_1^2 = \sigma_2^2$, H_o accepted

6. Two samples were drawn from the normal population and their values are

A	66	67	82	75	76	76	90	92	88	–	–
B	66	64	78	74	74	87	85	82	95	97	92

Test whether the two populations have the same variance at 5% level of significance.

Ans. The two populations have the same variance

6.11 Chi Square Test

In this section we discuss chi square test, which is used as a test of hypothesis. It is computer on the basis of frequency in a sample. Chi- square test is not a parametric test and is defined as follows

$$\chi^2 = \sum_{i=1}^{n} \frac{(O_i - E_i)^2}{E_i}$$

Conditions for using χ^2 –test:

1. The test is wholly dependent on degrees of freedom
2. Each of the observations making up the sample for this test should be independent of each other
3. The total number of observations must be large
4. The Chi-Square test applied in a fold found table will not give a reliable result with degree of freedom if the expected value in any cell is less than 5. In such cases Yates correction is necessary

Types of χ^2:

χ^2 test is of three types namely

(i) Goodness of fit

(ii) Contingency Chi-Square

(iii) Homogeneity Chi-Square

Chi-Square Distribution

Chi-Square distribution is a continuous distribution whose p.d.f is defined by

$$P(x^2) = y_0 (x^2)^{\frac{1}{2}(x-2)} . e^{-\frac{1}{2}x^2}$$

where y_o is a constant depending on the degrees of freedom r.

Proportion of χ^2 – Distribution

1. Chi-Square test is always positive and the value of χ^2 always lies between zero and infinity
2. The mean of the distribution is the number of degrees of freedom
3. The S.D of χ^2 distribution is $\sqrt{2v}$
4. For different degrees of freedom, the shapes of χ^2 – curve will be different
5. The shape of the curve of χ^2 – distribution depends on the degrees of freedom

Degrees of Freedom

If the number of data are given in the form of a series of variables in a row or column or the number of frequencies that are put in cells in a contingency table which can be calculated independently is called the degree of freedom

(i) If the data is given in the form of a row, the degrees of freedom is $v = n - 1$ where n denotes the number of observations in the row

(ii) If the data is given in the form of column then the degrees of freedom is $v = n - 1$, where n is the number of items in the column

(iii) If the data is in the form of a contingency table consisting of R rows and C columns then the degrees of freedom is

$$v = (R - 1)(C - 1)$$

In this case the frequencies are put in cells in the table

χ^2 – test for goodness of fit

***Example* 1:** A sample analysis of examination results of 500 students was mode. It was found that 220 students had failed, 170 secured a third class, 90 were placed in second class and 20 got a first class. Do these figures commensurate with the general examination result which is in the ratio 4 : 3: 2 : 1 for the various categories respectively.

Solution:

Null hypothesis H_o: The observed results commensurate with the general examination results

***Alternative hypothesis H_1*:** The observed results does not commensurate with general examination results

we have N = 500

The expected frequencies are in the ratio 4 : 3 : 2 : 1.

Hence we get 200, 150, 100 and 50 as the expected frequencies for various categories, we have

Class	Observed frequency O_i	Expected frequency E_i	$O_i - E_i$	$\left(\frac{O_i - E_i}{E_i}\right)^2$
Failed	220	200	20	2.00
Third	170	150	20	2.667
Second	90	100	– 10	1.000
First	20	50	–30	18.000
	500	500		23.667

Calculated value of $\chi^2 = \frac{\sum(O_i - E_o)^2}{E_i}$

$= 23.66$

Degrees of freedom = n –1 = 4 – 1 = 3

∴ v = 3

Level of significance = 5%

$X^2_{0.005}$ for 3 df = 7.81

Since the calculated value of χ^2 is greater than the table value at 5% level for 3 df we reject null hypothesis.

∴ The observed result does not commensurate with the general examination result.

***Example* 2:** The following table gives the number of aircraft accidents that occurred during the various days of the week. Test whether the accidents are uniformly distributed over the week.

Day	Mon	The	Wed	Thu	Fri	Sat
Number of Accidents	14	18	12	11	15	14

***Solution*:** Null hypothesis H_o: The accidents are uniformly distributed the week

Alternative hypothesis of the accidents are not uniformly distributed over the week

Degrees of freedom v = n – 1 = 6 – 1 = 5

Level of significance = 5%

Table value of $\lambda^2_{0.05}$ = for 5 df = 11.07

The expected frequency of accidents on each of the days is $\frac{84}{6} = 14$

Observed frequency 0	Expected frequency ∈	0- ∈	$\frac{(0-\in)^2}{\in}$
14	14	0	0
18	14	4	1.143
12	14	–2	0.286
11	14	–3	0.643
15	14	–1	0.71
14	14	0	0
84	84		2.143

$$\chi^2 = \frac{\Sigma(0-\in)^2}{\in}$$

$$= 2.143$$

The calculated value of χ^2 is less than the table value of x^2 0.05 for 5 d.f. Hence, we accept the null hypotheses.

∴ The accidents are uniformly distributed over the week

***Example* 3**: A die was thrown 498 times. Denoting x to be the number appearing on the top of it; the observed frequency of x is given below

x	1	2	3	4	5	6
f	69	78	85	82	86	98

What opinion your would form the accuracy of die

Solution: We have n = 498

$$E_i = \frac{498}{6} = 83$$

Null hypothesis H_o : Dies is unbiased

Alterative hypothesis H_1 : Die is biased

Level of significance = 5%, degrees of freedom

Critical value $\chi^2_{0.05}$ for 5 df = 11.07 $= \nu = 5$

$$X^2 = \frac{\sum(O_i - E_i)}{E_i}$$

$$= \frac{(69-83)^2}{83} + \frac{(78-83)^2}{83} + \frac{(85-83)^2}{83} + \frac{(82-83)^2}{83} + \frac{(88-83)^2}{83} + \frac{(98-83)^2}{83}$$

$$= \frac{1}{83}\ [\,196 + 25 + 4 + 1 + 9 + 225]$$

$$= \frac{460}{83} = 5.542$$

Calculated value of χ^2 at 5% level of significance for 5 df is less than the table value of χ^2. Hence, we accept null hypothesis

The die is unbiased.

***Example* 4:** A die is thrown 264 times with the following results. Show that the die is biased

No. appeared on the die	1	2	3	4	5	6
Frequency	40	32	28	58	54	60

Solution: Null hypothesis H_o : The die is un biased

Alternative hypothesis H_1 : The die is biased

Level of significance = 5%

$\chi^2_{0.05}$ for 6 –1 = 5 df = 11.07

Expected frequency for each out come $= \frac{264}{6} = 44$

Observed Frequency	**Expected Frequency**	**O.E**	$\frac{(O_i - E_i)^2}{E_i}$
40	44	– 4	0.3636
32	44	–12	3.2727
28	44	–16	5.8181
58	44	14	4.4545
54	44	10	2.2727
60	44	8	1.4545
264	264		17.6362

$$\chi^2 = \frac{\sum(O_i - E_o)^2}{E_i} = 17.6362$$

Since the calculated value of χ^2 is greater than the table value of χ^2 at 5% level for 5 df, we reject the null hypothesis and conclude that the die is biased.

***Example* 5:** Fit a Poisson distribution for the following data and test the goodness of fit.

x	0	1	2	3	4	Total
y	109	65	22	3	1	200

(given $\chi^2 0.05$ on df = 3.841)

***Solution*:** Here we have

$$\overline{x} = \frac{\sum f_i x_i}{\sum f_i}$$

$$= \frac{0\times109 + 1\times65 + 2\times22 + 3\times3 + 4\times1}{200}$$

$$= 0.61$$

$$\therefore \quad \lambda = 0.61$$

The expected frequencies are

$$N\,(v) = \frac{e^{-\lambda}\lambda^2}{r!}.N, \qquad r = 0, 1, 2, 3, 4$$

$$N\,(0) = e^{-0.61} \times 200 = 108.67$$

$$N\,(1) = N\,(0).\ \lambda = (108.61)\,(0.61) = 66.28$$

$$N\,(2) = N\,(1).\ \frac{\lambda}{2} = 66.28 \times \frac{0.61}{2} = 20.218$$

$$N\,(3) = N\,(2).\ \frac{\lambda}{3} = 20.218 \times \frac{0.61}{3} = 4.11$$

$$N\,(4) = N\,(3).\ \frac{\lambda}{4} = 4.11 \times \frac{0.61}{4} = 0.63$$

Thus, we have by pooling the data

X	0	1	2,3,4
O	109	65	26
E	108.7	66.3	25

$$\chi^2 = \frac{(109-108.7)^2}{108.7} + \frac{(65-66.3)^2}{66.3} + \frac{(26-25)^2}{25}$$

$$= 0.0663$$

$\therefore$ Calculated value if χ^2 is less than the table value at 5 % level of significance for 1 df

Hence, H_o is accepted poisson fit is good

***Example* 6:** 4 coins are tossed 100 times and the following results were obtained. Fit a binomial distribution for the data and test the goodness of fit

$(\chi^2_{0.05} = 9.49$ for 4 df)

Number of Heads	0	1	2	3	4
Frequency	5	29	36	25	5

Solution:

H_o The fit is good

H_1 The fit is not good

$$\therefore \quad \bar{n} = \frac{\sum n_i f_i}{\sum f_i} = \frac{0 \times 5 + 1 \times 29 + 2 \times 36 + 3 \times 25 + 4 \times 5}{100}$$

$$= \frac{196}{100} = 1.96$$

Since $\bar{x} = np$ i.e., $\lambda = np$

we get $4\,p = 1.96$

$$\therefore \quad p = \frac{1.96}{4} = 0.49$$

$$q = 1 - p = 1 - 0.49 = 0.51$$

The expected frequencies are

$$N\,P\,(0) = 100\,.\,(0.51)^4\,(0.49)^0 = 7$$

$$N\,P\,(1) = 100\,.\,4_{c_1}\,(0.51)^3\,(0.49)^1 = 26$$

$$N\,P\,(2) = 100\,.\,4_{c_2}\,(0.51)^2\,(0.49)^2 = 37$$

$$N\,P\,(3) = 100\,.\,4_{c_3}\,(0.51)\,(0.49)^3 = 24$$

$$N\,P\,(4) = 100\,.\,4_{c_4}\,(0.51)^0\,(0.49)^4 = 6$$

The excepted frequencies are 7, 26, 37, 24, 6

Hence, we have

O_i	5	29	36	25	5
E_i	7	26	37	24	6

$$\chi^2 = \frac{\sum (O_i - E_i)^2}{E_i} = \frac{(5-7)^2}{7} + \frac{(29-26)^2}{26} + \frac{(36-37)^2}{37} + \frac{(25-24)^2}{24} + \frac{(5-6)^2}{6}$$

$$= \frac{4}{7} + \frac{9}{26} + \frac{1}{37} + \frac{1}{24} + \frac{1}{6}$$

$$= 1.15$$

The degrees of freedom is 5 – 1 = 4

$$\chi^2_{0.05} \text{ for 4 df} = 9.49$$

Since calculated value of χ^2 is less than the table value of χ^{-2} at 4 df for 5 % level, the null hypothesis is accepted. We conclude that the fitness in good.

χ^2 – test for indepence of attributes:

chi-square test is used to test the indepence of attributes like blindness, smoking and drinking etc.

2 × 2 contingency table

2 × 2 contingences table is given below

a	B
c	D

a, b, c, d are known as cell frequencies. They are also the observed frequencies of two attributes. The total frequency in each row or column is called marginal frequency. The expected frequencies corresponding to the observed frequencies are

$$E(a) = \frac{(a+c)(a+b)}{(a+b+c+d)}, \qquad E(b) = \frac{(b+d)(a+b)}{a+b+c+d}$$

$$E(c) = \frac{(a+c)(c+d)}{a+b+c+d}, \qquad E(d) = \frac{(b+d)(c+d)}{a+b+c+d}$$

By the definition of χ^2 we have

$$\chi^2 = \Sigma\ \frac{(O_i - E_i)^2}{E_i}$$

$$= \Sigma\ \frac{(a - E(a))^2}{E(a)}$$

$$= \Sigma\ \frac{\left(a - \frac{(a+c)\ (a+b)}{a+b+c+d}\right)^2}{\frac{(a+c)\ (a+b)}{a+b+c+d}}$$

$$= \Sigma\ \frac{\frac{\left[a(a+b+c+d)\ - (a^2\ ab + ca + bc\right]^2}{(a+b+c+d)^2}}{\frac{(a+c)\ (a+b)}{(a+b+c+d)}}$$

$$= \Sigma\ \frac{(ad - bc)^2}{(a+b+c+d)\ (a+c)\ (a+b)}$$

Expanding we get

$$\chi^2 = \frac{(ad - bc)^2}{(a+b+c+d)}\left[\frac{1}{(a+c)\ (a+b)} + \frac{1}{(b+d)\ (a+b)} + \frac{1}{(a+c)\ (c+d)} + \frac{1}{(b+d)(c+d)}\right]$$

$$= \frac{(ad - bc)^2}{N}\left[\frac{(b+d)(c+d)\ + (a+c)(c+d) + (a+b)(b+d) + (a+c)\ (a+b)}{(a+c)\ (a+b)\ (b+d)\ (c+d)}\right]$$

where $N = a + b + c + d$

$$= \frac{(ad - bc)^2}{N}\left[\frac{(b+d)(a+b+c+d) + (a+c)\ (a+b+c+d)}{(a+b)\ (a+c)\ (b+d)\ (c+d)}\right]$$

$$= \frac{(ad - bc)^2[(a+b+c+d)(a+b+c+d)]}{N\ (a+b)\ (a+c)(b+d)(c+d)}$$

$$= \frac{(ad - bc)^2\ N^2}{N\ (a+b)\ (a+c)(b+d)(c+d)} = \frac{N(ad - bc)^2}{(a+b)\ (a+c)(b+d)(c+d)}$$

The degrees freedom for 2×2 contingency table is $r = (2 - 1)\ (2 - 1) = 1$

The table value of χ^2 at 5% level of significance for 1 df = 3.841

***Example* 7:** The following table gives the classification of 100 workers according to sex and the nature of the work. Test whether the nature of work in independent of the sex of the worker.

	stable	Un stable	Total
Males	40	20	60
Females	10	30	40
Total	50	50	100

Solution: H_o : the nature of the work is independent of the sex of the workers

We have

a = 40 b = 20

c = 10 d = 30

$$\chi^2 = \frac{N(ad - bc)^2}{(a + b)\,(a + c)(c + d)(b+d)} = \frac{100\,(40 \times 30 - 10 \times 20)^2}{50 \times 50 \times 60 \times 40}$$

$$= \frac{100\,(1200 - 200)^2}{50 \times 50 \times 60 \times 40} = \frac{100\,(1000)^2}{50 \times 50 \times 60 \times 40}$$

$= 16.66$

level of significance = 5%

$\chi^2_{0.05}$ or 1 dt = 3.841

Since the calculated value of χ^2 is greater than the table value at 5% level for 1 df, we reject null hypothesis.

∴ The nature of the work is not independent of the sex of the worker.

***Example* 8:** Given the following contingency table for hair colour and eye colour. Find the value of χ^2. Is there good association between two ?

		Hair colour			
		Fair	Brown	Black	Total
Eye colour	Blue	15	5	20	40
	Grey	20	10	20	50
	Brown	25	15	20	60
	Total	60	30	60	150

Solution: Null hypothesis H_o: The two attributes hair colour and eye colour are in dependent

$X_{0.05}$ for 4 df = 9.488

Table of expected frequencies

$\frac{60 \times 40}{150} = 16$	$\frac{30 \times 40}{150} = 8$	$\frac{60 \times 40}{150} = 16$
$\frac{60 \times 50}{150} = 20$	$\frac{30 \times 50}{150} = 10$	$\frac{60 \times 50}{150} = 20$
$\frac{60 \times 60}{150} = 24$	$\frac{30 \times 60}{150} = 12$	$\frac{60 \times 60}{150} = 24$

Computation of χ^2

O_i	E_i	$(O_i - E_i)^2$	$\frac{(O_i - E_i)^2}{E_i}$
15	16	1	0.0625
5	8	9	1.125
20	16	16	1.000
20	20	0	0
10	10	0	0
20	20	0	0
25	24	1	0.042
15	12	9	0.75
20	24	16	0.666

Total : 3.6458

$$\chi^2 = \frac{\sum(O_i - E_i)^2}{E_i} = 3.6458$$

∴ The calculated value of χ^2 at 5% level of significance is less than the table value. Hence we accept H_o and conclude that that hair colour eye colour are independent.

Exercise 6.3

1. The following show the distribution of digits in number at random from a telephone directory.

Digits	0	1	2	3	4	5	6	7	8	9
Frequency	1026	1107	997	966	1075	933	1107	922	964	853

Test whether the digits may be taken to occur equally frequently in the directory ($\chi^2_{0.05}$ for 9 df = 16.9.9)

Ans: The digits do not occur frequently in the directory

2. A pair of dice are thrown 360 times and the frequency of each sum is indicated below.

Sum	2	3	4	5	6	7	8	9	10	11	12
Frequency	8	24	35	37	44	65	51	42	26	14	14

Would you say that the dice are fair on the basis of the chi square list at 0.05 level of significance ($\chi^2_{0.05}$ for 11 df = 18.3).

Ans: The dice are fair

3. On the basis of information given below about the treatment of 200 patients suffering from a disease, state whether the new treatment is comparatively superior to the conventional treatment.

	Favourable	**Not Favourable**	**Total**
New	60	30	90
Conventional	40	70	110

($\chi^2_{0.05}$ for 1df = 3.541)

Ans: The new treatment is superior to the conventional treatment

4. In an investigation on the machine performance, the following results are obtained

	No. of units inspected	**No. of defectives**
Machine 1	375	17
Machine 2	450	22

Test whether there is any significant performance of two machines at $\alpha = 0.05$

Ans: There is significant performance of the two machines.

5. A die is thrown 120 times and the frequencies of various faces are as follows

Fall No	1	2	3	4	5	6
Frequency	10	15	25	25	18	27

Test whether the die was fair

Ans: Significant

6. Two salesmen A and B are working in a certain district. From a sample conducted by the head office, the following results were obtained. State whether there is any significant difference in the average sales between two salesmen.

No. of sales	20	18
Average sales (in Rs)	170	205
S. D (in Rs)	20	25

Ans: Significant

7. A large electronic firm that have many workers with disabilities wants to determine whether their disabilities affect such works performance. Use the level of significant $\alpha = 0.05$ to decide on the basing the following data, whether it is reasonable to maintain that the disabilities have no effect on the performance.

	Above average	average	Below average
Blind	21	64	17
Deaf	16	49	14
No. disability	29	93	28

Ans: H_o accepted

8. From the following data find whether there is any significant liking in the habit of taking soft drinks among the categories of employees.

Soft drinks	Employees			Total
	Clerks	Teachers	Offices	
Pepsi	10	25	65	100
Thumps lip	15	30	65	110
Fanta	50	60	30	140
Total	75	115	160	350

Ans: Null hypothesis rejected at 5% level of significance. Habit of taking soft drink depends on the category of the employee.

9. The following is the distribution of the hourly number of trucks arriving at a company's warehouse.

Tricks arriving at warehouse	0	1	2	3	4	5	6	7	8
Frequency	52	151	130	102	45	12	5	1	2

Fit a Poisson distribution and test for goodness of fit at the level of significance $\alpha = 0.05$ (JNTU 2007)

Ans: The fit is good

10. Four methods are under development for making discs of a super conducting material. Fifty discs are made by each method and they are checked for super conductivity when cooled with liquid nitrogen.

	Method I	Method II	Method III	Method IV	Total
Super conductor	31	42	22	25	120
Farcies	19	8	28	25	80
Total	50	50	50	50	200

Perform χ^2 – test with $\alpha = 0.05$ if there is significant difference between the proportions of super conductors produced. Plot the individual confidence internals

(JNTU 2008 Feb)

11. The following table gives the number of train accidents in a country that occurred during there various days of the week. Find whether the accidents are informly distributed over the week.

Days	Sunday	Monday	Tuesday	Wednesday	Thursday	Friday	Saturday
No. of accidents	20	18	13	23	26	11	15

Ans: Not significant

12. For the data given below age χ^2-test to test the effectiveness of inoculation in preventing the attack of small pox.

	Attacked	Not attacked	Total
Inoculated	25	220	245
Not-inoculated	90	160	250
Total	115	380	495

Ans: H_o is rejected

Correlation and Regression

7

7.1 Introduction

This chapter is devoted to the study of correlation and regression. Correlation measure the degree of relationship between two variables. Regression is used to predict the average value of one variable for a specified value of the other.

Definition:

Correlation is the relationship between two or more variables which vary is sympathy with the other in the same of opposite direction.

Coefficient of correlation

Definition

The extent or degree of relationship between the two variables is measured in terms of another parameter called coefficient of correlation. Coefficient of correlation is denoted by r.

The value of r lies between –1 and 1 i.e $-1 \leq r \leq 1$

Properties of r:

(a) If $r = 1$ then the correlation is perfect and positive

(b) If $r = -1$, then the correlation is perfect and negative

(c) If $r = 0$, there is no correlation.

When the coefficient of correlation is perfect, both the variables x and y increase or decrease in the same proportion.

When the coefficient of correlation is negative, the variables x and y are inversely proportional.

(d) If $0 < r < 1$, then there is partial positive correlation between the variables. Similarly if $-1 < r < 0$, we say that there is partial negative correlation between x and y .

7.2 Methods of Finding Coefficient of Correlation

(i) ***Direct method (Karl Pearson's method)***

If X and Y are two variates having their means $\bar{X}$ and $\bar{Y}$ respectively, then

$$r = \frac{\sum dx\, dy}{\sqrt{\sum dx^2 \sum dy^2}}$$

where $dx = X - \bar{X}$, $dy = Y - \bar{Y}$

$dx^2 = (X - \bar{X})^2$, $dy^2 = (Y - \bar{Y})^2$

It is also be written as

$$r = \frac{\sum dx\, dy}{n\, \sigma_x\, \sigma_y}$$

where n = number of observations in x or y series

σ_x = S.D of X, σ_y = S.D of Y

Alternative methods: The coefficient of correlation is also computed by formula

$$r = \frac{\sigma_x^2 + \sigma_y^2 + \sigma_z^2}{z\, \sigma_x x\, \sigma_y}$$

where $z = x - y$

Short cut method:

This method is used when $\bar{X}$ and $\bar{Y}$ are not integers

The formula is

$$\frac{\sum dx\, dy - \frac{\sum dx \sum dy}{n}}{\sqrt{\sum dx^2 - \left(\frac{\left(\sum dx^2\right)^2}{n}\right)}\sqrt{\sum dy^2 - \left(\frac{\left(\sum dy\right)^2}{n}\right)}}$$

where

$dx = X - A$, $dy = Y - B$

A,B are assumed means of X and Y series respectively

***Examples* 1:** Find the coefficient of correlation between X and Y for the following data

X	1	3	4	5	7	8	10
Y	2	6	8	10	14	16	20

***Solution*:** Let A = 5 be the assumed mean of X - Series

B = 14 be the assumed mean of Y -Series

X	dx = x – 5	dx^2	Y	dy = y – 14	dy^2	dx dy
1	–4	16	2	–12	144	48
3	–2	4	6	–8	64	16
4	–1	1	8	–6	36	6
5	0	0	10	–4	16	0
7	2	4	14	0	0	0
8	3	9	16	2	4	0
10	5	25	20	6	36	30
	3 $=\sum dx$	59 $=\sum dx^2$		$-22=\sum dy$	$\sum dy^2 =$ 300	106 $=\sum dx\ dy$

***Example* 2:** Calculate coefficient of correlation between X and Y for the following data

X:	1	2	3	4	5	6	7	8	9
Y:	10	11	12	14	13	15	16	17	18

***Solution*:** we have

$$\bar{X}=\frac{\sum X}{n}=\frac{1+2+3+4+5+6+7+8+9}{9}=\frac{45}{9}=5$$

$$\bar{Y}=\frac{\sum Y}{n}=\frac{10+11+12+14+13+15+16+17+18}{9}=\frac{126}{9}=14$$

X	**dx =X – $\bar{X}$**	**dx^2**	**Y**	**dy =Y– $\bar{Y}$**	**dy^2**	**dx dy**
1	–4	16	10	–4	16	16
2	–3	9	11	–3	9	9
3	–2	4	12	–2	4	4
4	–1	1	14	0	0	0
5	0	0	13	–1	1	0
6	1	1	15	1	1	1
7	2	4	16	2	4	4
8	3	9	17	3	9	9
9	4	16	18	4	16	16
45 = Σ x	0	60 = Σ dx^2	126 = Σ y	0	60 Σ dy^2	59 Σ dxdy

$$\text{Coefficient of correlation} = r = \frac{\sum dx\ dy}{\sqrt{\sum dx^2 \sum dy^2}} = \frac{59}{\sqrt{60 \times 60}} = \frac{59}{60} = 0.9833$$

***Example* 3:** Find the coefficient of correlation between the heights of fathers and sons from the following data

Height of Father	64	65	66	67	68	69	70
Height of Son	66	67	68	69	70	71	72

***Solution*:**

Let the height of father be denoted by X and the height of the son be denoted by Y.

Then, we have

$$\bar{x} = \frac{\Sigma x}{n} = \frac{64+65+66+67+68+69+70}{7} = \frac{469}{7} = 67$$

$$\bar{y} = \frac{\Sigma y}{n} = \frac{66+67+68+69+70+71+72}{7} = \frac{483}{7} = 69$$

x	dx	dx^2	Y	dy	dy^2	dx dy
64	$64 - 67 = -3$	9	66	$66 - 69 = 3$	9	9
65	$65 - 67 = -2$	4	67	$67 - 69 = -2$	4	4
66	$66 - 67 = -1$	1	68	$68 - 69 = -1$	1	1
67	$67 - 67 = 0$	0	69	$69 - 69 = 0$	0	0
68	$68 - 67 = 1$	1	70	$70 - 69 = 1$	1	1
69	$69 - 67 = 2$	4	71	$71 - 69 = 2$	4	4
70	$70 - 67 = 3$	9	72	$72 - 69 = 3$	9	9
$469 = \Sigma x$	0	$28 = \Sigma dx^2$	483 Σy		28 $= \Sigma dy^2$	$28 = \Sigma dx\ dy$

$$\text{Coefficient of correlation} = r = \frac{\Sigma dxdy}{\sqrt{\Sigma dx^2\ \Sigma dy^2}} = \frac{28}{\sqrt{28.28}} = \frac{28}{28} = 1$$

There is perfect positive correlation

$$r = \frac{\sum dx\,dy - \frac{\sum dx \sum dy}{n}}{\sqrt{\sum dx^2 - \left(\frac{\left(\sum dx\right)^2}{n}\right)}\sqrt{\sum dy^2 - \left(\frac{\left(\sum dy\right)^2}{n}\right)}}$$

$$= \frac{106 + \frac{(3)(-22)}{7}}{\sqrt{59 - \frac{3^2}{7}}\sqrt{300 - \frac{(-22)^2}{7}}}$$

$$= \frac{106 + \frac{60}{7}}{\sqrt{59 - \frac{9}{7}}\sqrt{300 - \frac{484}{7}}} = \frac{\frac{808}{7}}{\sqrt{\frac{404}{7}}\sqrt{\frac{1616}{7}}}$$

$$= \frac{808/7}{808/7} = 1$$

Karl Pearson's Product Moment Method:

In this method of coefficient of correlation is computed by

$$r = \frac{\sum\left(X - \bar{X}\right)\sum\left(Y - \bar{Y}\right)}{N\,\sigma_x\,\sigma_y}$$

where σ_x = S.D of X series

σ_y = S.D of Y series

N = number of observation

Alternative formula

$$r = \frac{\sigma_x^2 + \sigma_y^2 - \sigma_z^2}{2\,\sigma_x\,\sigma_y}$$

where $z = x - y$, σ_z = S.D of (x –y) series

Example

Find the coefficient of correlation for the following data

X	1	2	3	4	5
Y	2	5	3	8	7

Solution: We have the following table

x	y	z = x − y	x^2	y^2	z^2
1	2	−1	1	4	1
2	5	−3	4	25	9
3	3	0	9	9	0
4	8	−4	16	64	16
5	7	−2	25	49	4
$\sum x = 15$	$\sum y = 25$	$\sum z = -10$	$\sum x^2 = 55$	$\sum y^2 = 151$	$\sum z^2 = 30$

We get

$$\overline{x} = \frac{\sum x}{n} = \frac{15}{5} = 3, \qquad \overline{y} = \frac{\sum y}{n} = \frac{25}{5} = 5, \qquad \overline{z} = \frac{\sum z}{n} = \frac{-10}{5} = -2$$

$$\sigma_x^2 = \frac{\sum x^2}{n} - (\overline{x})^2 = \frac{55}{5} - 3^2 = 2$$

$$\sigma_y^2 = \frac{\sum y^2}{n} - (\overline{y})^2 = \frac{151}{5} - 5^2 = 5.2$$

$$\sigma_z^2 = \frac{\sum z^2}{n} - (\overline{z})^2 = \frac{30}{5} - (-2)^2 = 2$$

$$\therefore \quad r = \frac{\sigma_x^2 + \sigma_y^2 - \sigma_z^2}{2\,\sigma_x\,\sigma_y} = \frac{2 + 5.2 - 2}{2\sqrt{2}\sqrt{5.2}}$$

$$= 0.8062$$

Spearman's Rank Correlation:

In this method the individual series are ranked in order of merit. The rank coefficient of correlation coefficient is computed by the using the formula

$$\rho = 1 - \frac{6\sum d^2}{n\left(n^2 - 1\right)}$$

where $\quad d$ = difference in ranks of X from the ranks of Y

and $\quad \rho$ = rank correlation coefficient

Example: Karl Pearson's correlation coefficient between X and Y for the following data.

X:	43	54	59	68	76
Y:	105	98	84	63	50

Solution: We have n = 5

S. No	X	R_1	Y	R_2	$d = R_1 - R_2$	d^2
1	43	5	105	1	4	16
2	54	4	98	2	2	4
3	59	3	84	3	0	0
4	68	2	63	4	–2	4
5	76	1	50	5	–4	16
						$\Sigma d^2 = 40$

$$\rho = 1 - \frac{6\sum d^2}{n(n^2-1)} = 1 - \frac{6\times 40}{5(5^2-1)}$$

$$= 1 - \frac{240}{5\times 24} = 1 - 2 = -1$$

Example : In the following table recorded data shows the test scores made by 10 sales men on an intelligence test and their weekly sales

Sales men	1	2	3	4	5	6	7	8	9	10
Test scores	50	70	50	60	80	50	90	50	60	60
Sales (Rs)	25	60	45	50	45	20	55	30	45	30

salesman	Intelligence		Sales		D = difference in ranks of X and Y	d^2
	Test score	Rank	Sales	Rank		
1	50	8.5	25	9	– 0.5	0.25
2	70	3	60	1	2	4
3	50	8.5	45	5	3.5	12.25
4	60	5	50	3	2	4
5	80	2	45	5	– 3	9
6	50	8.5	20	10	– 1.5	2.25
7	90	1	55	2	– 1	1
8	50	8.5	30	7.5	1	1
9	60	5	45	5	0	0
10	60	5	30	7.5	2.5	6.25
						$\Sigma d^2 = 40$

$$R = 1 - \frac{6\left(\sum d^2 + \frac{\sum(t^3 - t)}{12}\right)}{n(n^2 - 1)}$$

$$= 1 - \frac{6}{10(10^2 - 1)} + \left(40 + \frac{4^3 - 4}{12} + \frac{3^3 - 3}{12} + \frac{3^3 - 3}{12} + \frac{2^3 - 2}{12}\right)$$

$$= 1 - \frac{6}{990}\ [40 + 9.5] = 1 - 0.3$$

$$= 0.70$$

Example :Ten competitors in a beauty contest are ranked by two judges in the following manner. Compute the coefficient of rank correlation

I	1	6	5	3	10	2	4	9	7	8
II	6	4	9	8	1	2	3	10	5	7

Solution: We have n = 10

$$\sum d^2 = (1 - 6)^2 + (6 - 4)^2 + (5 - 9)^2 + (3 - 8)^2 + (10 - 1)^2 + (2 - 2)^2$$
$$+ (4 - 3)^2 + (9 - 10)^2 + (9 - 10)^2 + (7 - 5)^2 + (8 - 7)^2$$

$$= 25 + 4 + 16 + 25 + 81 + 0 + 1 + 1 + 4 + 1$$

$$= 158$$

$$\therefore \rho = 1 - \frac{6\sum d^2}{n(n^2 - 1)}$$

$$= 1 - \frac{6(158)}{10(10^2 - 1)} = 0.042$$

7.3 Regression

The statistical method which helps us to estimate true unknown value of one variable from the known value of the related variable is called regression. The word 'Regression' was introduced by Sir Francis Galton, while studying the relationship about the heights of fathers and sons. Regression may be defined as the measure of the average relationship between two or more variables in terms of the original unit of the data.

Regression analysis is used to estimate the relation between two economic variables like income and expenditure. It predicts the value of dependent variables from the values of independent variables. Regression analysis is a mathematical measure average of the average relationship between two or more variables is terms of the original limit of the data. There are two methods of studying regression. Namely

(i) Graphic method and

(ii) Algebraic method.

In the graphic method a regression line is a straight line fitted to the data by the method least squares. It indicates the best probable value of variable corresponding to the mean value of the other. When two variables have relationship, then we can draw a regression line. If X and Y are the variables

We have two regression lines:

(i) Regression line of Y on X

(ii) Regression line of X on Y

***Regression Equation*:** Regression equation is an algebraic expression of the regression line. As there are two regression lines there are two regression equations.

(i) Regression equation of X on Y is given by

$$X = a + bY$$

where a and b are two unknown constants are parameters. By the lest square method, we can find the values of a and b. The formulae are

$$\sum X = na + b\sum Y$$

$$\sum XY = a\sum Y + b\sum Y^2$$

where n is the number of observed pairs of values

(ii) Regression equation Y on X is given by

$$Y = a + bX$$

To find the values of a and b we can use the normal equations.

$$\sum Y = na + b\sum X$$

$$\sum XY = a\sum X + b\sum X^2$$

Alternative method:

Let the equation of the line of regression be

$$Y = a + bX \qquad .....(1)$$

then we have

$$\overline{Y} = a + b\overline{X} \qquad .....(2)$$

subtracting (2) form (1) we get

$$Y - \overline{Y} = b(X - \overline{X}) \qquad ......(3)$$

The normal equations are

$$\sum Y = na + b\sum X \qquad .....(4)$$

$$\sum XY = a\sum X + b\sum X^2 \qquad .....(5)$$

Shifting the origin to ($\bar{X}, \bar{Y}$), equation (5) can be written as

$$\sum(X-\bar{X})(Y-\bar{Y}) = a\sum(X-\bar{X}) + b\sum(X-\bar{X})^2 \qquad .....(6)$$

Since $\quad r = \dfrac{\sum(X-\bar{X})(Y-\bar{Y})}{n\,\sigma_x\sigma_y}, \quad \sum(X-\bar{X}) = 0, \ \dfrac{1}{n}\sum(X-\bar{X})^2 = \sigma_x^2$

from (6) we get

$$n\,r\,\sigma_x\,\sigma_y = 0 + bn\,\sigma_x^2$$

or $\quad b = r\dfrac{\sigma_y}{\sigma_x}$

from (3), we get

$$(Y-\bar{Y}) = r\frac{\sigma_y}{\sigma_x}(X-\bar{X}) \qquad ......(I)$$

which is the regression of Y on X

$r\dfrac{\sigma_y}{\sigma_x}$ is called the regression coefficient of Y on X and is denoted by X

i.e., $\quad by_X = r\dfrac{\sigma_y}{\sigma_x}$

similarly, the line of regression of X on Y is

$$X - \bar{X} = r\frac{\sigma_y}{\sigma_x}\ (Y-\bar{Y})$$

where $r\dfrac{\sigma_y}{\sigma_x}$ is called the regression coefficient of X on Y and is denoted by b_{xy}

hence the regression equations are

$$Y - \bar{Y} = b_{yn}\ (X - \bar{X})$$

and $$X - \overline{X} = b_{xy}\ (Y - \overline{Y})$$

if, r = 0, the two lines of regressions become

$$Y - \overline{Y} \qquad \text{.....(7)}$$

and $$X - \overline{X} \qquad \text{.....(8)}$$

Which are straight lines parallel to the coordinate axes and passing through their means $\overline{Y}$ and $\overline{X}$.

The lines (7) and (8) are mutually perpendicular

If $r = \pm 1$, the two lines of regression coincide

Property 1

Correlation coefficient is the geometric mean between the regression coefficients

Proof

The regression coefficient x on y is $r\frac{\sigma_y}{\sigma_x}$, and

the regression coefficient of y on x is $r\frac{\sigma_y}{\sigma_x}$

the geometric mean between the regression coefficients is

$$\sqrt{r\ \frac{\sigma_y}{\sigma_x}\ .\ r\ \frac{\sigma_x}{\sigma_y}} = \sqrt{r^2} = r$$

= coefficient of correlation

Property 2

If one of the regression coefficient is greater than unity, the other must be less than unity

Proof

The regression coefficients are

$$b_{yx} = r\ \frac{\sigma_y}{\sigma_x} \text{ and } b_{xy} = r\ \frac{\sigma_x}{\sigma_y}$$

let $$b_{yx} > 1, \text{ then we have } \frac{1}{b_{yx}} < 1$$

but $b_{yx} \cdot b_{xy} = r^2 \leq 1$, (since $-1 \leq r \leq 1$)

$\therefore$ $b_{xy} \leq \dfrac{1}{b_{yx}} < 1$ (proved)

Similarly, if $b_{xy} > 1$, we can show that $b_{xy} < 1$

Property 3

Regression coefficients are independent of the origin but not of scale

Proof

Let $\mu \dfrac{x-a}{h}$, $v = \dfrac{y-b}{k}$

where a, b, h, k are constants

$$\therefore \quad b_{yx} = r\frac{\sigma_y}{\sigma_x} = r\frac{k\,\sigma_v}{h\,\sigma_u} = \frac{k}{h}\left(r\frac{\sigma_v}{\sigma_u}\right)$$

$$= \frac{k}{h}\left(r\frac{\sigma v}{\sigma u}\right) = \frac{k}{h} buv$$

Similarly $b_{xy} = \dfrac{h}{k} b_{uv}$

Hence, b_{yx} and b_{xy} are both independent of a and b but not of h and k

Property 4

The correlation coefficient and the two regression coefficients have the same sign

Proof

Regression coefficient of y on x = $b_{yx} = r\dfrac{\sigma_y}{\sigma_x}$

Regression coefficient of x on y = $b_{xy} = r\dfrac{\sigma_x}{\sigma_y}$

Since σ_x and σ_y are both positive b_{yx} and b_{xy} have the same sign.

***Example* 1:** For the following data, find the regression lines by applying the method of squares

X	5	10	15	20	25
Y	20	40	30	60	50

***Solution*:**

X	y	X^2	Y^2	XY
5	20	25	400	100
10	40	100	1600	400
15	30	225	900	450
20	60	400	3600	1200
25	50	625	2500	1250
75	200	1375	9000	3400

$\therefore \quad \sum x = 75, \sum y = 200, \sum x^2 = 1375, \sum y^2 = 9000, \sum xy = 3400$

Regression of Y on X

The normal equations are

$na + b\sum x = \sum y$

$a\sum x + b\sum x^2 = \sum xy$

$\therefore \quad 5a + 75b = 200$

$75a + 13756 = 3400$

Solving we get

$a = 16, b = 1.6$

$\therefore$ The regression of Y on X is

$Y = a + bx = 16 + 1.6\,x$

i.e., $\quad Y = 16 + 1.6\,x$

the regression of X on Y

the normal equations are

$n\,a + b\sum y = \sum x$

$a\sum y + \sum y^2 = \sum xy$

i.e $\quad 5\,a + 200\,b = 75$

$200\,a + 900\,b = 3400$

Solving the above equations we get

$a = -1, \quad b = 0.4$

∴ The regression of X on Y is

$$X = -1 + 0.4$$

Hence the equations of regression on line are

$$Y = 16 + 1.6X$$

and $X = -1 + 0.4\,Y$

***Example* 2:** Obtain the lines of regressions and hence find the coefficient correlation for the data

x	1	2	3	4	5	6	7
y	9	8	10	12	11	13	14

Solution: Here $\bar{x} = \frac{\sum x}{n} = \frac{1+2+3+4+5+6+7}{7} = \frac{28}{7} = 4$

$$\bar{y} = \frac{\sum y}{n} = \frac{9+8+10+12+11+13+14}{7} = \frac{77}{7} = 11$$

x	y	$X = x - \bar{x}$ $= n - 4$	$Y = y - \bar{y}$ = $y - (1)$	XY	X^2	Y^2
1	9	–3	–2	6	9	4
2	8	–2	–3	6	4	9
3	10	–1	–1	1	1	1
4	12	0	1	0	0	1
5	11	1	0	0	1	0
6	13	2	2	4	4	4
7	14	3	3	9	9	9
28	77			26	28	28

we have

$$\sum x = 28, \quad \sum y = 77, \quad \sum XY = 26, \quad \sum X^2 = 28, \quad \sum Y^2 = 28$$

$$b_{yx} = r\,\frac{\sigma_y}{\sigma_x} = \frac{\sum XY}{\sum X^2} = \frac{26}{28} = 0.93$$

$$b_{xy} = r\,\frac{\sigma_x}{\sigma_y} = \frac{\sum XY}{\sum Y^2} = \frac{26}{28} = 0.93$$

Regression of y on x is

$$y - \overline{y} = b_{yx}(x - \overline{x})$$

i.e $$y - 11 = 0.93\,(x - y)$$

or $$y = 0.93x + 7.28$$

Regression of x on y is

$$x - \overline{x} = b_{xy}(y - \overline{y})$$

$$x - 4 = 0.93\,(y - 11)$$

or $$x = 0.93x - 6.23$$

$$r = \sqrt{b_{yx}\, b_{xy}} = \sqrt{(0.93)(0.93)} = 0.93$$

***Example* 3:** Computer the correlation coefficient and the lines of regression for the data

x	1	2	3	4	5
y	2	5	3	8	7

x	y	z = x − y	x^2	y^2	z^2
1	2	–1	1	4	1
2	5	–3	4	25	9
3	3	0	9	9	0
4	8	–4	16	64	16
5	7	–2	25	49	4
15	25	–10	55	151	30

we have

$$\sum x = 15,\ \sum y = 25,\quad \sum z = -10,\quad \sum x^2 = \mathbf{55}$$

$$\sum y^2 = 151,\qquad \sum z^2 = 30,\qquad n = 5$$

$$\therefore\ \overline{x} = \frac{\sum x}{n} = \frac{15}{5} = 3,\qquad \overline{y} = \frac{\sum y}{n} = \frac{25}{5} = 5,\qquad \overline{z} = \frac{\sum z}{n} = \frac{-10}{5} = -2$$

$$\sigma_x^2 = \frac{\sum x^2}{n} - (\overline{x})^2 \qquad\qquad \sigma_y^2 = \frac{\sum y^2}{n} - (\overline{y})^2$$

$$= \frac{55}{5} = -3^2 = 11 - 9 \qquad\qquad = \frac{151}{5} - (5)^2$$

$$= 2 \qquad\qquad = 30.2 - 25 = 5.2$$

$$\sigma_z^2 = \frac{\sum z^2}{n} - (\bar{z})^2 = \frac{30}{5} = (-2)^2 = 6 - 4 = 2$$

$$\therefore \qquad \sigma_x = \sqrt{2}, \qquad \sigma_y = \sqrt{5.2}, \qquad \sigma_z = \sqrt{2}$$

$$r = \frac{\sigma_x^2 + \sigma_y^2 - \sigma_z^2}{2\,\sigma_x \sigma_y} = \frac{2 + 5.2 - 2}{2\sqrt{2}\sqrt{5.2}} = 0.8062$$

Regression equation of Y on X:

$$Y - \bar{Y} = r\,\frac{\sigma_y}{\sigma_x}\,(x - \bar{x})$$

$$y - 5 = (0.8062)\,\frac{\sqrt{5.2}}{\sqrt{2}}\,(x - 3)$$

or $\qquad y = (1.306)\,(x - 3) + 5$

i.e $\qquad y = 1.306\,x + 0.918$

Regression equation of X on Y is

$$X - \bar{X} = r\,\frac{\sigma_x}{\sigma_y}\,(y - \bar{y})$$

or $\qquad X - 3 = (0.8062)\,\dfrac{\sqrt{2}}{\sqrt{5.2}}\,(y - 5)$

or $\qquad x = 0.562\,y + 0.49$

Alternative method:

The regression coefficient of Y on X is given by

$$b_{YX} = \frac{N\sum XY - \sum X \sum Y}{N\sum X^2 - \left(\sum X\right)^2}$$

and, the regression coefficient of X on Y is given by

$$b_{XY} = \frac{N\sum XY - \sum X \sum Y}{N\sum Y^2 - \left(\sum Y\right)^2}$$

***Example* 1:** Find the regression of X on Y from the following data

$$\sum X = 24, \quad \sum Y = 44, \qquad \sum XY = 306, \quad \sum X^2 = 164, \quad \sum Y^2 = 574$$

and N = 4

Solution: Here we have $\bar{X} = \dfrac{\sum X}{N} = \dfrac{24}{4} = 6$

$$\bar{Y} = \frac{\sum Y}{N} = \frac{44}{4} = 11$$

Regression coefficient of X on Y is $b_{xy} = r\,\dfrac{\sigma_x}{\sigma_y}$

$$= \frac{N\sum XY - \sum X \sum Y}{N\sum Y^2 - \left(\sum Y\right)^2} = \frac{4(306) - (24)(44)}{4(574) - (44)^2}$$

$$= \frac{1224 - 1056}{2296 - 1936} = \frac{168}{360} = 0.466$$

The regression equation of X on Y is:

$$X - \bar{X} = r\,\frac{\sigma_x}{\sigma_y}\,(Y - \bar{Y})$$

i. e $\quad X - 6 = 0.466\,(Y - 11)$

or $\quad X = 0.466\,y - 5.126 + 6$

i.e $\quad X = 0.466\,Y + 0.874$

***Example* 2:** From the following data obtain the regression equation of Y on X

Variable	X	Y
Mean	47	96
Variance	64	81

Correlation coefficient r between X and Y = 0.36

Solution: We have $\bar{X} = 47, \qquad \bar{Y} = 96$

$$\sigma_x = \sqrt{64} = 8, \qquad \sigma_y = \sqrt{81} = 9$$

and $\quad r = 0.36$

regression equation of Y on X is

$$Y - \bar{Y} = r\,\frac{\sigma_y}{\sigma_x}\,(X - \bar{X})$$

i.e $$Y - 96 = 0.36 \left(\frac{9}{8}\right) (X - 47)$$

i.e $$Y - 96 = 0.405 (X - 47)$$

or $$Y = 0.405 X - 19.035 + 96$$

or $$Y = 0.405 X + 76.965$$

***Example* 3:** Computer $\bar{x}$, $\bar{y}$ and r from the following equation of regression lines :

$$2x + 3y + 1 = 0, \qquad x + 6y - 4 = 0$$

Solution: The regression lines pass through ($\bar{x}$, $\bar{y}$)

Therefore we get

$$2\bar{x} + 3\bar{y} + 1 = 0$$

$$\bar{x} + 6\bar{y} - 4 = 0$$

Solving these equations we obtain $\bar{x} = -2$, $\bar{y} = 1$

The equation $2x + 3y + 1 = 0$ can be written as

$$x = \frac{-3}{2} y \frac{-1}{2} \quad \text{.....(1)}$$

and the equation $x + 6y - 4 = 0$ can be written as

$$y = \frac{-1}{6} x + \frac{2}{3} \quad \text{.....(2)}$$

from (1), and (2)

$$b_{xy} = -\frac{3}{2}, \quad b_{yx} = -\frac{1}{6}$$

$$\therefore \; b_{yx} \times b_{xy} = \frac{-3}{2} \times \frac{-1}{6} = \frac{1}{4}$$

$$r^2 = \frac{1}{4} \quad \Rightarrow \quad r = \pm \frac{1}{2}$$

r is negative i.e

r = – 0.5

$$\therefore \quad \bar{x} = -2, \quad \bar{y} = 1, \quad r = -0.5$$

Exercise 7.2

1. Obtain the lines of regression and hence find the coefficient of correlation for the data

x	1	3	4	2	5	8	9	10	13	15
y	8	6	10	8	12	16	16	10	32	32

Ans. Y = 1.76 x + 2.68, x = 0.44 y + 0.4, r = 0.88

2. Compute the coefficient of correlation and the equation of the lines of regression for the data

x	1	2	3	4	5	6	7
y	9	8	10	12	11	13	14

Ans. (r = 0.93 , y = 0.93 x + 7.8, x = 0.93 y – 6.23)

3. Given

	X-Series	Y-Series
Mean	18	100
S.D	14	20

r = 0.8

Write down the equation of the lines of regression and hence find the most probable value of y when x = 70

Ans. y = 1.14 x + 79.48, x = 0.56 y – 38, 159.28

4. From the following equations of lines of regression compute $\overline{x}$, $\overline{y}$, r

$$y = 0.516\,x + 33.73, \qquad X = 0.512\,y + 32.52$$

Ans. $\overline{x} = 67.67$, $\overline{y} = 68.65$, r = 0.51

5. Computer $\overline{x}$, $\overline{y}$ and r form the equation of regression lines

$$3\,x + 2\,y - 26 = 0, \qquad 6x + y - 31 = 0$$

Ans. $\overline{x} = 4$, $\overline{y} = 7$, r = 0.5

6. Compute the coefficient of correlation and obtain the equation of regression lines

x	77	54	27	52	14	35	90	25	56	60
y	35	58	60	40	50	40	35	56	34	42

Ans. y = – 0.28 x + 58.67, x = – 1.56 y + 119.26, r = – 0.66

7. Obtain the lines of regression from the following data

x	17	18	19	19	20	20	21	22	21	23
y	12	16	14	11	15	19	22	15	16	20

Ans. y = 1.16x – 7.2, x = 0.32 y + 14.82, r = 0.39

8. Show that if θ is the angle between the lines of regression, then

$$\tan\theta = \frac{\sigma_x\,\sigma_y}{\sigma_x^2 + \sigma_y^2}\left(\frac{1-r^2}{r}\right)$$

9. Find the coefficient of correlation and obtain the least square regression line of y on x for the data

x	1	2	3	4	5	6	7	8	9
y	9	8	10	12	11	13	14	16	15

Ans. $y = 0.95\,x + 7.25$

10. Find the coefficient of correlation between x and y from the data

x	78	89	97	69	59	79	68	57
y	125	137	156	112	107	138	123	108

Ans. 0.96

11. If $r = 0$ show that the two lines of regression are parallel to the axes

12. Calculate the coefficient of correlation for the following ages of husbands and wives

Husbands age	23	27	28	28	29	30	31	33	35	36
Wives age	18	20	22	27	21	29	27	29	28	29

13. Two regression line are given by the equations

$$3x + 2y = 6 \quad \text{and} \quad 6x + y = 31$$

Find the mean of x and y and the coefficient of correlation

Ans. $r = 0.46, \quad \bar{x} = 9.06, \quad \bar{y} = 5.52$

Queuing Theory 8

8.1 Introduction

In this chapter we introduce queuing theorems. A group of items waiting to receive service are known as queues. At railway station booking counters, cinema hall, barbar shops and other places queues may be seen. Queues are formed to get service. When the demand for a service is more than the capacity of service facility. Queues are also known as waiting lines. A queue system consists of a group of customers waiting to be served and also the customer being served, at a particular time. The variables affecting the system are, arrival pattern, service pattern, number of service counters, queue discipline as the order in which the service is provided and customer behaviour. A queue model is developed considering all these variables. In this chapter we discuss probabilistic queuing models where both arrival and service rates are unknown and assumed to be random variables and the probability distribution is obtained on past experience.

8.2 Queuing Systems

Queuing systems are described by:

(i) the arrival pattern
(ii) the service pattern
(iii) the queue discipline
(iv) customer's behaviour

(i) *Arrival Pattern*: The way in which the customers arrive and join the system is called arrival pattern. Generally the customers in more or less random fashion. Therefore the arrival pattern can best be described in terms of probabilities and consequently the probability distribution for inter arrival times must be defined. We consider those queuing systems in which the customers in Poisson fashion. Mean arrival rate is denoted by λ.

(ii) *Service Pattern*: The service mechanism is specified when it is known how many customers can be served at a time. What is the statistical distribution of the service distribution and when the service is available. Service time may be a constant or it may be a random variable. Distribution service time is negative exponential distribution.

The mean service rate is denoted by μ.

(iii) The Queue discipline. The rule which determines the formation of queue, the manner of customer's behaviour while waiting and the manner in which they are chosen for service is known as queue discipline.

Some of the queue service disciplines are

FIFO – First in, First out (or FCFS)

LIFO – Lastin, First out (or LCFS)

SIRO – Service in Random order

(iv) *Customer's behaviour*: The customers may behave in one of following ways:

(a) *Balking*: A customer may leave the queue, if there is no waiting space

(b) *Reneging*: The customer may become impatient and leave the queue; which is called reneging.

(c) *Priorities*: In some cases the customers are served before others regardless of their order of arrival which known as priority.

(d) *Jockeying*: Customers may jump from one queue to another, which is called jockeying.

8.3 Transient State

A Queuing system is said to be in steady state when its operating characteristics are dependent of time.

8.4 Steady State

A queuing system is said to be in steady state when its operating characteristics are independent of time.

If $P_n(t)$ = n customers in the system at time t then,

then, $$\underset{t \to 0}{\mathrm{Lt}} P_n(t) = P_n$$

i.e., $$\frac{d}{dt} P_n(t) = \frac{dp_n}{dt}$$

8.5 Kendal's Notation

A queuing model may be completely specified and symbolically represented in the form

$$(a/b/c) : (d/e)$$

where

a = The type of distribution of the number of arrivals per unit time

b = The type of distribution of the service time or departure distribution

c = Number of servers

d = capacity of the system

e = Queue discipline

Notation used in this chapter are:

n = number of customers in the system

S_n = the state in which there are n customers in the system

$P_n(t)$ = steady state probability having n customers in the system

λ_n = mean arrival rate (when there are n customers in the system)

μ_n = mean service rate (when there are n customers in the system)

λ = mean arrival rate when λ_n is constant for all n

μ = mean service rate when $(n \geq 1)$

$\rho = \dfrac{\lambda}{\mu}$ = Traffic intensity ($P < 1$, for steady state)

$f_s(w)$ = P.d.f of waiting time in the system

$f_q(w)$ = P.d.f of waiting time in the queue

L_s = average (expected) number of customers in the system

L_q = average (expected) number of customers in queue

W_s = average waiting time of a customer in the system

W_q = average waiting time of a customer in the queue

W_w = average waiting time of a customer in the queue, if he has to wait

8.6 Queuing Models

Queuing models can be classified as follows:

(i) *Probability models*: When there is uncertainity in both arrival rate and service rate and are assumed to be random variables.

(ii) *Deterministic models*: Both arrival rate and service rate are constants.

(iii) *Mixed models*: When either the arrival rate or the service rate is known and the other is not known.

In this chapter we consider only probabilistic models which are denoted by the symbols: (M:M:1), (∞/F/F0), (M:M:S) : (∞ : F:F0), : M stands for Markov.

Arrivals and considered as 'births' into the system and departures are considered as 'deaths'.

8.7 Types of Service Systems

(a) A single channel, single phase system

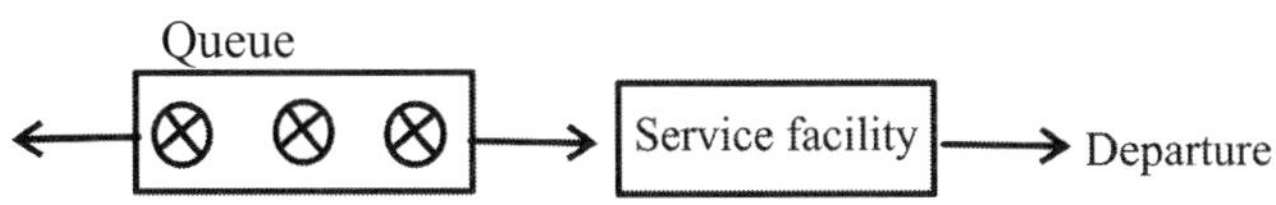

(b) Service facility in series

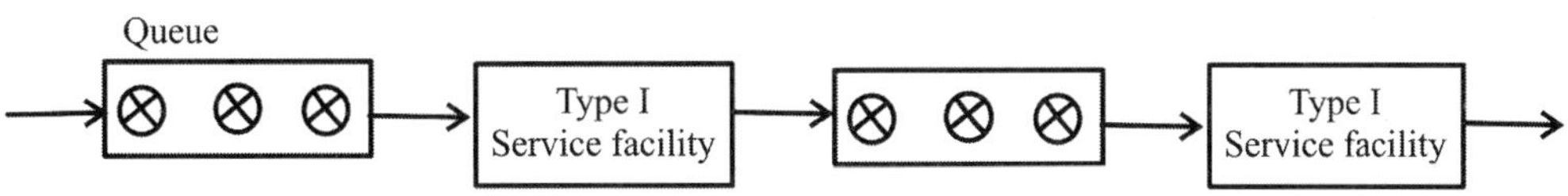

In this model a customer enters the queue and gets one kind of service and again moves to the next service station to get the service and so on and ultimately leaves the system.

8.8 Multiple, Parallel Facilities with Single Queue

In this model there are more than one server. Each server provides the same facilities.

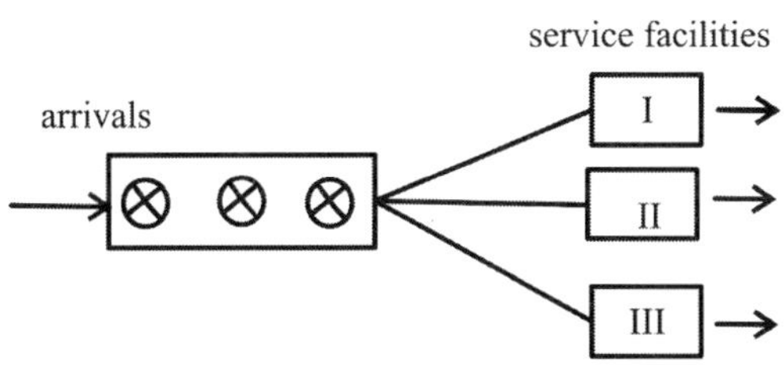

Multiple parallel facilities with multiple queues

In this model there are more queues which are parallel getting the same type of service facilities.

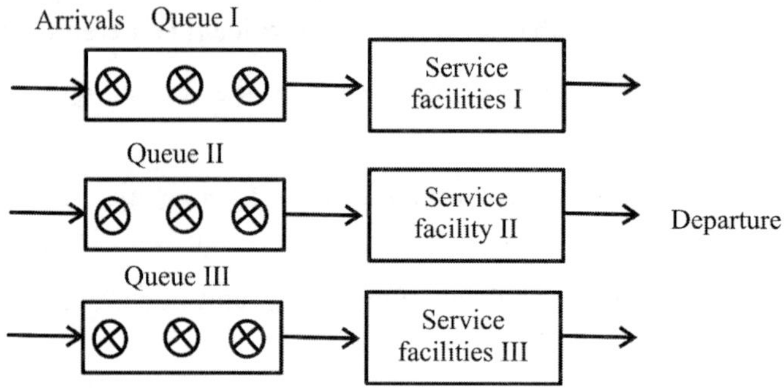

8.9 Arrival Theorem

Theorem:

If the arrivals are completely random, then the probability distribution of a number of arrivals in a fixed time interval follows a Poisson distribution.

Proof:

To prove the theorem we make the following assumptions

(i) Assume that there are n limits in the system at time t, and the probability that exactly are a arrival will occur during the small time interval Δt given by $\lambda \Delta t$.

(ii) Δt is considered to be so small that the probability of more than one arrival in time Δt is almost zero.

(iii) The process has independent increments. We wish to determine the probability of n arrivals in a time interval of length t, denoted by $P_n(t)$.

Case 1

When $n > 0$, these may be two mutually exclusive ways of having n units at time $t + \Delta t$.

(i) These are $(n - 1)$ units in the system at time t, and one arrival takes place during Δt.

Adding the two probabilities, we get

$$P_n(t + \Delta t) = P_n(t)(1 - \lambda \Delta t) + P_{n-1}(t) \lambda \Delta t \qquad .....(1)$$

Case 2

When $n = 0$

we have

$$P_0(t + \Delta t) = P_0(t)(1 - \lambda \Delta t) \qquad .....(2)$$

Rewriting the equations (1) and (2) and dividing throughout by Δt, we get

$$\frac{P_n(t + \Delta t) - P_n(t)}{\Delta t} = -\lambda P_n(t) + \lambda P_{n-1}(t)$$

and $$\frac{P_0(t+\Delta t) - P_0(t)}{\Delta t} = -\lambda\, P_0(t)$$

as $\Delta t \to 0$, we get

$$P_0^{'}(t) = -\lambda\, P_0(t) \qquad \text{for } n = 0 \qquad .....(3)$$

and $$P_n^{'}(t) = -\lambda\, P_n(t) + \lambda\, P_{n-1}(t) \qquad .....(4)$$

Equation (3) can be written as

$$\frac{P_0^{'}(t)}{P_0(t)} = -\lambda$$

or $$\frac{d}{dt}(\log P_0(t)) = -\lambda$$

integrating with respect to t, we get

$$\text{Log } P_0(t) = -\lambda t + A \qquad .....(5)$$

The constant A is determined such that

$$P_n(0) = \begin{bmatrix} 1, & n = 0 \\ 0, & n > 0 \end{bmatrix}$$

Substituting n = 0, $P_0(0) = 1$ in eq. (5) we get A = 0

$\therefore$ $$\log P_0(t) = -\lambda t$$

or $$P_0(t) = e^{-\lambda t}$$

Putting n = 1 in eq. (4) we get

$$P_1^{1}(t) = -\lambda\, P_1(t) + \lambda\, P_0(t)$$

or $$P_1^{1}(t) = -\lambda\, P_1(t) + \lambda\, e^{-pt}$$

or $$P_1^{1}(t) + \lambda\, P_1(t) = \lambda\, e^{-\lambda t}$$

which is a differential equation of order one

The integrating factor of the equation is

$$e^{\int \lambda\, dt} = e^{\lambda t}$$

Hence the solution of the equation is

$$P_1(t)\, e^{\lambda t} = \int \lambda\, e^{\lambda t}\, e^{-\lambda t}\, dt + B$$

i.e., $$P_1(t)\, e^{\lambda t} = \lambda t + B \qquad .....(6)$$

Putting t = 0 in eq. (6) we get B = 0

$$\therefore \qquad P_1(t) = \frac{\lambda t\, e^{-\lambda t}}{1!}$$

Similarly we get

$$P_2(t) = \frac{(\lambda t)^2\, e^{-\lambda t}}{2!}$$

$$P_3(t) = \frac{(\lambda t)^3\, e^{-\lambda t}}{3!}$$

$$P_n(t) = \frac{(\lambda t)^n\, e^{-\lambda t}}{n!}$$

Which is a Poisson distribution formula

8.10 Properties of Poisson Arrivals

(i) The arrival mean is λt and variance is λt

(ii) The probability that there are no arrivals

$$= P_0(\Delta t) = 1 - \lambda \Delta t$$

(iii) The probability that there is one arrival is

$$= P_1(\Delta t) = \lambda\, \Delta t$$

(iv) The probability that there are 2 or more arrivals

$$= P_n(\Delta t) = 0 \qquad (n \geq 2)$$

8.11 Pure Birth and Death Process

$$(M|M| : \infty FCFS)$$

Here the service discipline is first come first serve.

λ = Mean arrival rate

M = Mean service rate

8.12 Steady State Equations

The probability that there will be n units in the system at time $(t + \Delta t)$ is

$$P_n(t + \Delta t)$$

There are 4 Possibilities:

(i) These are (n – 1) units in the system at time t and one arrival occur in time Δt and nobody served in time Δt

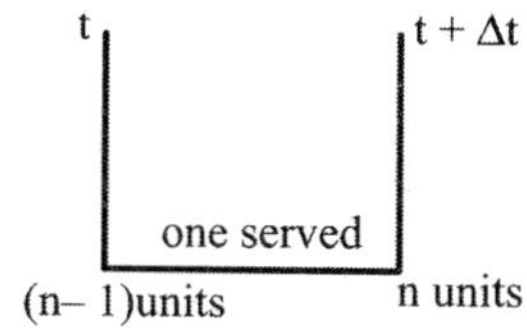

The probability in this case

$$= P_{n-1}(t)\ \lambda\Delta t\ (1 - \mu\ \Delta t)$$

The probability that no one is several in time Δt is $1 - \mu\ \Delta t$

(ii) These are n units in the system at time t, no arrival occur in time Δt and no units curved in time Δt

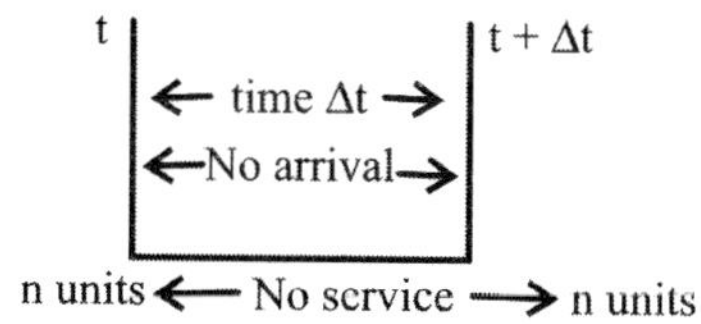

The probability in this was is

$$P_n\ (t)\ (1 - \lambda\ \Delta t)\ (1 - \mu\ \Delta t)$$

(iii) These are (n + 1) units in the system at time t, no unit arrived in time Δt and one unit is served is time Δt

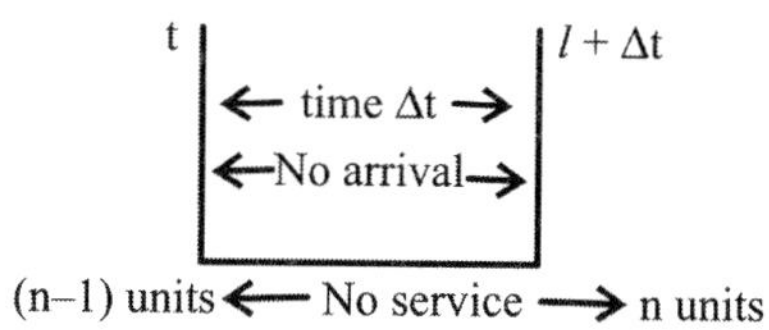

The probability is this case is $P_n(t)\ (1 - \lambda\ \Delta t)\ \mu\ \Delta t$

(iv) These are n units at time t, one arrived in time Δt and one served

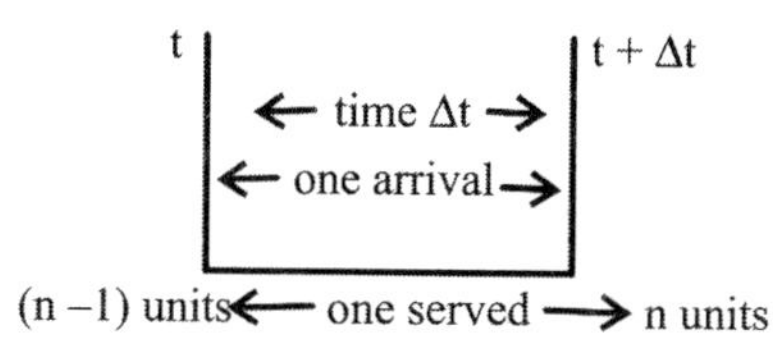

This case is not considered since $(\Delta t)^2$ occurs

We can write $P_n(t + \Delta t)$ as follows

$$P_n(t + \Delta t) = P_n(t)(1 - (\lambda + u)\Delta t) + P_{n-1}\lambda\Delta t + P_{n+1}(t)\mu\Delta t + P_n(t)(\lambda\mu)(\Delta t)^2$$

from the above equation we obtain

$$\underset{\Delta t \to 0}{\text{Lt}} \frac{P_n(t + \Delta t) - Pn(t)}{\Delta t} = -(\lambda + \mu)P_n(t) + \lambda P_{n-1}(t) + \mu P_{n+1}(t)$$

In the steady state $P_n^1(t) \to 0$, $P_n(t) \to P_n$

$$\therefore \qquad 0 = -(\lambda + \mu)P_n + \lambda P_{n-1} + \mu P_{n+1} \qquad .....(1)$$

Probability that there will be no unit at time $(t + \Delta t)$ will be the sum of the following independent probabilities

(i) Prob (that there is no unit in the system at time t and no arrival in Δt)

$$= P_0(t)(1 - \lambda\Delta t)$$

(ii) Prob (that there is one unit in the system at time t, are unit served in Δt, and no arrival in Δt)

$$= P_1(t)\mu\Delta t(1 - \lambda\Delta t)$$

adding these probabilities

$$P_0(t + \Delta t) = P_0(t)(1 - \lambda\Delta t) + P_1(t)\mu\Delta t(1 - \lambda\Delta t)$$

i.e.,

$$\frac{P_0(t + \Delta t) - P_0(t)}{\Delta t} = - >P_0(t) + P_1(t)u\Delta t \times (1 - \lambda\Delta t)$$

as $\Delta t \to 0$ we get

$$0 = -\lambda P_0 + \mu P_1$$

i.e.,

$$P_1 = \frac{\lambda}{\mu}P_0$$

taking n = 1 in eq. (1) we get

$$P_2 = \frac{\lambda}{\mu}P_1 = \left(\frac{\lambda}{\mu}\right)^2 P_0$$

:

$$P_n = \left(\frac{\lambda}{\mu}\right)^n P_0 \qquad \text{for } n \geq 0$$

since $$\sum_{n=0}^{\infty} P_n = 1$$

i.e., $$P_0 + \frac{\lambda}{\mu} P_0 + \left(\frac{\lambda}{\mu}\right)^2 P_0 + \ldots = 1$$

or $$P_0\left(1 + \frac{\lambda}{\mu} + \left(\frac{\lambda}{\mu}\right)^2 + \ldots..\right) = 1$$

or $$P_0\left(\frac{1}{1-\frac{\lambda}{\mu}}\right) = 1$$

for $\frac{\lambda}{\mu} < 1$ the series on LHS is an Infinite geometric series.

The first term = 1. The common ratio = $\frac{\lambda}{\mu} = \rho$

$$\therefore \qquad P_0 = 1 - \frac{\lambda}{\mu} = 1 - P$$

$$P_n = \left(\frac{\lambda}{\mu}\right)^n P_0 = \left(\frac{\lambda}{\mu}\right)^n \left(1 - \frac{\lambda}{\mu}\right)$$

i.e., $$P_n = \rho^n (1 - \rho)$$

The probability that queue size is greater than or equal to N.

We have $$\sum_{n=N}^{\infty} P_n = \sum_{n=0}^{\infty} P_n - \sum_{n=0}^{N-1}$$

$$= 1 - (P_0 + P_1 + P_2 + \ldots + P_{N-1})$$

$$= 1 - P_0(1 + \rho + \rho^2 + \ldots + \rho^{N-1})$$

$$= 1 - P_0 \frac{\left(1-\rho^N\right)}{1-\rho}$$

$$= 1 - \frac{(1-P)\left(1-\rho^N\right)}{1-\rho}$$

$$= 1 - (1 - P^N) = \rho^N$$

Pure birth process

Two cases arise

Case (i)

There are n units of time t in the system and no departure occurs in time Δt

The probability that there are n units in the system at time $1 + \Delta t$ is $P_n(t)\,(1 - \mu\,\Delta t)$

Where $1 - \mu\,\Delta t$ = The probability that there are no units served in time Δt

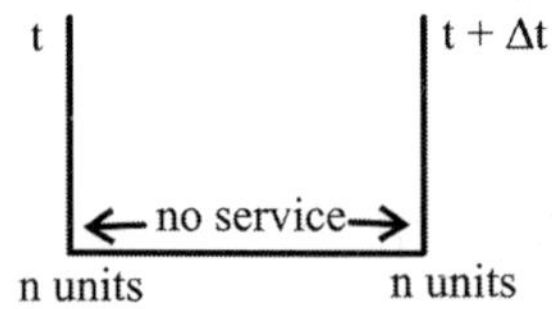

Case (ii)

These are (n + 1) limits in the system and are is served in Δt:

The probability in this case is $P_{n+1}(t)\,\mu\,\Delta t$

where $\mu\,\Delta t$ = probability that one is served in Δt

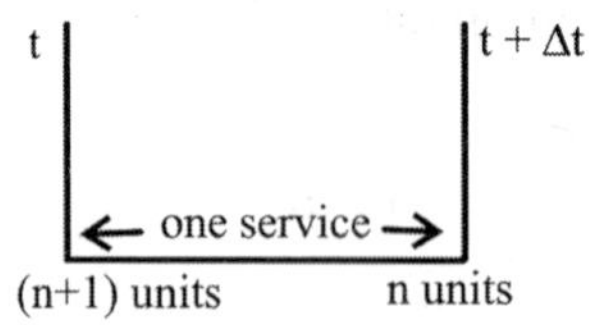

Therefore we get

$$P_n(t + \Delta t) = P_n(t)\,(1 - \mu\,\Delta t) + P_{n+1}(t)\,\mu\,\Delta t$$

$$\Rightarrow \quad P_n(t + \Delta t) - P_n(t) = -\mu\,P_n(t)\,\Delta t + P_{n+1}(t)\,\mu\,\Delta t$$

or $$\frac{P_n(t + \Delta t) - P_n(t)}{\Delta t} = -\mu\,P_n(t) + P_{n+1}(t)$$

taking limits as $\Delta t \to 0$ we get

$$P_n'(t) = -\mu\,P_n(t) + \mu\,P_{n+1}(t)$$

If these are exactly n units in the system, we have, $P_{N+1} = 0$

$$\Rightarrow \quad P_N(t + \Delta t) = P_N(t)\,.\,(1 - \mu\,\Delta t)$$

$$\Rightarrow \quad \frac{P_N(t + \Delta t) - P_N(t)}{\Delta t} = -\mu\,P_N(t)$$

taking limit as $\Delta t \to 0$, we get

$$P_N'(t) = -\mu\,P_N(t)$$

(i) There are no units and service in not possible

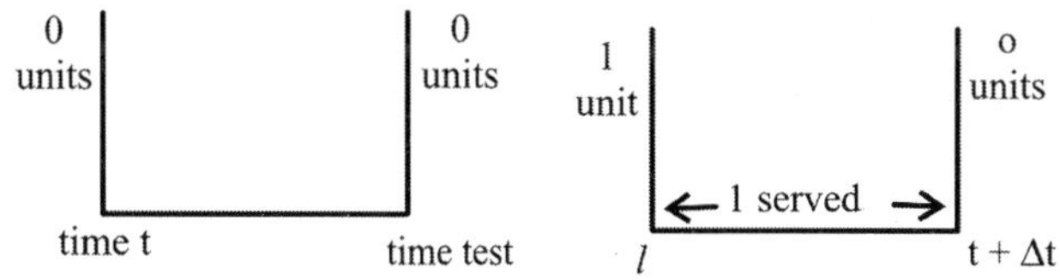

(ii) There is one unit at time t and one served in time Δt so 0 units at time $t + \Delta t$

The probability that there are 0 unit at time $t + \Delta t = P_o(t + \Delta t)$

$$= P_o(t)\,\mu\,P_1(t)$$

$$\therefore\; P_o(t + \Delta t) - P_o(t) = \mu\,\Delta t\,P_1(t)$$

$$\frac{P_o(t+\Delta t) - P_o(t)}{\Delta t} = \mu\,P_1(t)$$

Taking limit as $\Delta t \to 0$, we get

$$P_o'(t) = \mu\,P_1\,t)$$

The differential equations are

$$P_N'(t) = -\mu\,P_n(t) \qquad \text{when } n = N$$

$$P_n'(t) = \mu\,P_n(t) + \mu_{P_{n+1}}(t), \qquad 0 < n < N$$

$$P_o'(t) = \mu\,P_1(t), \qquad n = 0$$

Solving the equations

$$P_N(t) = -\mu\,P_N(t), \quad P_N(t) = ce^{-\mu t}$$

$$P_N(0) = 1$$

we get $c = 1$

$$\therefore \qquad P_N(t) = ce^{-\mu t}$$

Putting $n = N - 1$ in $P_n'(t) = \mu\,P_n(t) + \mu\,P_{n+1}(t)$

we get

$$P_{N-1}(t) = \mu\,P_{N-1}(t) + \mu\,P_N(t)$$

$$= -\mu\,P_N(t) + \mu\,e^{-\mu t} \qquad (\text{since } P_N(t) = e^{-\mu t})$$

$$\therefore \qquad P_{N-1} + \mu\,P_N(t) = \mu\,e^{-\mu t}$$

The above equation is a linear equation of the form

$$\frac{dy}{dx} + Py = Q$$

The integrating factor of the equation is

$$\int_e \mu\ dt = e^{\mu t}$$

The solution is $\quad P_{N-1}(t)\, e^{\mu t} = \int \mu\, e^{\mu t}\, e^{-\mu t}\, dt$

$$= \int \mu\ dt = \mu t + c$$

$\therefore \quad P_{N-1}(t) = \mu t\, e^{-\mu t} + ce^{-\mu t}$

$$P_N(0) = 0 \Rightarrow c = 0$$

$\therefore \quad P_{N-1}(t) = \mu t\, e^{-\mu t}$

If we put n = N–2, we get

$$P'_{N-2}(t) + \mu\, P_{N-2}(t) = \mu^2\, t\, e^{-\mu t}$$

The integrating factor of the equation is

$$e^{\int \mu\, dt} = e^{\mu t}$$

The solution of the equation is

$$P_{N-2}(t) = \int \mu^2 + dt = \mu^2\, \frac{t}{2} + c$$

$$P_{N-2}(0) = 0 \Rightarrow c = 0$$

$\therefore \quad P_{N-2}(t) = \dfrac{(\mu t)^2}{2!}\, e^{-\mu t}$

Proceeding in this way we get

$$P_{N-3}(t) = e^{-\mu t}\, \frac{(\mu t)^3}{4!}$$

$$P_{N-r}(t) = \frac{e^{-\mu t}(\mu t)^4}{r!}, \quad r = 0, 1, 2, \ldots\ldots, N-1$$

$$P_N(t) = \frac{e^{-\mu t}(\mu t)^{N-n}}{(N-n)!}$$

To find $P_o(t)$

since $$\sum_{n=0}^{\infty} P_n(t) = 1 = P_o(t) + \sum_{n=1}^{\infty} P_n(t)$$

i.e., $$P_0(t) = \sum_{n=0}^{N} P_n(t) - \sum_{n=1}^{N} P_n(t)$$

$$= 1 - \sum_{n=1}^{\infty} P_n(t)$$

$$\therefore \quad P_n(t) = \frac{(\mu t)^{N-n} e^{-\mu t}}{(N-n)!} \quad \text{for } n = 1, 2, \ldots\ldots\ldots\ldots, N$$

$$= 1 - \sum_{n=1}^{N} \frac{(\mu t)^{N-n} \; e^{-\mu t}}{(N-n)!} \quad \text{for } n = 0$$

Which is a truncated Poisson distribution

1. Expected number of units in the system, we have

$$L_s = \sum_{n=1}^{\infty} n \; p_n(t)$$

$$= \sum_{n=1}^{\infty} n \; \rho^n (1-\rho)$$

$$= \rho(1-\rho) \sum_{n=1}^{\infty} n \; \rho^{n-1}$$

$$= \rho(1-\rho)\left(1 + 2\rho + 3\rho^2 + \ldots..\right)$$

$$= \rho(1-\rho)(1-\rho)^2 = \frac{\rho}{1-\rho}$$

or $$L_s = \frac{\lambda}{\mu - \lambda}$$

2. Expected number of units in the Queue = L_q

   When there are n units in the system, one being served we have (n – 1) units in the Queue

$$\therefore \quad L_q = \sum_{n=1}^{\infty} (n-1)\rho_n$$

$$= \sum_{n=0}^{\infty} n\rho_n - \sum_{n=1}^{\infty} \rho_n$$

$$= \frac{\rho}{1-\rho} - \sum_{n=1}^{\infty} \rho_n + \rho_0$$

$$= \frac{\rho}{1-\rho} - 1 + (1-\rho)$$

$$= \frac{\rho^2}{1-\rho}$$

We no derive the following useful formulae

(i) Expected number of units in the system:

$$L_S = \sum_{n=1}^{\infty} n\ \rho_n(t) = \sum_{n=1}^{\infty} n\ \rho_n(1-\rho)$$

$$= \rho(1-\rho) \sum_{n=1}^{\infty} n\ \rho_{n-1}$$

$$= \rho(1-\rho)(1+2\rho+3\rho^2+......)$$

$$= \rho(1-\rho)(1-\rho)^{-2} = \frac{\rho}{1-\rho} \text{ or } \frac{\lambda}{\mu-\lambda}$$

(ii) Expected number of units in the Queue:

$$L_q = \sum_{n=1}^{\infty} (n-1)\rho_n = \sum_{n=0}^{\infty} n\rho_n - \sum_{n=1}^{\infty} \rho_n$$

$$= \frac{\rho}{1-\rho} - \sum_{n=1}^{\infty} \rho_n + \rho_0 = \frac{\rho}{1-\rho} - 1 + 1 - \rho$$

$$= \frac{\rho^2}{1-\rho}$$

(iii) Variance of Queue length

Since variance (X) = $E(X^2) - (E(X))^2$ we get

$$\text{Var}(n) = \sum_{n=1}^{\infty} n^2\rho_n - (L_s)^2 = \sum_{1}^{\infty} n^2\rho_n - \left(\frac{\rho}{1-\rho}\right)^2$$

$$= \sum_{1}^{\infty} n^2(1-\rho)\rho^n = \frac{\rho^2}{1-\rho^2}$$

$$= (1-\rho)\rho(1+2\rho+3^2\rho^2+.....) = \frac{X\mu}{(\mu-1)^2}$$

$$(\text{sin ce } \rho(1+2\rho+3\rho^2+.....)$$

(iv) Expected length of non-examples Queue $= \frac{L_s}{\rho} = \frac{\mu}{\mu-1}$

(v) Suppose that a customer arrives at w = 0. The probability that a unit is served in time dw is Ψ(w) where Ψ(w) is probability density function let Ψ(w) dw denote the probability that a customer begins to be served in the interval (w, w + dw), where w is measure from the time of his arrival. For convenience. We lable the customer as A

There are two possibilities

(i) When A arrives there are no customers in the system then the waiting time of A is zero. Hence the probability that the waiting time is 0 is given by ρ_0.

(ii) When A arrives, there are n customers in the system. Then before his service starts, all the n customer must leave the system that is (n – 1) customers must leave in (0, w) and the nth customer must leaving during (w, w + dw)

μ be the number of services that take place per unit time. Then, there will be mw services in time w. Probability that these are (n – 1) departure is n time is

$$\frac{(\mu w)^{n-1} e^{-\mu w}}{(n-1)1}$$

Thus in case (ii) the probability that there are (n – 1) services during (0, w) and one service during (w, w + dw) is

$$\Psi_n(w)dw = \frac{(\mu w)^{n-1}}{(n-1)!}\mu \, dw$$

Let w be the waiting time of a customer who has to wait such that $w \leq W \leq w +$ dw. Then we have

$$\Psi(w)dw = \text{prob}(w \leq W \leq w + dw)$$

= (Probability that there are n customers in the system)

(Probability that exactly n – 1 customers leave in (0, w)]. (The probability that nth customer leaves in (w, w + dw)]

$$= \sum_{n=1}^{\infty} \rho_n \psi_n(w)dw$$

$$= \sum_{n=1}^{\infty} \rho_n \frac{(\mu w)^{n \neq 1} e^{-\mu w} \mu dw}{(n-1)!}$$

$$= \sum_{n=1}^{\infty} \left(\frac{\lambda}{\mu}\right)^n \left(1 - \frac{\lambda}{\mu}\right) \frac{(\mu w)^{n-1} e^{-\mu w}}{(n-1)!} \mu dw$$

$$= \left(\frac{\lambda}{\mu}\right)\left(1 - \frac{\lambda}{\mu}\right) e^{-\mu w} \sum_{1}^{\infty} \frac{(\lambda w)^{n-1}}{(n-1)!} dw$$

$$= \lambda \left(1 - \frac{\lambda}{\mu}\right) e^{-\mu w} e^{\lambda w} dw$$

$$= \lambda \left(1 - \frac{\lambda}{w}\right) e^{-(\mu - \lambda)} dw$$

Therefore

$$\psi(w) = \lambda \left(1 - \frac{\lambda}{w}\right) e^{-(\mu-\lambda)w}, w > 0$$

Hence, the probability distribution density function of the waiting time distribution is

$$\psi(w) = \rho_0 = 1 - \rho$$

$$= 1 - \frac{\lambda}{\mu}, \text{ if } w = 0$$

and

$$\psi(w) = \lambda \left(1 - \frac{\lambda}{\mu}\right) e^{-(\mu-\lambda)w} \quad \text{if } w > 0$$

1. Probability that the waiting time exceeds w excluding service time is:

$$\int_0^w \psi(w) dw = \rho e^{-(\mu-\lambda)w}$$

2. The mean waiting time in the queue (excluding service time) is

$$w_q = \frac{\lambda}{\mu(\mu - \lambda)}$$

3. The mean waiting time in the system is

$$w_s = \frac{\mu}{\mu - \lambda}$$

***Example* 1:** In a public Telephone both the arrivals are on the average 15 per hour. A call on the average takes 3 minutes. If there is just one phone. Find (1) expected number of callers in the booth at any time (ii) The proportion of the time the booth is expected to be idle.

***Solution*:** Mean arrival rate $\lambda = 15$ per hour

Mean service rate $\mu = \frac{1}{3} \times 60 = 20$ per hour

(a) Expected length of the non-empty Queue

$$= \frac{\mu}{\mu - \lambda} = \frac{20}{20-15} = 4$$

(b) The service is busy $\frac{\mu}{4} = \frac{15}{20}$ hour

$\therefore$ The booth is expected to be idle $T - \frac{3}{4} = \frac{1}{4}$ hour

$= 15$ minutes

***Example* 2:** In a railway marshalling yard, goods trains arrive at a rate of 30 trains per day. Assuming that that the inter arrival time follows an exponential distribution and the service time distribution is also exponential, with an average of 36 minutes. Calculate the following

(a) The mean queue size

(b) The probability that queue size exceeds 10

(c) If the input of the train increases to an

average 33 per day.

what will be the changes in (a), (b)

***Solution*:** We have $\lambda = \frac{30}{60 \times 24} = \frac{1}{48}$

$$\mu = \frac{1}{36} \text{ trains/ minute}$$

***Example* 3:** Trains arrive at the marshalling yard at the rate 20 trains per day and the service time 40 minutes. If the time capacity of the yard is limited to 6 find

(a) The probability that the yard is empty

(b) The average number of trains in the system

Solution: The mean arrival rate = $\lambda = \dfrac{20}{60 \times 24}$

$$= \frac{1}{72} \text{ per minute}$$

Mean service rate

$$\mu = \frac{1}{40} \text{ trains/ minute}$$

$$\rho = \frac{\lambda}{\mu} = \frac{1}{72} \times \frac{40}{1} = \frac{5}{9}$$

(a) The probability that there are no trains in the yard = $P_o = 1 - \rho = 1 - \dfrac{5}{9} = \dfrac{4}{9}$

(b) The average number of trains in the system

$$= L_s = \frac{\lambda}{\mu - \lambda}$$

$$= \frac{\frac{1}{72}}{\frac{1}{40} - \frac{1}{72}} = \frac{5}{4}$$

***Example* 4:** A PC repairman finds that the time spent on jobs has an exponential distribution with mean 30 minutes. If the sets are repaired in the order, in whose they come in and if the arrival of sets is approximately Poisson with average of 10 per 8 hours per day, what is the repair man's expected time each day? How many jobs are ahead of the average set just brought in?

Solution: Mean arrival rate = $\dfrac{10}{8} = \dfrac{5}{4}$ per hour

$$\therefore \qquad \lambda = \frac{5}{4}$$

Mean service rate = $\dfrac{1}{30}$ per minute

$$\mu = \frac{1}{30} \times 60 = 2 \text{ per hour}$$

$$\rho = \frac{\lambda}{\mu} = \frac{5}{8}$$

The probability that there is no unit in the system $= P_o = 1 - \rho = 1 - \frac{5}{8} = \frac{3}{8}$

The idle time in a day $= 8\ P_o = 8 \times \frac{3}{8} = 3$ hours

Expected number of jobs $= \frac{\lambda}{\mu - \lambda} = \frac{5/4}{2 - 5/4} = \frac{5}{3}$

***Example* 5:** A computer shop has a laser printer. The jobs for laser printing are randomly distributed, approximately a Poisson distribution with mean service rate of 10 jobs per hour. Since job pages vary in length, the jobs arrive at a rate of 6 per hour during the entire 8 hours work a day. If the laser printer is valued Rs 30/- per hour, determine

(a) The percent time an arriving job has to wait

(b) Average system time

(c) Average idle time cost of the printer per day [JNTU 2007]

***Solution*:** Mean arrival rate = 6 per hour $\therefore \lambda = 6$

Mean service rate $\mu = 10$ per hours

Traffic intensity $= \rho = \frac{\lambda}{\mu} = \frac{6}{10} = 0.6$

(a) The percent time an arriving job has to wait

$$= \rho \times 100 = 0.6$$

(b) Average system time $W_s = \frac{1}{\mu - \lambda} = \frac{1}{10 - 6} = \frac{1}{4} = 0.25$

(c) idle time $= 1 - \rho = 1 - 0.6 = 0.4$

Idle time per day $= (1 - \rho)\ 8 = 0.4 \times 8 = 3.2$

The cost of the per day $= 3.2 \times 30$

$= \text{Rs } 96$

$$\rho = \frac{\lambda}{\mu} = \frac{36}{48} = 0.75$$

$\therefore$ (a) length i.e mean queue size

$$= \frac{\rho}{1 - \rho} = \frac{0.75}{1 - 0.75} = \frac{0.75}{0.25} = 3 \text{ trains}$$

(b) $P(\geq 10) = (0.75)^{10}$

$= 0.056$

(c) When the input increases to 33 trains per day, we have

$$\lambda = \frac{33}{60 \times 24} = \frac{1}{480}$$

$$\mu = \frac{1}{36} \text{ trains / minute}$$

$$\therefore \quad \rho/\mu = 0.825$$

$$\text{Mean queue size} = \frac{\rho}{1-\rho} = \frac{0.825}{1-0.825} = \frac{0.825}{0.175} = 5 \text{ (approx)}$$

$$\therefore \quad P(\geq 10) = \rho^{10} = (0.825)^{10} = 0.1460$$

***Example* 6**: In a colour TV manufacturing plant, a loading unit takes exactly 10 minutes to load two TV sets into a wagon and again comes back to the position to load another set of TVs. If the arrival of TV's is a Poisson stream at an average of 2 TVs every 20 minutes. Calculate the average waiting time of 2 TV sets in a stationary state.

(JNTU 2006)

Solution:

$$\text{The mean arrival rate} = \lambda = \frac{1}{20}$$

$$\text{The mean service rate} = \mu = \frac{1}{10}$$

$$\text{The average waiting time} = \frac{\lambda}{\mu(\mu - \lambda)} = \frac{\frac{1}{20}}{\frac{1}{10} - \frac{1}{20}}$$

$$= 10 \text{ minutes}$$

***Example* 7**: On an average 96 patients per 24 hour day require the service of an emergency clinic. Also on average a patient requires 10 minutes of active attention. Assume that the facility can handle only one emergency at a time. Suppose that it costs the clinic Rs. 100 per patient treated to obtain an average servicing time of 10 minutes and that each minute of decrease in this average time would cost Rs. 10 per patient treated, how much would have to be budgeted by the clinic to decrease the average of the Queue from $1\frac{1}{3}$ patients to $\frac{1}{2}$ patient

Solution:

We have $\lambda = \frac{96}{24} = 4$ patients per hour

$$\mu = \frac{1}{10} \times 60 = 6 \text{ patients per hour}$$

Average number of patients in the Queue

$$L_q = \frac{\chi}{\mu} \cdot \frac{\chi}{\chi - \mu} = \frac{4}{6} \times \frac{4}{6-4}$$

$$= 1\frac{1}{3}$$

The number is to be reduced from $1\frac{1}{3}$ to $\frac{1}{2}$

Therefore $$L_q' = \frac{\chi}{\mu'} \cdot \frac{\chi}{\mu' - \chi}$$

i.e. $$\frac{1}{2} = \frac{\lambda^2}{\mu'^2 - \mu'\lambda}$$

or $$\frac{1}{2} = \frac{16}{\mu'^2 - 4\mu'}$$

or $$\mu'^2 - 4\mu' - 32 = 0$$

or $$(\mu' - 8)(\mu' - 4) = 0$$

$$\mu' = 8 \text{ or } -4$$

Since μ' cannot be negative, we consider $\mu' = 8$

$\therefore$ Average time required by each patient $= \frac{1}{8}$ hrs $= \frac{15}{2}$ minutes

Hence, the decrease in the time required by each patient $= 10 - \frac{15}{2} = \frac{5}{2}$ minutes

Therefore the budget required for each patient $= 100 + \frac{5}{2} \times 10$

$$= \text{Rs. } 125.00$$

***Example* 8:** Consider a self service store with one cashier. Assume poisson arrivals and exponential service times. Suppose that 9 customers arrive on the average of every 5 minutes and the cashier can serve 19 in 5 minutes, find

(a) The average number of customers Queuing for service

(b) The probability of having more than 10 customers in the system

(c) The probability that the customer has to Queue for more than 2 minutes

Solution: The mean arrival rate $= \lambda = \frac{9}{5}$ per minute

The mean service rate $\mu = \frac{10}{5} = 2$ per minute

$$\rho = \frac{\lambda}{\mu} = \frac{9}{5} \times \frac{1}{2} = \frac{9}{10} = 0.9$$

(a) The average number of customer in the Queue $= \frac{\rho^2}{1-\rho} = \frac{(0.9)^2}{1-0.9} = \frac{0.81}{0.1} = 8.1$

$\therefore$ The average number of customers = 8

(b) The probability of more than 10 customers in the system $= \rho^{10} = (0.9)^{10} = 0.3487$

(c) The probability that the customer has to queue for more than 2 minutes

$$= \int_2^{\infty} \frac{\lambda}{\mu}(\mu - \lambda) e^{-(\mu-\lambda)t} dt$$

$$= \rho e^{-(\mu-\lambda)t} = 0.9 e^{-0.4}$$

$$= 0.6033$$

Littles Formula

(Relations between L_s, L_q, w_s and w_q)

From the above formulae we have

$$L_s = \lambda\, w_s \qquad .....(8.1)$$

$$L_q = \lambda\, w_q \qquad .....(8.2)$$

But by definition. $w_s = w_q + \frac{1}{\mu}$ .....(8.3)

Multiplying (8.3) by λ, we see

$$\lambda\, w_s = \lambda\, w_q + \frac{\lambda}{\mu}$$

i.e.,
$$L_s = L_q + \frac{\lambda}{\mu}$$

Which is known as Littles formula.

***Example* 1:** Four counters are being mn on the frontier of a counters to check the passports of the tourists. The tourists choose a counter at random. If the arrives at the frontiers in poisson at the rate λ and the service time is exponential with parameter $\lambda/2$ find the steady average queue at each counter.

Solution:

$$p_o = \left[\sum_{n=0}^{3} \frac{1}{n!}\left(\frac{\lambda}{\mu}\right)^n + \frac{1}{s!}\left(\frac{\lambda}{\lambda}\right)^s \frac{\mu s}{\mu s - \lambda}\right]^{-1}$$

$$= \left[1 + 2 + \frac{2^2}{2} + \frac{2^3}{6} + \frac{1}{4!}.2^4 \frac{2\lambda}{2\lambda - \lambda}\right]^{-1}$$

$$= \left[1 + 2 + 2 + \frac{4}{3} + \frac{2}{3} - (2)\right]^{-1} = \left(\frac{23}{3}\right)^{-1}$$

$$= \frac{3}{23}$$

$\therefore$
$$L_q = \frac{1}{s.s!} \frac{\left(\frac{\lambda}{\mu}\right)^{s+1}}{\left(1 - \frac{\lambda}{\mu s}\right)} . \frac{3}{23}$$

$$= \frac{1}{4.4!} \frac{25}{\left(1 - \frac{\lambda}{2\lambda}\right)^2} . \frac{3}{23}$$

$$= \left(\frac{1}{3}\right).(4).\left(\frac{3}{23}\right) = \frac{4}{23} = 0.1739$$

***Example* 2:** A Supermarket has two gives ringing up sales at the counters. If the service time for each customer in exponential with mean 4 minutes and if the people arrive the poisson fashion at the rate 10/hr.

(a) What is the probability of having to wait for service (b) What is the expected percentage of idle time for each girl.

Solution:

(a) Probability of having to wait for service is $p(w > 0) = \dfrac{\left(\frac{\lambda}{\mu}\right)^s p_o}{s!(1-\rho)}$

We have $s = 2,\ \mu = \dfrac{1}{4},\ \lambda = \dfrac{1}{6},\ \rho = \dfrac{\lambda}{s\,\mu} = \dfrac{1}{3}$

$$p_w = \left(\sum_{n=0}^{s-1} \frac{(s\rho)^n}{n!} + \frac{(s\rho)^2}{s!(1-\rho)}\right)^{-1}$$

$$= \sum_{n=0}^{1} \frac{\left(2.\frac{1}{3}\right)^2}{n!} + \frac{\left(2.\frac{1}{3}\right)^2}{2!\left(1-\frac{1}{3}\right)}\Bigg]^{-1}$$

$$= \left(1 + \frac{2}{3} + \frac{\frac{4}{9}}{2\left(\frac{2}{3}\right)}\right)^{-1}$$

$$\therefore \qquad p(w > 0) = \frac{\left(\frac{4}{6}\right)^2\left(\frac{1}{2}\right)}{2!\left(1-\frac{1}{3}\right)} = \frac{1}{6}$$

(b) The fraction of the time, the service is busy

$$= \frac{\lambda}{s\,\mu} = \frac{1}{3}$$

The fraction of the time service remains i μ_e

$$= 1 - \frac{1}{3} = \frac{2}{3} = 67\%$$

***Example* 3:** A petrol station has two pumps. The service time follows the exponential distribution with mean 4 minutes and loss arrive for service in a poisson process at the rate of ten cars per hour. Find the probability that a customer has the wait for service what proportion of time the pump remains idle.

Solution:

We have

$$s = 2, \lambda = 10/\text{hr} \ \mu = \frac{1}{4} \text{ per minute}$$

$$= \frac{6v}{4} = 15 \text{ per hour}$$

$$\therefore \qquad \rho = \frac{\lambda}{s\mu} = \frac{10}{(2)(15)} = \frac{1}{3}$$

Therefore the proportion of the time, the pump remains busy $= \frac{1}{3}$

And, the proportion of time, the pump remains idle $= 1 - \frac{1}{3} = \frac{2}{3}$

Percentage idle period $= \frac{2}{3} \times 100$

$$= 66.66 \simeq 67\% \text{ (approximately)}$$

Probability $(w > 0) = \dfrac{p_s}{1-\rho} = \dfrac{\left(\frac{\lambda}{u}\right)}{s!} \dfrac{p_0}{1-\rho}$

$$p_0 = \left[\sum_{n=0}^{s-1} \left(\frac{s\rho}{n!}\right)^n + \frac{(s\rho)^s}{s!(1-\rho)}\right]^{-1}$$

$$= \left[\sum_{n=0}^{1} \left(\frac{\rho s}{n!}\right)^n + \frac{(\rho s)^2}{2!(1-\rho)}\right]^{-1}$$

$$= \left[1 + \frac{(\rho s)^n}{n!} + \frac{(\rho s)^2}{2!(1-\rho)}\right]^{-1}$$

$$= \left[1+\left(\frac{1}{3}\right)^2+\frac{\left(\frac{1}{3}(2)\right)}{2!\left(1-\frac{1}{3}\right)}\right]^{-1}$$

$$= \frac{1}{1+\frac{2}{3}+\frac{3}{4}.\frac{4}{\rho}} = \frac{1}{1+\frac{2}{3}.\frac{1}{3}}$$

$$= \frac{3}{3+2+1} = \frac{1}{2}$$

$$\text{Probability} = \frac{p_s}{1-\rho} = \frac{\left(\frac{\lambda}{\mu}\right)^s p_o}{s!(1-\rho)} = \frac{\left(\frac{2}{3}\right)^2\left(\frac{1}{2}\right)}{2!\left(1-\frac{1}{3}\right)}$$

$$= \frac{\left(\frac{4}{\rho}\right)\left(\frac{1}{2}\right)}{2!\left(\frac{2}{3}\right)} = \left(\frac{1}{9}\right)\left(\frac{3}{2}\right) = \frac{1}{6} = 0.1667$$

***Example* 4:** A telephone exchange has two long distance operators. The telephone company finds that during the peak load long distance calls arrive in a poisson fashion at an average rate of 15 per hour. Then length of service on these calls in approximately exponentially distributed with mean length 5 minutes.

(a) What is the probability that a subscriber will have to wait for his long distance call during the peak loass of the day.

(b) If the subscribers will wait and are serviced in turn, what is the expected waiting time.

Solution:

Here, we have

$$s = 2, \lambda = \frac{15}{60} = \frac{1}{4} \text{ and } \mu = \frac{1}{5}$$

$$\rho = \frac{\lambda}{s\mu} = \frac{5}{2\times 4} = \frac{5}{6}$$

$$p_o = \left[\sum_{n=0}^{s-1} \frac{(s\rho)^n}{n!} + \frac{(s\rho)^s}{s!(1-\rho)}\right]^{-1}$$

$$= \left[\sum_{n=0}^{1} \frac{\left(\frac{5}{4}\right)^n}{n!} + \frac{\left(\frac{5}{4}\right)^s}{2!\left(1-\frac{5}{8}\right)}\right]^{-1}$$

$$= \frac{1}{1+\frac{5}{4}+\left(\frac{5}{4}\right)^2 \cdot \left(\frac{1}{2}\right)\left(\frac{8}{3}\right)} = \frac{3}{13}$$

(i) Probability $(w > 0) = \dfrac{\left(\frac{\lambda}{\mu}\right)^s}{s!(1-\rho)} p_o$

$$= \frac{\left(\frac{5}{4}\right)^2 \left(\frac{3}{13}\right)}{2!\left(1-\frac{5}{8}\right)} = \frac{25}{52}$$

$= 0.48$

(ii) $w_q = \dfrac{L_w}{\lambda}$

$$= \frac{1}{\lambda} \cdot \frac{\rho(s\rho)^2}{(1-\rho)^2} p_o$$

$$= 4 \cdot \frac{\left(\frac{5}{8}\right)\left(\frac{5}{4}\right)^2}{2!\left(1-\frac{5}{8}\right)} \times \frac{3}{13}$$

$$= \frac{4 \times \frac{5}{8} \times \frac{25}{16}}{2 \cdot \left(\frac{3}{8}\right)} \cdot \left(\frac{3}{13}\right)$$

$$= \frac{125}{39} = 3.2 \text{ minutes}$$

***Example* 5:** Consider a box office window being manned by a single server customers arrive to purchase tickets according to poisson input process with a mean rate of 30 per hour. The time required to serve a customer has an exponential distribution with a mean of 910 seconds. Determine the following

(i) fraction of time the server is busy

(ii) the average number of customers queuing for service

Solution:

$$\text{Mean arrive rate 30/hr} \quad \therefore \lambda = \frac{30}{60} = \frac{1}{2}$$

$$\text{Mean service rate} = \frac{60}{1.5} = \frac{60}{3/2} = \frac{120}{3} = \mu = \frac{60}{1.5}/\text{hr}$$

i.e., $\mu = \frac{60}{90} = \frac{6}{9} = \frac{2}{3}$

(since 1.5 minutes = 90 seconds)

(i) fraction of the time the service is busy $= \rho = \frac{\lambda}{\mu}$

$$= \frac{\left(1/2\right)}{2/3} = \frac{3}{2 \times 2} = \frac{3}{4} = 0.75$$

(ii) Average number of customers waiting for service

$$w_q = \frac{\lambda}{\mu(\mu - \lambda)} = \frac{1/2}{2/3\left(2/3 - \frac{1}{2}\right)}$$

$$= 1/2 \times \frac{3}{2} \times \frac{1}{\left(\frac{4-3}{6}\right)} = \frac{18}{4} = 4.5$$

Exercise 8.2

1. Weavers in a textile mill arrive at a department store room to obtain spare parts needed for keeping the 100 ms running. The store is manned by one attendant. The average arrival rate of weavers per hour is 10 and service rate hour is 12. Both arrival service rate follow Poisson process. Determine

   (a) Average length of waiting time

   (b) Average time a machine spends in the system

(c) Percentage idle time of department store room

(a) 25/6 (b) 30 minutes (c) 16.67%

2. A computer shop has a laser printer. The jobs for laser printer are randomly distributed approximately a Poisson distribution with mean service rate of 10 jobs per hour. Since jobs very in length, the jobs arrive at a rate of 6 per hour during 8 hours work day. If the laser printer is valued Rs. 30/- per hour, determine

(a) The percent time an arriving job has to wait

(b) Average system time

(c) Average idle time, cost of the printer per day

Ans. (a) 60 (b) 15 minutes (c) 3.2, Rs. 96

3. Trains arrive at the marshalling yard, 20 trains per day and the service time is 40 mts. If the line capacity of the yard is limited to 6, find

(i) Probability that the yard is empty

(ii) The average number of trains in the system

Ans. (i) $\frac{4}{8}$ (ii) $\frac{5}{4}$

4. In a colour TV manufacturing plant, a loading unit takes exactly 10 minutes to load two TV sets into a wagon and again comes back to the position to load another set of TVs. If the arrival of TVs is a Poisson stream at an average of 2 TVs every 20 minutes, calculate the average waiting time of 2 TV units in a stationary state

Ans. 10 minutes

5. A super market has a cashier. During peak hours, customers arrive at a rate of 20/hour. The average number of customers that can be processed by the cashier is 24/hr. Calculate

(a) The probability that the cashier is idle

(b) The average number of customers in the queuing system

(c) The average time customer spends in the system

(d) The average number of customers in the Queue

Ans. (a) $\frac{5}{6}$ (b) 5 (c) 15 mts (d) $\frac{25}{6}$

6. Assuming the at customers arrive in a poisson fashion to the counter at super market at an average rate of 15 per hour and the service by the clerk has an exponential distribution. Determine at what average rate must a dark in order to

ensure a probability of 0.90 that the customer will not wait longer than 12 minutes.

Ans. 24.135

7. A self financing college has only one typist. Since the typing work varies in length the typing rate is randomly distributed approximately a poisson distribution with mean service rate of 8 letters per hour. The letters arrive at a rate of 5 per hour during the entire 8 hour work day. If the equipment is valued at Rs. 2 per hour and typist earns Rs. 3 per hour determine the following. (a) equipment utilization (b) the percentage of idle time of the equipment (c) the percentage of time an arrival of letter has to wait (d) expected system time (e) the average idle time cost of the equipment typist per day.

Ans. (a) 0.625 (b) 0.375 (c) 62.5% (d) 0.33 hr (e) Rs. 6

8. Customers arrive at a box office windows busy manned by a single individual, accordingly to a poisson input process with a mean rate of 20 per hour. The time requires to serve a customer has an exponential distribution with a mean of 90 seconds. Find the average waiting time of a customer in the queue. Also determine the average number of customers in the system and average queue length.

Ans. $w_q = 4.489$ min/customers $L_s = 3$ customers $L_q = 2$ customers

9. If for a period of 2 hours in the day (10 Am to 12 Am) trains arrive at the yard every 20 minutes but the service time continues to remain 36 mts. Calculate the following for the above said period.

(a) probability that the yard is empty

(b) average number of trains on the assumption that the line capacity of the yard is limited to 4 trains only

Ans. 0.0449, 3 trains

10. Machines in a factory breakdown at an exponential rate of six per hour. There is a single repair man who fixes machines at an exponential rate of eight per hour. The cost incurred in lost production when machines are out of service 10 per/hour per machine. What is the average cost rate incurred due to failed machines.

Ans. $ 20/hr]

11. Assume that the mean duration of a telephone conversation is 3 mts, and no more than 3 mts wait for the phone may be tolerated.

(i) what is the largest amount of incoming traffic that can be supported

(ii) determine the maximum call rate that can be supported

Ans. (i) $\frac{1}{2}$ (ii) $\frac{1}{6}$ calls/min

Stochastic Processes 9

9.1 Introduction

In this chapter, we study stochastic processes. The concept of Markov processes (chains) will be introduced and illustrated.

In a random experiment if a real variable X is associated, with every outcome, then X is called a stochastic variable or a random variable. It is a real valued function defined on the sample space S of the random experiment. If the value of a random variable defined on S depends not only on st S, but also on a real parameter t that varies over a set T of real numbers. We denote such a random variable by X(t) or X_t. That is corresponding to each $t \in T$ there is defined a random variable X(t) on S. The collection of all such random variables, i.e., $\{X(t) ; t \in T\}$ is called a stochastic process defined on S with t is a parameter. The set T over which t varies is called the index set of the process. For a specified value of t, the values $X_s(t)$ taken by x(t) as s sums over S are called the states of the process. The set of all possible values of X(t) form the state space of the process.

A stochastic process is said to be discrete if its state space is discrete. A discrete state process is also called a chain. Also, if the index set T is discrete, then we have a discrete parameter process. Otherwise we have a continuous parameter process. A discrete parameter process is also called stochastic sequence $\{X_n\}$, $n \in T$.

Classification of (random processes) Stochastic processes: Stochastic processes can be divided into four types:

1. Continuous stochastic process
2. Discrete stochastic process
3. Deterministic (Random process) stochastic process
4. Non-deterministic stochastic process.

9.2 Markov Process

A stochastic process { X(t) : t $\in$ T} is called a Markov process if for any $t_0 < t_1 < t_2 < \ldots < t_n < t$, the conditional distribution of X(t) for given vlues of $X(t_0)$, $X(t_1)$, $X(t_2)$, ….$X(t_n)$ depends only on $X(t_n)$

i.e.,

$$P \ X(t) \leq n \mid X(t_n) = X_n \ ; \ X(t_{n-1}) = X_{n-1}, \ X(t_0) = X]$$

$$= P(X(t) \leq X \mid X(t_n) = X_n]$$

In stochastic processes, we have two types of Markov processes.

(i) Markov Process with discrete state space

(ii) Markov process with continuous state space

9.3 Markov Chain

Let X(t) be a Markov process which possess Markov property which takes only discrete values whether t is discrete or continuous is called as Markov chain.

For example, consider the number of heads obtained in the first n tosses of a coin. The possible values are 0, 1, 2,….n.

Let

$$S_{n+1} = \begin{cases} x+1 & \text{if}\,(n+1)^{th} \text{ trial results in head} \\ x & \text{if}\,(n+1)^{th} \text{ trial result in tail} \end{cases}$$

From this we have

$$S_n = X_0 + X_1 + \ldots + X_n$$

i.e., the conditional probability of S_{n+1} given S_n depends on S_n but not on the manner how the value of S_n is derived.

If we let

$$P[X_n = a_n/X_{n-1} = a_{n-1}/X_{n-2} = a_{n-2}, \ldots, X_n = a_n\}$$

such that

$$P[X_n = a_n / X_{n-1} = a_{n-1}\} \ \forall \ n$$

then this process x_n j n = 0, 1, 2, …. is called as Markov chain.

9.4 Homogeneous Markov Chain

If P_{ij} (n –1, n) = P_{ij}(n– 1, m), then the Markov chain is called homogeneous Markov chain.

i.e., the chain is said to have stationary transition probabilities then it is called as homogeneous Markov chain.

The transition probability of Markov chain is called stochastic Matrix if

(i) $P_{ij} > 0$

(ii) $\sum_j P_{ij} = 1 \forall i$

9.5 Matrix of Transition Probabilities

The transition probabilities, will be arranged in a matrix called the matrix of transition probabilities.

$$P = \begin{bmatrix} p_{11} & p_{12} & \cdots & p_{1j} & \cdots \\ p_{21} & p_{22} & \cdots & p_{2j} & \cdot\cdot \\ \vdots & & & & \\ p_{i1} & p_{i2} & \cdots & p_{ij} & \cdots \\ \cdots & \cdots & \cdots & & \end{bmatrix}$$

9.6 Classification of States

1. State j is said to be accessible from state i if $P_{ij}^n > 0$ for some $n \geq o$.
2. Two states i and j which are accessible to each other are said to communicate
   (i) State i communicates with itself for all $i \geq 0$.
   (ii) If state i communicates with state j and state j communicate with state k, then state i communicate with state k.
3. Two states that communicates are in the same class, two states are either identical or disjoint.
4. The Markov chain is irreducible if there is only one class.
5. A state is said to be an absorbing state if no other state is accessible from it i.e., from absorbing state i, $p_{ij} = 1$.

   Markov chain is absorbing if

   (i) it has atleast one absorbing state
   (ii) It is possible to go from every non-absorbing state to atleast one absorbing state.
6. State i is said to be recurrent if starting in state *i*, the process will reenter state i with probability $P_i = 1$.

A state i is recurrent if $\sum_{n=1}^{\infty} P_{ij}^{n} = \infty$

A state i is positive recurrent, if starting in i, the expected time until the process returns to state i is finite. For, a process, a recurrent state need not be positive recurrent. Such states are called null recurrent.

7. State i is said to be transient, if starting from state i, the process will ever reenter with probability $i < 1$.

8. A state i is called an essential state if it communicates with every state it leads to

9. State is said have a period d if $P_{ij}^{n} = 0$,whenever n is not divisible by d and d is the largest integer with this property.

   If a state i is periodic with period d, the g.c.d of the set $\{n \mid P_{ij}^{n} > 0, n \geq 1\}$ is $d > 1$.

   A state is said to be a periodic if its period is 1.

10. Positive recurrent, aperiodic states called periodic.

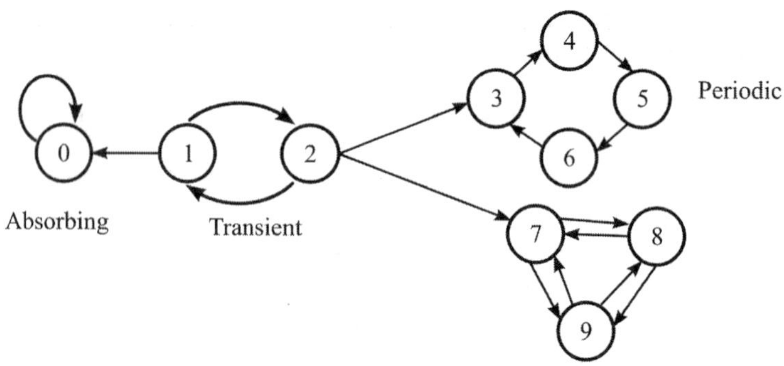

Fig. 9.1 Classification of states.

9.7 Examples of Markov Chains

(a) A random walk on the line is a Markov chain

(b) Random placement of balls. Consider a sequence of independent trials each consisting in placing a ball at random in one of the P given cells.

We say that the system is in state $\in_n$ if exactly k cells are occupied. This determines a Markov chain with states $\in_0$, $\in_1$, ... $\in_p$ and transition probabilities such that

$$Pji = \frac{j}{P}, \qquad P_{j,j+1} = \frac{P-j}{P}$$

$$P_{jk} = 0 \text{ for all other combinations of j and k}$$

If initially all cells are empty, the distribution $\{a_k\}$ is determined by $a_0 = 1$ and $a_k = 0$ for $k > 0$.

9.8 Probability Vector

A vector $v = (v_1, v_2, \ldots, v_n)$ is called the probability vector if the components are non-negative and their sum is equal to 1.

Stochastic Matrix

A square matrix $P = (P_{ij})$ is called the stochastic matrix if each of the rows is a probability vector and if each entry P is non-negative and the sum of entries in each rows is 1

Solved Examples

***Example* 1:** The matrix

$$P = \begin{bmatrix} 0 & 1 & 0 \\ \frac{1}{2} & \frac{1}{6} & \frac{1}{3} \\ \frac{1}{3} & \frac{2}{3} & 0 \end{bmatrix} \text{ is a stochastic matrix}$$

***Example* 2**:

The matrix $$A = \begin{bmatrix} 0 & 1 \\ \frac{1}{2} & \frac{1}{2} \end{bmatrix} \text{ is a stochastic matrix}$$

9.9 Limiting Distribution

The limiting distribution $\{v_k\}$ of an aperiodic irreducible Markov chain whether it is descrete or continuous parameter with a finite number of states is given by

$$v_k = \frac{c_k}{\Sigma_j c_j}$$

where $$c_j = \Sigma w_i(T_j)$$

9.10 Regular Stochastic Matrix

A stochastic matrix P is said to be regular if all the entries of some power P_n are positive.

9.11 Probability Distribution

Consider the Markov Chain $\{X_1, X_2, \ldots)\}$ for which X_1 in the first member. X_1 is called initial random variable of the process.

Let $P_1^{(0)}$ denote the probability that x_1 takes the value a_1, $P_2^{(0)}$ denote the probability that x_1 takes the value a_2, and so on. Then the probability distribution of x_1 may be represented by the row matrix

$$A^{(0)} = \left[P_1^{(0)}, P_2^{(0)}, \ldots P_m^{(0)}\right] \qquad \ldots\ldots(9.1)$$

This is called the initial probability distribution of the chain. If the probability distribution of x_1 is known, then the probability distribution of x_{n+1} referred as the nth step probability distribution of the system and is represented by the row matrix

$$A^{(n)} \qquad \ldots\ldots(9.2)$$

where $A^{(n)} = A^o P^n$

Since $A^{(0)}$ is a row matrix of order m and P^n is an $m \times m$ matrix, we observe that $A^{(n)}$ is a row matrix of order m, of the form

$$A^{(n)} = (P_1^{(n)}, P_2^{(n)}, \ldots P_m^{(n)})$$

Suppose $\underset{n+\infty}{Lt} \rightarrow P$

$$\lim_{n\to\infty} P_i^{(n)} = v_i,\ i = 1, 2, \ldots m \qquad \ldots\ldots(9.3)$$

where v_i are non-negative, independent of $P_i^{(0)}$, and $\sum_{i=1}^{\infty} v_i = 1$ .....(9.4)

Then the row matrix

$$A^{(\infty)} = (v_1, v_2, \ldots\ldots v_m) = V \qquad \ldots\ldots(9.5)$$

represents what is called a steady-state distribution of the process. The row matrix V is called a stationary probability vector of the chain.

For a given chain, the steady state distribution is determined by the formulae

$$V = vP \qquad \ldots\ldots(9.6)$$

Solved Examples

***Example* 1**: Show that the matrix

$$A = \begin{bmatrix} 0 & 1 \\ \frac{1}{2} & \frac{1}{2} \end{bmatrix}$$

is a stochastic matrix. Check whether it is regular.

Solution: Consider
$$A = \begin{bmatrix} 0 & \frac{1}{2} \\ \frac{1}{2} & \frac{1}{2} \end{bmatrix}$$

All the entries of A are positive.

and sum of all entries in each row is equal to 1

$\therefore$ A is a stochastic matrix.

Now
$$A^2 = \begin{bmatrix} 0 & 1 \\ \frac{1}{2} & \frac{1}{2} \end{bmatrix}\begin{bmatrix} 0 & 1 \\ \frac{1}{2} & \frac{1}{2} \end{bmatrix}$$

$$= \begin{bmatrix} 0+\frac{1}{2} & 0+\frac{1}{2} \\ 0+\frac{1}{4} & \frac{1}{2}+\frac{1}{4} \end{bmatrix}$$

$$= \begin{bmatrix} \frac{1}{2} & \frac{1}{2} \\ \frac{1}{4} & \frac{3}{4} \end{bmatrix}$$

Each entry in A^2 is positive and sum of all entries in each row is equal to 1

i.e.,
$$\sum_{i=1}^{\infty} a_i = 1$$

Hence, A is regular.

***Example* 2:** Three boys A, B and C are throwing a ball to each other. A always throws the ball to B and B always throws the ball to C. But C just as likely to throw the ball to B as to A. If C was the first person to throw the ball, find the probabilities that (i) A has the ball (ii) B has the ball (iii) C has the ball after three throws.

***Solution*:** We have

P_{11} = Probability that the ball is thrown from A to A = ∞

P_{12} = Probability that the ball is thrown from A to B = 1

P_{13} = Probability that the ball is thrown from A to C = 0

P_{21} = Probability that the ball is thrown from B to A = 0

P_{22} = Probability that the ball is thrown from B to B = 0

P_{23} = Probability that the ball is thrown from B to C = 1

P_{31} = Probability that the ball is thrown from C to A = $\frac{1}{2}$

P_{32} = Probability that the ball is thrown from C to B = $\frac{1}{2}$

P_{33} = Probability that the ball is thrown from C to C = 0

The transition matrix is

$$P = \begin{bmatrix} 0 & 1 & 0 \\ 0 & 0 & 1 \\ \frac{1}{2} & \frac{1}{2} & 0 \end{bmatrix}$$

Hence the 3-step transition matrix is

$$P^3 = \begin{bmatrix} 0 & 1 & 0 \\ 0 & 0 & 1 \\ \frac{1}{2} & \frac{1}{2} & 0 \end{bmatrix} \begin{bmatrix} 0 & 1 & 0 \\ 0 & 0 & 1 \\ \frac{1}{2} & \frac{1}{2} & 0 \end{bmatrix} \begin{bmatrix} 0 & 1 & 0 \\ 0 & 0 & 1 \\ \frac{1}{2} & \frac{1}{2} & 0 \end{bmatrix}$$

$$= \begin{bmatrix} \frac{1}{2} & \frac{1}{2} & 0 \\ 0 & \frac{1}{2} & \frac{1}{2} \\ \frac{1}{4} & \frac{1}{4} & \frac{1}{2} \end{bmatrix}$$

Now if the ball was first thrown by C, the initial probability distribution is given by the row matrix

$$A^{(0)} = [P_1^{(0)}, P_2^{(0)}, P_3^{(0)}] = [0, 0, 1]$$

After 3 throws, the probability distribution is given by

$$[P_1^{(3)}, P_2^{(3)}, P_3^{(3)}] = [A^{(0)} P^3]$$

$$= [0, 0, 1] \begin{bmatrix} \frac{1}{2} & \frac{1}{2} & 0 \\ 0 & \frac{1}{2} & \frac{1}{2} \\ \frac{1}{4} & \frac{1}{4} & \frac{1}{2} \end{bmatrix}$$

$$= \begin{bmatrix} \frac{1}{4} & \frac{1}{4} & \frac{1}{4} \end{bmatrix}$$

Thus after three throws the probability that the ball is with

(i) A is $\frac{1}{4}$

(ii) B is $\frac{1}{4}$

(iii) C is $\frac{1}{2}$

***Example* 3:** In a cascade of binary communication channels the symbols 1 and 0 are transmitted in successive stages. In any stage the probability of transmitted 1 is received as a 1 is 0.75 and the probability of a 0 is received as a 0 is 0.5. Find the probability that

(i) 1 is transmitted in the first stage is received correctly, and

(ii) 0 is transmitted in the first stage is received as 1 after the third stage.

***Solution*:** We have

P_{11} = Probability that a transmitted 1 is received as 1 = $\frac{3}{4}$

P_{12} = Probability that a transmitted 1 is received as 0 = $\frac{1}{4}$

P_{21} = Probability that a transmitted 0 is received as 1 = $\frac{1}{2}$

P_{22} = Probability that a transmitted 0 is received as 0 = $\frac{1}{2}$

The transition matrix is

$$P = \begin{bmatrix} \frac{3}{4} & \frac{1}{4} \\ \frac{1}{2} & \frac{1}{2} \end{bmatrix}$$

Hence, we get

$$P^3 = \begin{bmatrix} \frac{43}{64} & \frac{21}{64} \\ \frac{21}{32} & \frac{11}{32} \end{bmatrix}$$

$$= \begin{bmatrix} 0.6719 & 0.3281 \\ 0.6563 & 0.3437 \end{bmatrix}$$

Therefore,

(i) The probability that 1 is transmitted in the first stage is received correctly as 1 after the third states is $\frac{43}{64} = 0.6719$.

(ii) The probability that 0 transmitted in the first stage is received as a 1 after the third stage is $\frac{21}{32} = 0.6563$

***Example* 4:**

A raining process is considered as a two state Markov chain. If it rains it is considered to be in state 0 and if it does not rain the chain is in state 1. The transition probability of the Markov chain is defined as

$$P = \begin{bmatrix} 0.6 & 0.4 \\ 0.2 & 0.8 \end{bmatrix}$$

Find the probability that is will rain for three days from today assuming that is raining today. Find also the unconditional probability that it will rain after three days. Assume the initial probabilities of state 0 and 1 as 0.4 and 0.6 respectively.

Solution: The one step transition probability matrix is

$$P = \begin{bmatrix} 0.6 & 0.4 \\ 0.2 & 0.8 \end{bmatrix}$$

$$\therefore \qquad P^2 = P_{(2)} = \begin{bmatrix} 0.6 & 0.4 \\ 0.2 & 0.8 \end{bmatrix} \begin{bmatrix} 0.6 & 0.4 \\ 0.2 & 0.8 \end{bmatrix}$$

$$= \begin{bmatrix} 0.44 & 0.56 \\ 0.28 & 0.72 \end{bmatrix}$$

$$P^3 = P_{(3)} = P^2.P = \begin{bmatrix} 0.44 & 0.56 \\ 0.28 & 0.72 \end{bmatrix} \begin{bmatrix} 0.6 & 0.4 \\ 0.2 & 0.8 \end{bmatrix}$$

$$= \begin{bmatrix} 0.376 & 0.622 \\ 0.312 & 0.688 \end{bmatrix}$$

The probability that it will rain on third day given that it will rain today is 0.376

The conditional probability that it will rain after 3 days =

$$P(X_3 = 0) = (0.4)P_{00}^{\ 3} + (0.6)P_{10}^{\ 3}$$

$$= 0.4 \times 0.376 + 0.6 \times 0.312$$

$$= 0.3376$$

***Example* 5:** Evaluate $P_{(2)}$ and $P_{(3)}$ for the homogeneous Markov chain given by the transition probability matrix

$$P_{(1)} = \begin{bmatrix} 0.1 & 0.6 & 0.3 \\ 0.5 & 0.1 & 0.4 \\ 0.1 & 0.2 & 0.7 \end{bmatrix}$$

Solution: We have

$$P_{(2)} = \left(P_{(1)}\right)^2$$

$$= \begin{bmatrix} 0.1 & 0.6 & 0.3 \\ 0.5 & 0.1 & 0.4 \\ 0.1 & 0.2 & 0.7 \end{bmatrix} \begin{bmatrix} 0.1 & 0.6 & 0.3 \\ 0.5 & 0.1 & 0.4 \\ 0.1 & 0.2 & 0.7 \end{bmatrix}$$

$$= \begin{bmatrix} 0.34 & 0.18 & 0.48 \\ 0.14 & 0.35 & 0.47 \\ 0.18 & 0.22 & 0.60 \end{bmatrix}$$

$$P(3) = \left(P(1)\right)^3 = \begin{bmatrix} 0.34 & 0.18 & 0.48 \\ 0.14 & 0.35 & 0.47 \\ 0.18 & 0.22 & 0.60 \end{bmatrix} \begin{bmatrix} 0.1 & 0.6 & 0.3 \\ 0.5 & 0.1 & 0.4 \\ 0.1 & 0.2 & 0.7 \end{bmatrix}$$

$$= \begin{bmatrix} 0.172 & 0.318 & 0.51 \\ 0.256 & 0.217 & 0.527 \\ 0.188 & 0.25 & 0.562 \end{bmatrix}$$

***Example* 6:** Consider the transition probability matrix of a Markov chain as

$$\begin{bmatrix} 0.3 & 0.7 & 0 \\ 0.1 & 0.4 & 0.5 \\ 0 & 0.2 & 0.8 \end{bmatrix}$$

Check whether the chain is irreducible

Solution: It we assume the states as 0, 1 and 2, it is possible to go from 0 to 1 with a probability 0.7 and from state 1 to 2 with probability 0.5. Hence it is possible to go from 0 to 2. In this way all the states communicate with each other in the given Markov chain thus, the given chain is irreducible.

***Example* 7:** A person owning a scooter has the option to switch over to scooter, bike or a car next time with the probability of (0.3, 0.5, 0.2). If the transition probability matrix is

$$\begin{bmatrix} 0.4 & 0.3 & 0.3 \\ 0.2 & 0.5 & 0.3 \\ 0.25 & 0.25 & 0.5 \end{bmatrix}$$

what are the probabilities of vehicles related to his fourth purchase

Solution:

$$\text{we have } P(1) = \begin{bmatrix} 0.4 & 0.3 & 0.3 \\ 0.2 & 0.5 & 0.3 \\ 0.25 & 0.25 & 0.5 \end{bmatrix}$$

$$\therefore \qquad P^3 = (P(1))^3 = \begin{bmatrix} 0.4 & 0.3 & 0.3 \\ 0.2 & 0.5 & 0.3 \\ 0.25 & 0.25 & 0.5 \end{bmatrix} \begin{bmatrix} 0.4 & 0.3 & 0.3 \\ 0.2 & 0.5 & 0.3 \\ 0.25 & 0.25 & 0.5 \end{bmatrix} \begin{bmatrix} 0.4 & 0.3 & 0.3 \\ 0.2 & 0.5 & 0.3 \\ 0.25 & 0.25 & 0.5 \end{bmatrix}$$

$$= \begin{bmatrix} 0.277 & 0.351 & 0.372 \\ 0.269 & 0.359 & 0.372 \\ 0.275 & 0.345 & 0.380 \end{bmatrix}$$

$\therefore$ Probabilities of his fourth purchase = $(0.3 \quad 0.5\ 0.2)\ P^3 = (0.2726,\ 0.3538,\ 0.3736)$

***Example* 8:** In the transition Matrix

$$P = \begin{bmatrix} 1 & 0 & 0 \\ 0 & \frac{1}{2} & \frac{1}{2} \\ 0 & \frac{1}{3} & \frac{2}{3} \end{bmatrix}$$

An absorbing Markov Chain

***Solution*:**

We have

$$P = \begin{bmatrix} 1 & 0 & 0 \\ 0 & \frac{1}{2} & \frac{1}{2} \\ 0 & \frac{1}{3} & \frac{2}{3} \end{bmatrix}$$

S_1 is the only absorbing state and this cannot be reached from S_2 or S_3

Hence P is not an absorbing Markov Chain

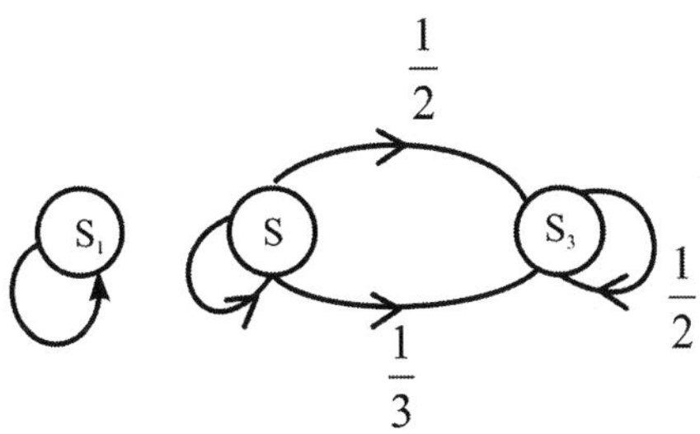

Exercise 9.1

1. Consider the Markov chain with transient probability matrix $\begin{bmatrix} 0.4 & 0.6 & 0 & 0 \\ 0.3 & 0.7 & 0 & 0 \\ 0.2 & 0.4 & 0.1 & 0.3 \\ 0 & 0 & 0 & 1 \end{bmatrix}$

Is it irreducible. If no find the classes. Find the nature of states.

Ans: Not irreducible. The classes are [0, 1], [2], [3]. State 3 is absorbing state.

2. Find P(n), for the homogenous Markov chain with the following transition probability matrix

$$P = \begin{bmatrix} 1-a & a \\ b & 1-b \end{bmatrix}$$

where $\quad 0 < a < 1, 0 < b < 1$

Ans: The limiting transition matrix is

$$\underset{n\to\infty}{\text{Lt}}\ P(n) = \begin{bmatrix} \frac{b}{a+b} & \frac{a}{a+b} \\ \frac{b}{a+b} & \frac{a}{a+b} \end{bmatrix}$$

3. Check whether the following Markov chain is regular $\begin{bmatrix} 0 & \frac{1}{2} & \frac{1}{2} & 0 \\ \frac{1}{2} & 0 & 0 & \frac{1}{2} \\ \frac{1}{2} & 0 & 0 & \frac{1}{2} \\ 0 & \frac{1}{2} & \frac{1}{2} & 0 \end{bmatrix}$

4. A student's study habits are as follows

If he studies one night he is 60% sure not to study next night. In the other hand if he does not study one night, he is 80% sure to study the next night. In the long run how often does he study.

Ans: [57% of the time]

5. Define (i) stochastic process (ii) Markov chain

6. Define the terms

(i) Absorbing state (ii) Irreducible Merkov chain (iii) Recurrent state

7. Check whether the following matrices are stochastic matrices.

(a) $A = \begin{bmatrix} \frac{2}{3} & 0 & \frac{1}{3} \\ \frac{-1}{2} & \frac{1}{2} & \frac{3}{4} \\ \frac{1}{3} & \frac{1}{3} & \frac{1}{3} \end{bmatrix}$ (b) $A = \begin{bmatrix} \frac{3}{4} & \frac{1}{4} \\ \frac{1}{3} & \frac{1}{3} \end{bmatrix}$

Ans: (a) no (b) no

8. Show that the matrix $A = \begin{bmatrix} 0 & 1 \\ \frac{1}{2} & \frac{1}{2} \end{bmatrix}$ is regular

9. Consider the Markov chain with TPM

$$P = \begin{bmatrix} 0 & 1 & 0 \\ \frac{1}{2} & 0 & \frac{1}{2} \\ 0 & 1 & 0 \end{bmatrix}$$

Show that $P^2n = P^2$

10. A drilling process is considered to be state Markov chain. If process is there in the production company it is in the state 0 and if the process is not there it is in state 1.

The TPM is $P = \begin{bmatrix} 0.1 & 0.2 \\ 0.3 & 0.4 \end{bmatrix}$.

Find the probability that the drilling process will be then for 3 days from 1 day.

Ans: $P(3) = \begin{bmatrix} 0.037 & 0.054 \\ 0.081 & 0.218 \end{bmatrix}$

TABLE

Significance points of F

(5% values)

Degree of freedom (n_2)	Degree of freedom (n_1) 1	2	3	4	5	6	7	8	9	∝
1	161.4	199.5	215.7	224.6	230.2	234.0	236.8	238.9	240.5	245.3
2	18.51	19.00	19.16	19.35	19.30	19.33	19.35	19.37	19.38	19.50
3	10.13	9.55	9.28	9.12	9.01	8.94	8.89	8.85	8.81	8.53
4	7.71	6.94	6.59	6.39	6.26	6.16	6.09	6.04	6.00	5.63
5	6.61	5.79	5.41	5.19	5.05	4.95	4.88	4.82	4.77	4.36
6	5.99	5.14	4.76	4.53	4.39	4.28	4.21	4.15	4.10	3.67
7	5.59	4.74	4.35	4.12	3.97	3.87	3.79	3.73	3.68	3.23
8	5.32	4.46	4.07	3.84	3.69	3.58	3.50	3.44	3.39	2.93
9	5.12	4.26	3.86	3.63	3.48	3.37	3.29	3.23	3.18	2.71
10	4.96	4.10	3.71	3.48	3.33	3.22	3.14	3.07	3.02	2.54
11	4.84	3.98	3.59	3.36	3.20	3.09	3.01	2.95	2.90	2.40
12	4.75	3.88	3.49	3.26	3.11	3.00	2.91	2.85	2.80	2.30
13	4.67	3.80	3.41	3.18	3.02	2.92	2.83	2.77	2.71	2.21
14	4.60	3.74	3.34	3.11	2.96	2.85	2.76	2.70	2.65	2.13
15	4.54	3.68	3.29	3.06	2.90	2.79	2.71	2.64	2.59	2.07
16	4.49	3.63	3.24	3.01	2.85	2.74	2.66	2.59	2.54	2.01
17	4.45	3.59	3.20	2.96	2.81	2.70	2.61	2.55	2.49	1.96
18	4.41	3.55	3.16	2.93	2.77	2.66	2.58	2.51	2.46	1.92
19	4.38	3.52	3.13	2.90	2.74	2.63	2.54	2.48	2.42	1.88
20	4.35	3.49	3.10	2.87	2.71	2.60	2.51	2.45	2.39	1.84
30	4.17	3.32	2.92	2.69	2.53	2.42	2.33	2.27	2.21	1.62
∝	3.84	3.00	2.60	2.37	2.21	2.10	2.01	1.94	1.88	1.00

TABLE

Significance points of F

(1% *values*)

Degree of freedom (n_2)	1	2	3	4	5	6	7	8	9	∝
	Degree of freedom (n_1)									
1	4052	4999	5403	5625	5764	5859	5928	5981	6022	6366
2	98.50	99.00	99.17	99.25	99.30	99.33	99.36	99.37	99.39	99.50
3	34.12	30.82	29.46	28.71	28.24	27.91	27.67	27.49	27.35	26.13
4	21.20	18.00	16.69	15.98	15.52	15.21	14.98	14.80	14.66	13.46
5	16.26	13.27	12.06	11.39	10.97	10.67	10.46	10.29	10.16	9.02
6	13.75	10.92	9.78	9.15	8.75	8.47	8.26	8.10	7.98	6.88
7	12.25	9.55	8.45	7.85	7.46	7.19	6.99	6.84	6.72	5.65
8	11.26	8.65	7.59	7.01	6.63	6.37	6.18	6.03	5.91	4.86
9	10.56	8.02	6.99	6.42	6.06	5.80	5.61	5.47	5.35	4.31
10	10.04	7.56	6.55	5.99	5.64	5.39	5.20	5.06	4.94	3.91
11	9.65	7.21	6.22	5.67	5.32	5.07	4.89	4.74	4.63	3.60
12	9.33	6.93	5.95	5.41	5.06	4.82	4.64	4.50	4.39	3.36
13	9.07	6.70	5.74	5.21	4.86	4.62	4.44	4.30	4.19	3.17
14	8.86	6.51	5.56	5.04	4.69	4.46	4.28	4.14	4.03	3.00
15	8.68	6.36	5.42	4.89	4.56	4.32	4.14	4.00	3.89	2.87
16	8.53	6.23	5.29	4.77	4.44	4.20	4.03	3.89	3.78	2.75
17	8.40	6.11	5.18	4.67	4.34	4.10	3.93	3.79	3.68	2.65
18	8.29	6.01	5.09	4.58	4.25	4.01	3.84	3.71	3.60	2.57
19	8.18	5.93	5.01	4.50	4.17	3.94	3.77	3.63	3.52	2.49
20	8.10	5.85	4.94	4.43	4.10	3.87	3.70	3.56	3.46	2.42
30	7.56	5.39	4.51	4.02	3.70	3.47	3.30	3.17	3.07	2.01
∝	6.63	4.61	3.78	3.32	3.02	2.80	2.64	2.51	2.41	1.00

Table: The probabilities of exceeding different chi-square values for degrees of freedom from 1 to 50 when the expected hypothesis is true

	Probabilities									
df	.95	.90	.70	.50	.30	.20	.10	.05	.01	.001
1	.004	.016	.15	.46	1.07	1.64	2.71	3.84	6.64	10.83
2	.10	.21	.71	1.39	2.41	3.22	4.61	5.99	9.21	13.82
3	.35	.58	1.42	2.37	3.67	4.64	6.25	7.82	11.35	16.27
4	.71	1.06	2.20	3.36	4.88	5.99	7.78	9.49	13.28	18.47
5	1.15	1.61	3.00	4.35	6.06	7.29	9.24	11.07	15.09	20.52
6	1.64	2.20	3.83	5.35	7.23	8.56	10.65	12.59	16.81	22.46
7	2.17	2.83	4.67	6.35	8.38	9.80	12.02	14.07	18.48	24.32
8	2.73	3.49	5.53	7.34	9.52	11.03	13.36	15.51	20.09	26.13
9	3.33	4.17	6.39	8.34	10.66	12.24	14.68	16.92	21.67	27.88
10	3.94	4.87	7.27	9.34	11.78	13.44	15.99	18.31	23.21	29.59
11	4.58	5.58	8.15	10.34	12.90	14.63	17.28	19.68	24.73	31.26
12	5.23	6.30	9.03	11.34	14.01	15.81	18.55	21.03	26.22	32.91
13	5.89	7.04	9.93	12.34	15.12	16.99	19.81	22.36	27.69	34.53
14	6.57	7.79	10.82	13.34	16.22	18.15	21.06	23.69	29.14	36.12
15	7.26	8.55	11.72	14.34	17.32	19.31	22.31	25.00	30.58	37.70
20	10.85	12.44	16.27	19.34	22.78	25.04	28.41	31.41	37.57	45.32
25	14.61	16.47	20.87	24.34	28.17	30.68	34.38	37.65	44.31	52.62
30	18.49	20.60	25.51	29.34	33.53	36.25	40.26	43.77	50.89	59.70
50	34.76	37.69	44.31	49.34	54.72	58.16	63.17	67.51	76.15	86.66

Table: Distribution of *t* values ("Student's" distribution)*

df	Probabilities .90	.70	.50	.30	.10	.05	.01	.001
1	.16	.51	1.00	2.00	6.31	12.70	63.66	636.62
2	.14	.44	.82	1.39	2.92	4.30	9.92	31.60
3	.14	.42	.76	1.25	2.35	3.18	5.84	12.92
4	.13	.41	.74	1.19	2.13	2.78	4.60	8.61
5	.13	.41	.73	1.16	2.02	2.57	4.03	6.87
6	.13	.40	.72	1.13	1.94	2.45	3.71	5.96
7	.13	.40	.71	1.12	1.90	2.36	3.50	5.41
8	.13	.40	.71	1.11	1.86	2.30	3.36	5.04
9	.13	.40	.70	1.10	1.83	2.26	3.25	4.78
10	.13	.40	.70	1.09	1.81	2.23	3.17	4.59
11	.13	.40	.70	1.09	1.80	2.20	3.10	4.44
12	.13	.40	.70	1.08	1.78	2.18	3.05	4.32
13	.13	.39	.69	1.08	1.77	2.16	3.01	4.22
14	.13	.39	.69	1.08	1.76	2.14	2.98	4.14
15	.13	.39	.69	1.07	1.75	2.13	2.95	4.07
16	.13	.39	.69	1.07	1.75	2.12	2.92	4.02
17	.13	.39	.69	1.07	1.74	2.11	2.90	3.96
18	.13	.39	.69	1.07	1.73	2.10	2.88	3.92
19	.13	.39	.69	1.07	1.73	2.09	2.86	3.88
20	.13	.39	.69	1.06	1.72	2.09	2.84	3.85
21	.13	.39	.69	1.06	1.72	2.08	2.83	3.82
22	.13	.39	.69	1.06	1.72	2.07	2.82	3.79
23	.13	.39	.68	1.06	1.71	2.07	2.81	3.77
24	.13	.39	.68	1.06	1.71	2.06	2.80	3.74
25	.13	.39	.68	1.06	1.71	2.06	2.79	3.72
26	.13	.39	.68	1.06	1.71	2.06	2.78	3.71
27	.13	.39	.68	1.06	1.70	2.05	2.77	3.69
28	.13	.39	.68	1.06	1.70	2.05	2.76	3.67
29	.13	.39	.68	1.06	1.70	2.04	2.76	3.66
30	.13	.39	.68	1.06	1.70	2.04	2.75	3.65
40	.13	.39	.68	1.05	1.68	2.02	2.70	3.55
60	.13	.39	.68	1.05	1.67	2.00	2.66	3.46
120	.13	.39	.68	1.04	1.66	1.98	2.62	3.37
∞	.13	.38	.67	1.04	1.64	1.96	2.58	3.29

LOGARITHMS TABLES

	0	1	2	3	4	5	6	7	8	9	Mean Differences								
											1	2	3	4	5	6	7	8	9
10	0000	0043	0086	0128	0170	0212	0253	0294	0334	0374	4	8	12	17	21	25	29	33	37
11	0414	0453	0492	0531	0569	0607	0645	0682	0719	0755	4	8	11	15	19	23	26	30	34
12	0792	0828	0864	0899	0934	0969	1004	1038	1072	1106	3	7	10	14	17	21	24	28	31
13	1139	1173	1206	1239	1271	1303	1335	1367	1399	1430	3	6	10	13	16	19	23	26	29
14	1461	1492	1523	1553	1584	1614	1644	1673	1703	1732	3	6	9	12	15	18	21	24	27
15	1761	1790	1818	1847	1875	1903	1931	1959	1987	2014	3	6	8	11	14	17	20	22	25
16	2041	2068	2095	2122	2148	2175	2201	2227	2253	2279	3	5	8	11	13	16	18	21	24
17	2304	2330	2355	2380	2405	2430	2455	2480	2504	2529	2	5	7	10	12	15	17	20	22
18	2553	2577	2601	2625	2648	2672	2695	2718	2742	2765	2	5	7	9	12	14	16	19	21
19	2788	2810	2833	2856	2878	2900	2923	2945	2967	2989	2	4	7	9	11	13	16	18	20
20	3010	3032	3054	3075	3096	3118	3139	3160	3181	3201	2	4	6	8	11	13	15	17	19
21	3222	3243	3263	3284	3304	3324	3345	3365	3385	3404	2	4	6	8	10	12	14	16	18
22	3424	3444	3464	3483	3502	3522	3541	3560	3579	3598	2	4	6	8	10	12	14	15	17
23	3617	3636	3655	3674	3692	3711	3729	3747	3766	3784	2	4	6	7	9	11	13	15	17
24	3802	3820	3838	3856	3874	3892	3909	3927	3945	3962	2	4	5	7	9	11	12	14	16
25	3979	3997	4014	4031	4048	4065	4082	4099	4116	4133	2	3	5	7	9	10	12	14	15
26	4150	4166	4183	4200	4216	4232	4249	4265	4281	4298	2	3	5	7	8	10	11	13	15
27	4314	4330	4346	4362	4378	4393	4409	4425	4440	4456	2	3	5	6	8	9	11	13	14
28	4472	4487	4502	4518	4533	4548	4564	4579	4594	4609	2	3	5	6	8	9	11	12	14
29	4624	4639	4654	4669	4683	4698	4713	4728	4742	4757	1	3	4	6	7	9	10	12	13
30	4771	4786	4800	4814	4829	4843	4857	4871	4886	4900	1	3	4	6	7	9	10	11	13
31	4914	4928	4942	4955	4969	4983	4997	5011	5024	5038	1	3	4	6	7	8	10	11	12
32	5051	5065	5079	5092	5105	5119	5132	5145	5159	5172	1	3	4	5	7	8	9	11	12
33	5185	5198	5211	5224	5237	5250	5263	5276	5289	5302	1	3	4	5	6	8	9	10	12
34	5315	5328	5340	5353	5366	5378	5391	5403	5416	5428	1	3	4	5	6	8	9	10	11
35	5441	5453	5465	5478	5490	5502	5514	5527	5539	5551	1	2	4	5	6	7	9	10	11
36	5563	5575	5587	5599	5611	5623	5635	5647	5658	5670	1	2	4	5	6	7	8	10	11
37	5682	5694	5705	5717	5729	5740	5752	5763	5775	5786	1	2	3	5	6	7	8	9	10
38	5798	5809	5821	5832	5843	5855	5866	5877	5888	5899	1	2	3	5	6	7	8	9	10
39	5911	5922	5933	5944	5955	5966	5977	5988	5999	6010	1	2	3	4	5	7	8	9	10
40	6021	6031	6042	6053	6064	6075	6085	6096	6107	6117	1	2	3	4	5	6	8	9	10
41	6128	6138	6149	6160	6170	6180	6191	6201	6212	6222	1	2	3	4	5	6	7	8	9
42	6232	6243	6253	6263	6274	6284	6294	6304	6314	6325	1	2	3	4	5	6	7	8	9
43	6335	6345	6355	6365	6375	6385	6395	6405	6415	6425	1	2	3	4	5	6	7	8	9
44	6435	6444	6454	6464	6474	6484	6493	6503	6513	6522	1	2	3	4	5	6	7	8	9
45	6532	6542	6551	6561	6571	6580	6590	6599	6609	6618	1	2	3	4	5	6	7	8	9
46	6628	6637	6646	6656	6665	6675	6684	6693	6702	6712	1	2	3	4	5	6	7	7	8
47	6721	6730	6739	6749	6758	6767	6776	6785	6794	6803	1	2	3	4	5	5	6	7	8
48	6812	6821	6830	6839	6848	6857	6866	6875	6884	6893	1	2	3	4	4	5	6	7	8
49	6902	6911	6920	6928	6937	6946	6955	6964	6972	6981	1	2	3	4	4	5	6	7	8
50	6990	6998	7007	7016	7024	7033	7042	7050	7059	7067	1	2	3	3	4	5	6	7	8

(Contd.)

LOGARITHMS

	0	1	2	3	4	5	6	7	8	9	Mean Differences								
											1	2	3	4	5	6	7	8	9
51	7076	7084	7093	7101	7110	7118	7126	7135	7143	7152	1	2	3	3	4	5	6	7	8
52	7160	7168	7177	7185	7193	7202	7210	7218	7226	7235	1	2	2	3	4	5	6	7	7
53	7243	7251	7259	7267	7275	7284	7292	7300	7308	7316	1	2	2	3	4	5	6	6	7
54	7324	7332	7340	7348	7356	7364	7372	7380	7388	7396	1	2	2	3	4	5	6	6	7
55	7404	7412	7419	7427	7435	7443	7451	7459	7466	7474	1	2	2	3	4	5	5	6	7
56	7482	7490	7497	7505	7513	7520	7528	7536	7543	7551	1	2	2	3	4	5	5	6	7
57	7559	7566	7574	7582	7589	7597	7604	7612	7619	7627	1	2	2	3	4	5	5	6	7
58	7634	7642	7649	7657	7664	7672	7679	7686	7694	7701	1	1	2	3	4	4	5	6	7
59	7709	7716	7723	7731	7738	7745	7752	7760	7767	7774	1	1	2	3	4	4	5	6	7
60	7782	7789	7796	7803	7810	7818	7825	7832	7839	7846	1	1	2	3	4	4	5	6	6
61	7853	7860	7868	7875	7882	7889	7896	7903	7910	7917	1	1	2	3	4	4	5	6	6
62	7924	7931	7938	7945	7952	7959	7966	7973	7980	7987	1	1	2	3	3	4	5	6	6
63	7993	8000	8007	8014	8021	8028	8035	8041	8048	8055	1	1	2	3	3	4	5	5	6
64	8062	8069	8075	8082	8089	8096	8102	8109	8116	8122	1	1	2	3	3	4	5	5	6
65	8129	8136	8142	8149	8156	8162	8169	8176	8182	8189	1	1	2	3	3	4	5	5	6
66	8195	8202	8209	8215	8222	8228	8235	8241	8248	8254	1	1	2	3	3	4	5	5	6
67	8261	8267	8274	8280	8287	8293	8299	8306	8312	8319	1	1	2	3	3	4	5	5	6
68	8325	8331	8338	8344	8351	8357	8363	8370	8376	8382	1	1	2	3	3	4	4	5	6
69	8388	8395	8401	8407	8414	8420	8426	8432	8439	8445	1	1	2	2	3	4	4	5	6
70	8451	8457	8463	8470	8476	8482	8488	8494	8500	8506	1	1	2	2	3	4	4	5	6
71	8513	8519	8525	8531	8537	8543	8549	8555	8561	8567	1	1	2	2	3	4	4	5	5
72	8573	8579	8585	8591	8597	8603	8609	8615	8621	8627	1	1	2	2	3	4	4	5	5
73	8633	8639	8645	8651	8657	8663	8669	8675	8681	8686	1	1	2	2	3	4	4	5	5
74	8692	8698	8704	8710	8716	8722	8727	8733	8739	8745	1	1	2	2	3	4	4	5	5
75	8751	8756	8762	8768	8774	8779	8785	8791	8797	8802	1	1	2	2	3	3	4	5	5
76	8808	8814	8820	8825	8831	8837	8842	8848	8854	8859	1	1	2	2	3	3	4	5	5
77	8865	8871	8876	8882	8887	8893	8899	8904	8910	8915	1	1	2	2	3	3	4	4	5
78	8921	8927	8932	8938	8943	8949	8954	8960	8965	8971	1	1	2	2	3	3	4	4	5
79	8976	8982	8987	8993	8998	9004	9009	9015	9020	9025	1	1	2	2	3	3	4	4	5
80	9031	9036	9042	9047	9053	9058	9063	9069	9074	9079	1	1	2	2	3	3	4	4	5
81	9085	9090	9096	9101	9106	9112	9117	9122	9128	9133	1	1	2	2	3	3	4	4	5
82	9138	9143	9149	9154	9159	9165	9170	9175	9180	9186	1	1	2	2	3	3	4	4	5
83	9191	9196	9201	9206	9217	9217	9222	9227	9232	9238	1	1	2	2	3	3	4	4	5
84	9243	9248	9253	9258	9263	9269	9274	9279	9284	9289	1	1	2	2	3	3	4	4	5
85	9294	9299	9304	9360	9315	9320	9325	9330	9335	9340	1	1	2	2	3	3	4	4	5
86	9345	9350	9355	9360	9365	9370	9375	9380	9385	9390	1	1	2	2	3	3	4	4	5
87	9395	9400	9405	9410	9415	9420	9425	9430	9435	9440	0	1	1	2	2	3	3	4	4
88	9445	9450	9455	9460	9465	9469	9474	9479	9484	9489	0	1	1	2	2	3	3	4	4
89	9494	9499	9504	9509	9513	9518	9523	9528	9533	9538	0	1	1	2	2	3	3	4	4
90	9542	9547	9552	9557	9562	9566	9571	9576	9581	9586	0	1	1	2	2	3	3	4	4
91	9590	9595	9600	9605	9609	9614	9619	9624	9628	9633	0	1	1	2	2	3	3	4	4
92	9638	9643	9647	9652	9657	9661	9666	9671	9675	9680	0	1	1	2	2	3	3	4	4
93	9685	9689	9694	9699	9703	9708	9713	9717	9722	9727	0	1	1	2	2	3	3	4	4
94	9731	9736	9741	9745	9750	9754	9759	9763	9768	9773	0	1	1	2	2	3	3	4	4
95	9777	9782	9786	9791	9795	9800	9805	9809	9814	9818	0	1	1	2	2	3	3	4	4
96	9823	9827	9832	9836	9841	9845	9850	9854	9859	9863	0	1	1	2	2	3	3	4	4
97	9868	9872	9877	9881	9886	9890	9894	9899	9903	9908	0	1	1	2	2	3	3	4	4
98	9912	9916	9921	9926	9930	9934	9939	9943	9948	9952	0	1	1	2	2	3	3	4	4
99	9956	9961	9965	9969	9974	9978	9983	9987	9991	9996	0	1	1	2	2	3	3	3	4